Portrait of Henry IV, about 1600, by an unknown painter

From the Bibliothèque Nationale, Paris

Frontispiece

ḢENRY
OF NAVARRE

HENRY DWIGHT SEDGWICK
Author of Cortés, Lafayette

ILLUSTRATED

THE BOBBS-MERRILL COMPANY
PUBLISHER   INDIANAPOLIS

DC
122.8
.S4
1930   944.03†
        H518S

Printed in the United States of America

PRESS OF
BRAUNWORTH & CO., INC.
BOOK MANUFACTURERS
BROOKLYN, N. Y.

PREFACE

Most people think of Henry IV as the hero of Ivry with *panache blanc* blazing amidst the thickest carnage, as Macaulay puts it, like a guiding star, or as the lawgiver of the *Edict of Nantes,* or as the *Vert Galant* sporting with the Charmante Gabrielle. In deference to these romantical, Protestantish or sexually minded, possible readers, I have concentrated my attention upon such conceptions, and left out of the background all I could of what is usually called history—those national, ethical and intellectual changes summed up under the title Reformation; also, the political aspects of dying feudalism; and also, the general condition of bourgeoisie, peasants, women, and so on, at the close of the sixteenth century, such as the more curious might ask for. And in order to avoid my own prejudices and idiosyncrasies, I have quoted letters and proclamations and, where possible, conversations and sayings by contemporaries. These conversations and sayings are probably not verbally correct, but they were recorded for the most part by the persons that heard them; and constitute a better basis for readers to draw their own conclusions as to Henry's character and disposition, than any inferences of my own.

I have, without regard to nice accuracy, spoken of all Henry's territories, Navarre, Béarn, Foix, et cetera, as Navarre or Béarn.

H. D. S.

CONTENTS

ILLUSTRATIONS

ILLUSTRATIONS—*Continued*

HENRY OF NAVARRE

HENRY OF NAVARRE

CHAPTER I

GRANDPARENTS AND PARENTS

MARGUERITE D'ANGOULÊME, sister to François I and grandmother of Henry of Navarre, is the most sympathetic woman in French history of the century. Tender, compassionate and intellectual, both melancholy and gay, she stands out from the society of her time, as made of more delicate clay and more finely modeled. She was scholarly in her tastes, curious for new ideas, on tiptoe with the desire for a wider horizon, for a greater understanding of the interdependence of all things, and she was eager for affection. The deepest sentiment of her life was her love for her brother, the King, two years younger than herself. At the age of seventeen she married the Duc d'Alençon a husband quite unworthy of her, who, it is said, by incompetence or cowardice, was in great part responsible for the defeat at Pavia. Nature had given her a tendency to religion and mysticism, and this tendency was deepened by the lack of satisfaction, to heart or head, in her marriage. She wrote verses of a mystical character, steeped in Platonic ideas, and tender with a melancholy yearning for divine comradeship. She was much interested in the new religious thought, and went to visit the Reformers when they were in fear from the intolerance of Paris. She comforted

13

them: "I assure you," she wrote, "that the King and the Queen Mother are firm in their decision to make it understood that the truth of God is not heresy, and that, more than ever, they are intent upon the reformation of the Church." (1521.) So close was her relation to these Reformers, and so great her interest in their ideas, that she was suspected of heresy.

But the great solicitude of her life was her brother, François Premier. When he was a prisoner and ill at Madrid, she journeyed there to take care of him, and tried to persuade the Emperor, Charles V, not to exact harsh terms. She was friendly and kind to his mistresses. His death was a great blow, which she sought to ease by a sojourn in a most austere retreat, and by sad religious verses. She was tall, her carriage stately, and her manner full of royal dignity. She was not beautiful, but in spite of the likeness to her brother, there was a fine seriousness and winsome pathos in her face, a gentle resignation, as of one who, as she said, had had more than her share of the burdens of life; at least, the artists saw something of this and put it in their crayon sketches of her, and Clément Marot said that she possessed *"une douceur assise en belle face,"* that "sweetness resided in her beautiful face."

In all this there is no trace of her distinguished grandson. If there is any likeness between the two, it lies in what Monsieur René Doumic calls her *humeur libre, vive, enjouée.* Of this free gaiety of spirit the chief evidence is the *Heptameron,* a collection of tales grouped together very much as in Boccaccio's *Decameron.* By her apologists the love-stories are said to be, at least as explained by the dialogues that accompany them, edifying; but it was edification of a sort limited to the needs of the sixteenth century. To-day, according to Monsieur Doumic, for it is safer to take a French opinion, "they shock us by their crudity, by the liveliness of details and sometimes by the most repulsive grossness, *par la plus ré-butante grossièreté.*" Here certainly we put our finger on a trait of Henry IV; and we must remember in his excuse, that his grandmother, a very distinguished and high-bred lady, of irreproachable conduct, treated certain matters in writing as frankly as he did in fact.

The Duc d'Alençon died in 1525, and Marguerite, for her second husband, married Henri d'Albret, King of Navarre. The marriage was dictated by French policy. The Kingdom of Navarre, less than twenty years before, had extended on both sides of the Pyrenees, with Pau and Nérac, its chief cities to the north, and Pamplona to the south. In 1512, Ferdinand of Aragon had laid violent hold of the provinces south of the mountains and annexed them. Ever since then the despoiled kings, Jean d'Albret up to his death, and his son and successor Henri, after him, had had but one thought, the recovery of the lost lands. So, Henri married Marguerite, who was eleven years older than he, in the hope that François would help him; while François favored the marriage, out of fear lest Henri might come to terms with Charles V, and open the passes of the Pyrenees to a Spanish army.

Of this marriage, the only child to grow up was Jeanne, born in 1528, and destined, according to the plans both of her father and her Uncle François, to be a pawn in their political game. Each proposed to use her to his advantage. She was a delicate child, and passed her early youth at her mother's castle in Angoulême, where she played in a park, attended by a squirrel, a parrot, six turkey cocks, six turkey hens, and for human companionship by a little girl, whom she used to slap but who adored her. When she was about ten or eleven years old, her Uncle François deemed it prudent to have this political pawn in his possession, and invited her to the castle of Plessis-lès-Tours. There she stayed while her uncle and her father made their respective plans for her marriage. Already, when she was but six or seven, the King her uncle had suggested the First Prince of the Blood, Antoine de Bourbon, who was ten years her senior, but her mother held off, and her father, having discovered that he would not be likely to get any help from France, was privily trying to betroth her to young Prince Philip, son and heir to Charles V. But other plans intervened, and nothing final was done. François I died in 1547. His son Henri II succeeded him, and in his turn, fearful lest Henri d'Albret should make an alliance with the Emperor, again brought forward the project of a match between Jeanne and Antoine de Bourbon, while the King of Navarre, as before, secretly nursed his pet plan of a Spanish marriage.

The princely house of Bourbon was descended from Saint Louis. Its credit had been hurt by the defection of the Connétable de Bourbon, but Antoine's branch had remained faithful. Antoine himself was a good-looking, attractive man, somewhat of a dandy—in his wardrobe was a nightgown of cloth of silver, damasked with gold and crimson silk—of charming address, ready of speech, with a debonair, nonchalant manner, and unquestioned bravery. Jeanne fell in love with him. Her father, with the Spanish bee in his bonnet, shuffled and tried to procrastinate, but the King was firm and, according to his own report of the conversation, spoke out roundly; *"Je luy dys quy falloyt quy le fyt et que ce fut dedans dymanche; se quy m'a acordé,*—I told him that it must be done, and done before Sunday; to which he agreed." Henri II repeated the familiar promise to send an army to help recover Spanish Navarre, which Henri d'Albret affected to believe, and he also promised to pay him fifteen thousand livres a year, and actually made one payment. The marriage was celebrated in October, 1549; the bride was twenty, the bridegroom thirty. Ronsard wrote the epithalamium. One stanza touches our hero:

> *Le ciel fera beaucoup*
> *Pour tout le monde ensemble,*
> *Si tu conçois un coup*
> *Un fils qui te resemble,*
> *Où l'honneur de ta face*
> *Soit peint, et de tes yeux,*
> *Et ta celeste grace*
> *Qui tenteroit les Dieux.*
> > *O Hymen, Hymenée,*
> > *Hymen, O Hymenée.*

> Heaven will do much
> For all the world together,
> If you conceive a son
> That shall resemble you;
> In whom the glory of your face
> Shall painted be, and of your eyes
> And your celestial grace
> That could seduce the Gods.
> > O Hymen.

Hymen heard the prayer, and Jeanne conceived a son, who, if he did not inherit the face that found so much favor in Ronsard's verses, inherited much of her strong character and ardent temperament. Jeanne was happy; Antoine, also, because he was partly in love and had the prospect of a kingly title upon his father-in-law's death. Henri II was content because the marriage barred the passes of the Pyrenees against Spain; but there the satisfaction ended. Henri d'Albret recognized that he was no nearer to the recovery of Spanish Navarre, and had lost his pawn, and poor Marguerite wept to part from her daughter, for she was now old and did not like Antoine, and her husband was rude and tyrannical to her and went dangling after other women.

Jeanne was a delightful person in her youth, *amazone hardie et courageuse; la mignonne des rois,* so pleasant-spirited and gay that her conversation would dispel *ennui,* or any disturbance from anybody's mind. Like her mother she was highly educated; she knew Spanish, Italian, Latin and Greek, she wrote verses and enjoyed the society of learned and cultivated men. At the beginning her married life was very happy, she was deep in love with her husband, and he as much in love with her as his vain self-complacent nature would permit. He was away from home most of the time, in the field, serving against the Spanish on the Flemish border; the two exchanged frequent letters, and his are very affectionate: "I pray God, my Darling, to keep you in health and grant you a long happy life, Your very true and affectionate husband, Antoine. . . . I never would have believed that I should love you as much as I do. Another time I shall take good care when I go on a long journey to have you always with me, for when I am alone it is no fun at all. . . . *Ma mie* . . . please send me news of your health as often as possible, no news in the world interests me so much. From your good friend and your better husband." He repeats that he can't live without her, and that never a husband loved his wife so much as he does, that he can no more live without her than a body without its soul. Her letters are those of the dutiful wife to her far superior husband, she signs herself *Vostre très humble et très obeissante fille et mignonne, et femme et metresse, Jehanne de Navarre.*

Their first child was born while Jeanne was in the north, at

LA·ROYNE·DE·NAVARRE

Marguerite d'Angoulême, grandmother of Henry of Navarre

Coucy, September 24, 1551, and a second was on its way in the summer of 1553. When Henri d'Albret heard of this second baby he wrote:

July [?], 1553.

Dear Daughter:

I can't tell you how happy I am over your *beaus maus,* your blessed troubles, for you are so near and dear to me that you must be aware of all I feel, good or bad. For the present there is little that I can do to comfort your troubles; but for yourself let me counsel amusements, and for the fruit you bear, I recommend the patience of women. Please take good care of yourself, and *don't be afraid of losing your place through any of the persons you may hear of,* for I should never get the happiness from them that I get from you, and I shall be very fond of the baby. I have written this letter to you with my own hand on account of the pleasure I saw you got from my last. If it only depends on me for you to have all you desire, you shall have it soon, for I want you to be as happy as any father alive could wish his child to be. I should be glad if I could jump to you, but the jump is pretty long; nevertheless, if my health will bear it, after going to the baths, I shan't fail to go to see you, and meantime, I am

Your good father and friend,

HENRY.

The first child was not destined to live long. The lady in charge of him was very sensitive to cold, and kept the nursery so hot that the baby sweated to death. The grandfather was frightened by this and, distrustful of northern midwives and nurses, wrote to Jeanne urging her to come to Pau for the

delivery of her second child. Antoine wished her to stay near
him in the north, and bade her write to her father how good
the shooting was at Vendôme. But the old King was in-
sistent, and Jeanne may well have been disquieted by the
rumors, to which her father's letter had referred, that one of
several importunate ladies might beguile him, for he was not
over fifty, into marrying her for the sake of a son and heir
of his own. So she went to Pau. The old King made his will,
leaving the Kingdom to her, put it in a little gold box, and
said that he would give it to her as soon as the child was born,
on the condition that she would sing a Béarnais song during
her labor, so that the child should not be born a cry-baby.
Accordingly when the pains were upon her, Jeanne sang a song
to *Our Lady at the head of the Bridge,* to whom the women
of Pau prayed when in labor:

> *Nouste Dame deü cap deü poun*
> *Adjudat me a d'aqueste hour!*

> Our Lady of the head of the bridge
> Help me at this time!

As soon as the child was born, the grandfather, overjoyed
that it was a boy, took it in his arms, wrapped it in a flap of
his dressing-gown, rubbed its lips with a bit of garlic and held
a cup of Jurançon from the vineyards across the river, to its
mouth. The baby wiggled its head. "Ah," he cried, "you will
be a true Béarnais," and laid it (December 14, 1553) in the
tortoise-shell cradle that you may still see in the castle at Pau.

CHAPTER II

CHILDHOOD

THE mother could not nurse her baby, and seven wet-nurses followed one another before a satisfactory nurse was found. After the baby had been weaned, he was taken to the Château of Coarraze in the valley of the Gave de Pau, and there brought up after the fashion of a peasant's child. But the old King did not live to enjoy his grandson for long. He fell ill in the beginning of 1555. At this news, Antoine wrote to his wife:

Ma Mie,

I have received the letter you wrote to tell me of the sickness of the King, our father. I hope that God will not help him less now than he has helped him in other times of need. And do you, my Love, betake yourself to the sovereign Physician and supplicate him by processions and prayers to be pleased to give him health and all that he needs; and let me know from hour to hour how matters go, and don't let it appear that you are forsaken by the courage that has served you so faithfully in other trials, nor that it grows less rather than greater at this time. I write this for I am afraid,— because you love him so much more than any one else except me, and because his loss will be greater to you than any you have experienced—I am afraid lest nature should constrain you to some outburst. I beg you to show yourself mistress of your-

21

self and to assure you that you have a husband who, if such mischance befall, will be father, mother, brother and husband to you, for I am sure that no matter what happens to you you will always be an obedient wife, and I promise that whatever happens to me, I shall be the most affectionate and gentle husband in the world.

As to the other matter (that you are not with child), I thank God; for I shall see you the sooner, and I think you will be very wrong if you are downcast, seeing that God has given us a fine, handsome baby, that gives us as much happiness as a dozen would to other parents. . . . There is nothing to do but leave all to God, in supplicating Him to grant to us all what is most necessary, and a very happy long life.

Your true friend and very affectionate husband,

ANTOINE.

The old King died in May, 1555. Jeanne went back to Pau and took charge of young Harry's education. She held her father's theories; and the boy was brought up out-of-doors, running barefoot, climbing the hills, scrambling over rocks, wrestling and romping with shepherd boys, playing their games, talking their dialect, feeding on black bread and cheese, beef and onions, and fitting his body for his adventurous life. And he was well whipped when he needed it.

Husband and wife were on very affectionate terms, and the discords of the future were still unsuspected.

Paris, 7 July, 1556.

Ma Mie,

    . . . For the rest, I am sending you a melon that seems

ripe. I hope that it will be very good; if it isn't I am very sorry, for I should like everything that comes from me to be of the same quality as my good wishes, so that it may be worthy of you and acceptable. . . . I have decided to tell Seigneur de Descars, in case the King appears well disposed to us, to venture to ask for a troop of fifty men at arms for our son [Henry, aged two]. It will be as God may dispose, if it doesn't succeed this time, we'll try again. You say our son is splendid; I do not doubt that, so long as he is with you and in your hands, he will be the finest in the world. It would be odd if the workwoman that made him, when she put her hand to it, should not bring him to perfection better than another. For my part I am sure of it, and all sensible people will be too. . . .

Your affectionate friend and most faithful husband

ANTOINE.

Ma Mie,

I have received your letter by the bearer, in which you ask me to indicate a place to plant your mulberry trees. I will try. It seems to me that there is no better place than along the border of the fields where we play pitching the bar. As for mine, please plant them at the end of the bridge across the Gave, where there are ditches already digged, those which President Bertomio had made. So much for the mulberry trees; as for the upper garden, leave it as it is unless Perguade brings the trees, for we must first lay out a plan for the buildings. But if the trees have come, plant them along the middle alley and the alleys that cross it.

Your very affectionate friend and most loyal husband,

ANTOINE.

Ma Mie,

I can't write better news from this place than that to-morrow we start for Pontacq and the next day for Pau, where I shall hope to find you in as fine fettle as you say you are. As for us, we have a grand time from morning to night on horseback, with all the fun of hawking that one could wish. But that does not please me as much as being comfortably tucked up in bed beside you which, please God, shall be on Saturday.

I end with a prayer to God to grant you a long, happy life.

Your very faithful husband

ANTOINE.

The little Prince's peasant régime in the Valley of the Gave was interrupted by a visit to Paris in the winter of 1556-1557. The boy, just three years old, robust and comely, was presented to Henri II, who was greatly taken by the little fellow, so different from his own delicate, pale-cheeked children. He picked him up, kissed him, and asked him if he would like to be his son. Harry answered in his Béarnais patois, pointing to Antoine de Bourbon, *"Aquet es lo seigne pay."* (That is the gentleman my father.) "Well," said the King, "if you don't wish to be my son, will you be my son-in-law?" *"Obé,"* Harry answered. (Oh, yes.) And a match was soon arranged between young Harry and Margot, the King's daughter, who was then three and a half. Politics dictated this betrothal. Henri II had but lately renewed the war with Spain, and he felt no great confidence in the First Prince of the Blood, who held the passes of the Pyrenees, more especially as rumor had

Jeanne d'Albret, mother of Henry of Navarre

it that Charles V was trying to arrange a marriage between his niece and young Henry of Navarre. There might be good and there could be no harm in binding an uncertain Prince by a compact that was of no unbreakable nature. Antoine's vanity was greatly gratified. He wrote the news to his sister, the Duchess of Nevers:

Chantilly, 21 March, 1557.

Dear Sister,

I am told that one should hide nothing from one's friends, and as I believe that I have no friend nearer or better than you, owing to the bond that unites us, I should be sorry to tell good news without telling it to you the very first. For that reason, as I am sending Captain Beauvais, the bearer of this, to Monsieur the Cardinal my brother, I have also bidden him communicate to you the favor it has pleased the King to show me by the compact between us of the marriage of Madame Marguerite, his daughter, with my oldest son, which I take as a very singular mark of his favor, so that I am now happily satisfied of what I could most wish for in this world. I am sure that you will agree with me, and think highly of the advantage and honor that we all can get from it, in which you share as well as I myself. I commend myself with all my heart to your favor, and I pray God to give you what you most wish.

Your affectionate brother and best friend,

ANTOINE.

There is one other glimpse of the little Prince during this visit to Paris shortly before his mother took him back to Pau:

Abbey de Saint Taurin, near Evreux

3 May, 1557.

Monsieur de Tignonville [her maître d'hôtel],

. . . I beg you to start as soon as possible to join me in Paris where I am going to take my son. Do not fail me, and bring your wife with you. In the meantime, I beg the Creator, Monsieur de Tignonville, to have you in his holy keeping.

Votre bonne metresse

JEHANNE DE NAVARRE

My son is in good condition in every particular, and you will find him strong and with a good likelihood to become more so.

CHAPTER III

FROM this time, there is no news of young Harry for several years. He lived with his mother in their little Kingdom, while his father spent part of his time there and part in France, as they expressed it, in attendance upon the French court, or engaged in military duties. Henri II died in 1559; François II reigned for a year, and on his death, Charles IX, a boy of ten, succeeded to the throne, and his mother, Catherine de Médicis became Regent.

It was quiet enough in Béarn, where the Reformers were teaching and preaching in a reasonably discreet manner; but out in the great world of France these were stormy times. The Huguenots had become numerous; members of the gentry and of the high nobility had come flocking to them, and Calvin had organized their scattered congregation into an ecclesiastical and political party, which was preparing itself to resist persecution and to compel the government to grant it freedom of conscience and freedom of worship. The Catholics did not look with unconcern upon the swelling greatness of the heretics. The House of Guise, a younger branch of the reigning House of Lorraine, stepped forward as champion of orthodoxy.

Of this House the two oldest brothers were the leaders, François, Duc de Guise, and Charles, Cardinal de Lorraine. They were the most brilliant men in public affairs in France. Even now, as we see them through the mists and prejudices of

27

history, they show like well-graced actors on the stage, with something of the same charm that has won so many admirers for their niece, Mary Stuart, Queen of Scots. François, defender of Metz, and conqueror of Calais, was also the staunchest champion of the Mother Church; and he gave an outward luster to his glory by his dress, and by the state he kept. He would ride into Paris on a coal-black horse, with black saddle-cloth and caparisons, dressed all in scarlet, with a white plume in his bonnet, the idol of the populace. The Cardinal of Lorraine was very clever, quick, insinuating, suave and courteous; a measure of his talents and address is afforded by the hatred of the Protestants. They never tired of reviling him: "crocodile tears," "foxy subtlety," "bloodthirstiness," a man who "neither the fear of God, honor, chivalry, nor the ties of blood or friendship, nor shame, nor any other obligation," can deter from his natural cruelty, a "mad tiger," a "venomous viper," a "detestable monster," a "sepulcher of abomination," et cetera.

Over against the Guises stood the House of Bourbon, with three brothers at its head, Antoine, Charles, Cardinal de Bourbon, and the Prince de Condé. History would have gained in simplicity, if the three brothers had put themselves at the head of the Protestant party; but Antoine was vacillating, and had his mind set on the recovery of Spanish Navarre, and the Cardinal was a man of mediocre parts, who felt that his position committed him to orthodoxy, and Condé was not only much younger than his brothers, but was poor and fond of pleasure. In the end, Antoine joined the Guises and became one of the Catholic leaders, while Condé, out of ambition and vanity, became head of the Huguenots. All efforts at reconciliation between the two parties failed; an accidental fracas

ended in a massacre of a Huguenot conventicle by the Duke
of Guise's men, and civil war followed on the heels of the
massacre. The poor Regent was confronted by a situation
that would have nonplused any ruler.

Catherine dei Medici, de Médicis, as the French call her,
was the great-granddaughter of Lorenzo the Magnificent and
grandniece of Leo X; her mother, Madeleine de la Tour
d'Auvergne, was a French woman. In 1531 she was betrothed
for political reasons to Henri, second son of François I. Two
years later, when both had attained the age of fourteen, they
were married. The bride was not pretty, her face was broad,
her eyes were prominent, her nose was overemphasized, her
lower lip thick, but in spite of these defects, she seems to have
had a certain *beauté du diable,* and to have made a favorable
impression on people, for she did not lack spirit nor intelligence, and her manners were excellent.

In childhood she was educated in the school of adversity,
and at the French court during the first years of her married
life she was but little noticed; her husband was stout of limb
but sluggish of mind, and took small pleasure in her company.
When the King's oldest son died, her husband became Dauphin,
and she must have entertained hopes that now she would occupy a position of importance; but her hopes were dashed, for
Henri fell in love with the beautiful widow, Diane de Poitiers,
a lady nearly twenty years his senior, and remained her lover
until his death. This eclipse, and the fact that for ten years
she bore no children, coupled with suggestions that her husband had better divorce her and marry a fertile wife, embit-
tered her early womanhood. She hated Diane, and once tried
to persuade the young Duc de Nemours to throw vitriol in her
face, but except for that she bore herself well and uttered no

complaint; and as time went on, after she had borne children, she, her husband and Diane lived *à trois* very amicably.

She seems to have loved her husband, and been fond of all her children, as long as they were infants, but the only deep affection of her life was for her son Henri. On the accession of François II she was forty-one. A foreign ambassador describes her then as a "tall stout woman with a red face, hair that looked like a wig, pale eyes, big mouth and a rough way of speaking, almost like a peasant woman." But Brantôme, the courtier, looked with kinder eyes; to him her figure though ample—*un embonpoint très riche*—was of a noble carriage, her throat was white and well-rounded, her complexion pink, her countenance agreeable and her hands beautiful,—*la plus belle main qui fut jamais veue.* Evidently she bore herself with dignity, and when she wished, she was gentle and affable. She dressed richly and with care, always wearing something new and attractive, perhaps a hood embroidered with pearls, perhaps wide sleeves of silver cloth trimmed with fur. She was a bold rider and fond of hunting, and though frequently thrown and several times badly hurt, she continued to ride till she was sixty. She enjoyed gaiety, and in her times of good humor she used to chaff and bandy repartees; she also liked good food,—one hears of French dishes, *ratatouille de crêtes, rognons de coq et fonds d'artichauts*—and often ate too much. One might think that a Medici, who had passed her earliest impressionable years in Florence and Rome, who had seen Michelangelo's statue of her father, *Il Penseroso,* and the frescoes in the Sistine Chapel, who was daughter-in-law to François I, would have had a marked taste for art and beautiful things. It seems doubtful if she cared for anything of the sort. She liked jewelry, and she followed the influences of

Catherine de Médicis

Portrait in the Louvre

the prevailing fashion among potentates and princes so far as
to dispossess Diane de Poitiers of the Château de Chenonceaux,
and to do there with greater extravagance, thanks to her
greater means, what Diane would have done; she employed
Philibert Delorme to build a gallery on the bridge across the
river, she doubled the size of the gardens, fetched gardeners
from Italy, and commanded Bernard Palissy to make artificial
rocks for ornamental grottoes.   She bought pictures and
furnishings for her palaces; but there her concern with art
ended.   In her kitchen garden, however, she was much interested, and asked her cousin, the Grand Duke of Tuscany, to
send her Italian gardeners and dairymen, who knew about
cheeses and other products from milk, and about jams, pre-
serves, salads and fruits.

She was very feminine, not as a woman in relation to men,
not as a mother, for she was deficient in these deep elementary
instincts, but in her guiles and blandishments, in her falsehoods
and persuasion, and in her intuitions.

The great interest of her life was power, and the pursuit
of power by political intrigue.   She had scanty imagination,
and little foresight, but delighted in the petty opportunism that
one associates, perhaps wrongly, with sacerdotal politics.   She
flattered, she cajoled, she fawned, she showed her pretty well-
modeled hands, and spoke softly, she blew hot and cold, she
bullied, she browbeat, she promised, she lied, she shifted,
twisted, doubled in her course, and never doubted but that she
was well justified in all she did.   She had no care for the welfare of the Kingdom apart from her, and her sons', rights over
it, nor was she concerned about the religious schism, except as it
upset peace and quiet.   In the attainment of her ends she was
persistent and tenacious; from the very first she sought to

bind persons to her by favors or hopes of favors, and she was tireless; you find these traits throughout the mass of letters that she wrote. One of her practises was to keep in attendance, and take about with her, a great troop of ladies, *l'Escadron volant* as it was called; some thought that the Queen Mother hoped by means of their bright eyes to confirm doubtful followers and win over adversaries, and the Huguenots spoke rudely of these ladies, but Brantôme testifies that Catherine's court was irreproachable and most delightful—*sa cour estoit un vray paradis du monde et escolle de toute honnestete, de vertu, l'ornement de la France,*—and young Montmorency, Vicomte de Turenne, confirms him, and certainly one of these ladies, Hélène de Surgères, whom Ronsard vainly courted, behaved with puritanical propriety.

CHAPTER IV

In 1560 young Henry of Navarre was with his mother in Béarn, aged seven, old enough to perceive that things were going wrong. His parents were drifting rapidly apart; under the stress of the religious crisis their characters revealed a deep incompatibility. While Antoine shilly-shallied and tergiversated, Jeanne's temper became firmer, she took the road her mother had started upon and went farther. She gave attentive ear to Théodore de Bèze and on Christmas Day, 1560, she made public profession of the Protestant faith: "It has pleased God of His mercy," she said, "to drag me out of the idolatry in which I was deeply plunged and to receive me in His church." Calvin wrote her a letter of approval: "Though some good seed was sown in you long ago, you understand now how choked those seeds were by the thorns of this world. Unless we betake ourselves daily to the Holy Scriptures the truth that we once knew oozes away little by little till it is all gone, except that God shall come to our aid. In His infinite wisdom He has seen fit to prevent you from descending to such a pass."

From this time on Jeanne became a champion of the Huguenot cause. Her husband—*suggetto debolissimo* as the Venetian ambassador reported—showed himself as unstable as water. Passed over in the Treaty of Cateau-Cambrésis (1559) which had arranged the quarrels between France and

33

Spain without a word concerning the ravished province of
Spanish Navarre, he had turned to the Protestants. He
gathered their clergy about him and appointed a Calvinist
tutor to his boy. A little later, still inspired by the vain hope
of recovering Spanish Navarre, he took communion in the
Catholic Church (April, 1561) ; and yet, having gone to Paris,
while fasting on Fridays and attending mass on Sundays, he
was writing to his wife to encourage Calvinism in Navarre.
At the same time he was making diligent love to ladies of the
court. Calvin wrote, *"Totus est Venereus,* he is all for women." In June he was a Protestant again; poor man, he
wished to gain provinces or a weightier crown, and did not
know which way to go about it. But decide he must. The
current of events swung him again into Catholicism, and there
he stayed.

That summer, his wife, whether concerned about her husband's behavior or about the fate of the Huguenots, came to
the court at Saint-Germain, bringing her son with her. She
avowed herself a Huguenot, and would not put up with any
pretense, she had her clergy preach to her with all doors open.
She declared that "she would not go to mass if they killed her,
she would sooner throw her son and her kingdom into the sea
than yield . . . that she had liefer endure death than obey
the creature in place of the Creator." She planned a national
Reformed Church, and tried to influence the boy King, young
Charles IX. The Catholics hated her, and heaped epithets on
her head: this "mad Slut," this "furious She Beast," this
"Jezebel," this "Enemy of God," et cetera. But as the Queen
Mother was pursuing a policy of tolerance and balance, and for
the moment even leaning toward the Protestants, Jeanne was
left unmolested. She nailed her flag to the mast, and went so

far as to ask the Queen Mother to bring up Margot as a
Protestant, affecting to show a distaste for the marriage on the
ground that the daughter of a Medici was not a good enough
match for her son.

By this time Henry of Navarre's childhood was over, and a
troubled boyhood lay before him. His body had greatly
profited by his country life and peasant fare; he was not tall,
but supple and sinewy, he had learned to drink hot, drink
cold; to give buffets and take them, and to make light of sun,
wind and rain. He came to court a staunch little Huguenot.
One day when the Queen Mother was receiving the Cardinal
of Ferrara, the door burst open, and a troop of little boys on
donkeys rode into the room, Henry of Navarre at their head,
dressed up as prelates with cassocks, rochets and mitres. The
Spanish ambassador wrote a solemn account of the affair to
Philip II. For his studies, Henry of Navarre had a most respectable tutor, La Gaucherie, a Calvinist, an intelligent teacher,
austere and possibly a little priggish. In order to learn Latin
and conduct simultaneously, Henri was made to copy out pious
sentences: "The prince that reigns over a great kingdom, but
lets his passions tyrannize over him, is but a crowned slave"
and such. He made a translation of Cæsar's *Commentaries,*
which the famous humanist, old Casaubon, so he says, looked
at with admiration. And Julius Scaliger testified that Henry
was well aware if Latin was spoken badly in his presence.
But these compliments were paid after Henry became King.
He also read Plutarch's *Lives,* I presume in Jacques Amyot's
translation; and he learned from his pious tutor to use no more
objectionable oath than *Ventre-saint-gris.*

This régime lasted but a year; for political troubles, that
interrupted much else, interrupted it also. The Massacre at

Vassy had been followed by the flight of Condé, and by the submission of the Queen Mother to the Catholic leaders. Antoine ordered his wife to leave the court. She obeyed, and was obliged to leave her boy behind. Both were distressed by the separation. The boy wrote to one of the officers of her escort:

Paris, September 26, 1562.

Larchant,

Write me news of the Queen, my mother, in order to put me out of anxiety, for I am very much afraid that some harm may come to her on this journey. The greatest pleasure you can give me is to send me news frequently. God speed you and bring you back safe. Good-by.

HENRY.

At parting Jeanne had adjured him to remain firm in the new faith. But no sooner had she gone, than Antoine took control. He dismissed La Gaucherie, put a Catholic in his place, sent the boy to the very orthodox Collège de Navarre, in company with young Henri, Duc d'Anjou, who afterward, as Pierre Matthieu says, *"fut son Roy,"* and young Henri de Guise *"qui le voulait estre,"* and in short, spared no pains to force him back into Catholicism. For two months the boy held out against blandishments, scoldings and whippings, but at last yielded, and swore to live and die in the holy Catholic faith; he was rewarded by being made a King of the Order of Saint Michael. He was nine years old.

The parents had parted for ever. Jeanne was collecting men and money in Béarn for the Prince de Condé, while Antoine as Lieutenant-General assumed command of the

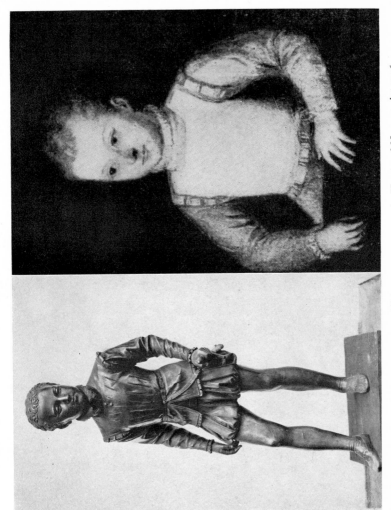

a. Statue of Henry of Navarre as a child

In the Louvre

b. Henry of Navarre in 1556

Catholic forces. The country was upside down; there were "stabbings, stonings, stranglings, burnings, deaths from hunger, burials alive, drownings and smotherings"; and yet both sides shrank from actual battle. The two brothers entered into negotiations and were near an agreement, but Philip II dangled Sardinia before Antoine's eyes, and his personal interest blinded him. Fighting began; the Royalists captured Bourges and advanced to the siege of Rouen. Old Montmorency and the Duc de Guise served under Bourbon. During the slow progress of the siege, Antoine, whose personal bravery was beyond question, went up to the front trench; his page, while handing him a cup, was killed, then a captain by his side, and he, in his turn, was hit by a bullet in the shoulder. Ten days later the city was taken and sacked; Huguenots and Catholics, men, women and children, churches and shops, were all treated alike. Bourbon was carried in on a litter through a breach in the walls; but his end was near. Even on his death-bed he was still negotiating with King Philip, while his latest love, Louise de la Béraudière de l'Isle-Rouet ministered to him. A Huguenot physician attended the dying man, and read to him from the Bible the passage in which Saint Paul bids wives obey their husbands. "You see," said the sick man, "that God wishes wives to obey their husbands." "Yes," the physician answered, "but he also says, 'Husbands, love your wives.'" The King listened to further counsels, and said that, if God permitted him to live, he would have the Gospel preached according to the Augsburg Confession throughout his Kingdom. His last words were to an attendant: "Serve my son well, and let him serve his King well." (November 16, 1562.)

CHAPTER V

IT IS said that on the news of her husband's wound Jeanne proposed to hurry to his bedside, but delay in obtaining a safe-conduct, or knowledge that other hands were taking care of him, delayed her until it was too late. She then gave herself up wholly to the Huguenot cause, collecting men, money and materials for the army. So bitter was she, that in moments of leisure she ripped up a design in her mother's tapestry that depicted a priest elevating the host, and crocheted a fox in the priest's place. Her support of the pastors from Geneva enabled them to multiply their flocks. The Catholics in Béarn sent up cries of alarm: in one town they said, "there are six thousand blasphemers" here; in a second, "the wolf has entered into our garden, he protests that he will not listen to the stinking mass"; in a third "this region is the worst of all, *le plus infecté de cette vilenie.*"

Nevertheless, the Queen Mother, still trying to conciliate, would not break with Jeanne. She refused to let her have her son, but allowed her to reassume control of his education, with the consequence that La Gaucherie was reinstated as tutor, and she conferred on the boy the governorship of Guyenne (a derisive appointment, to be sure, as it was coupled with that of Montluc a zealous Catholic as Lieutenant-Governor), gave him also pay as captain of fifty men-at-arms, and a little later the command of a hundred lances, posts and emoluments that his

father had held before him. As Henry was but ten years old,
these honors and offices made no difference in his life. Except
for temporary indisposition from an attack of measles, for
which his physicians administered rhubarb and pills in bouillon,
he passed his days as before, with Latin, Plutarch, riding, *jeu
de paume* and other exercises, until the Queen Mother took
him traveling with her. She and Chancellor l'Hôpital had conceived a plan for strengthening the royal authority. She
should make a tour of France, show the young King to his
subjects, and win sympathy for his youth and inexperience, or,
as officially expressed, *pour coignoistre ses bons et loyaux subjects, et pour soy donner à coignoistre à eulx.*

Young Harry of Navarre went with them, as the Queen
Mother was unwilling to leave him behind, and on the tour,
which lasted two years, got the beginnings of that knowledge
of the French provinces as well as certain precocious political
experience, both of which were to serve him in such good stead
in later life. After the journey Harry, now thirteen years
old, returned to his mother and his native Kingdom.

Béarn is a little country, some fifty miles from north to
south and sixty from east to west, and lies at the foot of the
Pyrenees shut in between them and Gascony, which bounds it on
the north. Little rivers or torrents, the Gave de Pau, Gave
d'Oloron, Gave de Mauléon, the Nive and their fellows, run
down from the mountains through the valleys between the
foot-hills, and empty into the Adour, which, starting above the
Bagnères-de-Bigorre, circles north of Béarn round through
Gascony to the ocean. In Roman times the route from Spain
crossed the Pyrenees at the Somport, near the source of the
Gave d'Aspe; and all through the Middle Ages the Pilgrims'
Road to St. James of Compostela traversed the pass of Ron-

cevaux. These and other passes into Spain gave the little kingdom whatever political importance it had; but the upper valleys of alluvial soil made admirable pastures, and the plains below, gay with grassy meadows, fields of grain, and poplar groves, were fertile and rich. Farther down the Gave de Pau, near Orthez, quarries of limestone furnished excellent material for castles, walls and ramparts. There were forests well stocked with wild beasts and birds; there were vineyards at Jurançon and elsewhere. So that the little well-watered state of mountain and plain was well-nigh self-sufficient.

Here Harry stayed for a year and a half. He studied with Florent Chrétien, a man of letters, whom he did not like much, received religious instruction from Huguenot divines, rode, hunted, and led the healthy, rough, outdoor life that he loved so dearly. His mother set about her self-imposed task of uprooting Catholicism, and planting the reformed religion in its place, with redoubled vigor. And she might have abolished Catholicism altogether, if her council had not been afraid of a general uprising. As it was, she destroyed the holy images in several places; and in many ways outraged the feelings of some Catholic gentlemen more than they could bear. A plot was contrived. Some said that it proposed to get possession of the Queen and her two children, and to suppress Protestant worship. Others went further and said that the conspirators meant to massacre the Protestants while taking communion at Pentecost. The country was much disturbed, and an open revolt actually occurred. Here young Harry had his first military experience. The Queen gave him command, nominally at least, of the royal troops, and he rode against the rebels at the head of a goodly company of loyal gentry. The rebels took fright, and fled across the Spanish border at Val Carlos between Roncevaux and Saint-Jean-Pied-de-Port. Young Harry ordered the people of the neighborhood to come together and, by means of a Basque interpreter, harangued them. They had done very wrong, he said, to follow or abet these seditious men, who at the mere whiff and wind of the coming of the Queen's troops had fled, frightened still more by their consciences, and had left the countryside exposed to the depredations of alien soldiers. Happily for them the merciful Queen had taken them under her protection. Had the Queen refused to listen to their complaints, there might have been some justification for taking up arms, but as her doors and ears were always open, they had no excuse whatever. Nevertheless, if they would show themselves good subjects, the Queen would not change their laws or customs, nor interfere with their religion, until God of His mercy should bring them to a knowledge of the truth, for which he prayed devoutly. The people listened attentively, cheered loudly and promised never to be misled again. Three ringleaders among the gentry were hanged, but the rest were pardoned at the intercession of Charles IX.

If Jeanne could now feel easy as to her enemies in Béarn, it was not so with respect to her enemies outside. There was Catherine de Médicis in France, and Philip II in Spain. She was especially apprehensive of the Cardinal of Lorraine, who was the Huguenot arch-bugbear; she believed the "damnable" Cardinal of Lorraine capable of "all felonies and execrable wickedness," and whenever news came, as it often did, of "massacres, acts of injustice, or violations of the *Edict of Pacification*," she attributed them to the "plots, the treacheries, the comings and goings of the Cardinal and of our sly, Hispanified politicians." Another evil-doer was Blaise Montluc, the Lieu-

tenant-Governor of Guyenne, who paid no deference whatever to his nominal chief, Henry of Navarre, but was aiding
the Catholics and harrying the Protestants to the best of
his ability. Jeanne, although she had already remonstrated in
vain with Catherine, now wrote to the King a letter of complaint. "My son," she said, "is old enough now to take part in
the government of Guyenne, and he should, so that when he is
older he shall be more competent," and she begged their
Majesties to permit him to make a tour through the principal
cities of the province in order to enforce the *Edict of Pacification.* Young Harry wrote, also; he was beginning to wish to
be his own master:

July 7, 1568.

Monseigneur:

I do not wish to fail so far in my duty as not to send a
letter together with my mother's to recall myself to your
favor, and to beg to remind you very humbly, that, if there
are some persons who do not entertain the affection for me
that you do, and under pretext of my youth try to prevent me
from exercising the honorable charge of the government of
Guyenne, which you conferred on me, you will nevertheless
permit me to refer to this matter, in accordance with my
mother's explanation and request. It seems to me, Monseigneur, since I have the honor to be First Prince of the
Blood, and feel an extreme desire to be of service to your
Majesty, like my predecessors, that it is high time for me to
prove my good-will; as I will do always with my life and all
the means that God gives me.

Monseigneur, I beg our Creator to bestow upon you perfect

health and happiness and a long life. I present my very humble
respects.

Your very humble and obedient servant
HENRY.

As was to be expected, the Queen Mother replied that
Harry was too young, he should be at court with the King,
amusing himself with games and sports appropriate to his age,
and she invited the Queen to bring him. She also sent an
envoy, La Mothe-Fénelon, to urge persuasive arguments:
Jeanne should be mediatrix between the two religious parties,
and so forth. But Jeanne not only did not believe what
Catherine and her envoy said, but on the contrary she and
all the Huguenots were convinced that this invitation to Paris
was another plot to catch her and her children.

It was now toward the end of the summer of 1568, and
her suspicions were confirmed, for word reached her at Nérac,
about the first of September, that her brother-in-law, the
Prince de Condé, and Admiral Coligny had narrowly escaped
being kidnaped by the Royalists, and had fled to La Rochelle
for safety. She promptly decided that that was the safest
place, too, for Harry and her. Besides, she was tired, she
said, to see her son at his age among petticoats, *parmy les
femmes,* and wished him to draw his sword "for the glory of
God, the service of his King and the good of his Country."
La Mothe-Fénelon tried to persuade Harry not to go. Harry
replied that he was going to join his Uncle Condé in order to
save the expenses of family mourning, for if the Princes of
the Blood were put to death one by one, mourning would cost
the survivors much money, but if they were all killed together,
there would be no expense whatever. And, he added, "I know

who started this conflagration in France, and I could put it out
with one bucket of water." "How so?" "By making the
Cardinal de Lorraine drink till he burst."

So Jeanne went, taking Harry and her young nephew,
Condé's son. On their way to La Rochelle she wrote another
letter to the Queen Mother:

Bergerac, September 16, 1568.

Madam:

Here are my motives for going to La Rochelle: First; for
God's service, since it is clear that M. le Cardinal de Lorraine
and his accomplices wish to sweep from the earth all who prefer the true religion: Second, for the King's service even at the
expense of life and property, in order that the *Edict of Pacification* shall be observed according to his will, and that our
country, France, mother of so many noble men, shall not be
sucked dry and her children die; Third: for the tie of blood,
that calls us to the aid of M. le Prince, my brother, since he
contrary to the King's wish has been chased away by malignant
men, who have too long usurped places not theirs by right,
who shut your eyes to their wickedness, and stop your ears
from hearing our complaints."

When they reached La Rochelle the magistrates of the
town came out to felicitate the young Prince of the Blood:
"Gentlemen," Harry replied, "I have not followed my studies
far enough to be able to speak as well as you do, but take my
word for it, if I do not speak well, I shall act better, for I
know much better how to act than to speak." He had a hard
road ahead of him, but for his age he was well prepared. His

Gaspard de Coligny, Admiral of France

wit was ready. His constitution was excellent; his body had
the physical vigor of a young mountaineer, it had been developed and hardened by all sorts of exercise, he was accustomed to spend hours in the saddle, and come home disgust-
ingly wet and sweating, *tout dégoûtant de pluie et de sueur.*
He was not yet fifteen but he was now a man; and at La
Rochelle his mother felt that it was time for him and her to
part. She said: "Those who think of me only as a woman and
a mother, and my son as a boy delicately nurtured at home,
will imagine that many tears were shed at our parting. But,
that everybody may learn my feelings in consecrating him to
so noble a work, I will say that joy laughed in our eyes and
was stamped on our faces. The satisfaction of parting in such
a cause quite overcame all the weakness of sex, of age and
relationship. He went his way, and I stayed at La Rochelle
only too happy to suffer for my God."

The campaign of *les troisièmes troubles* as this third civil
war is called, began as soon as the rigor of winter had abated.
The two armies met at Jarnac, on the Charente (March 13,
1569). The Huguenot army was too far extended; the
Catholics, under the actual guidance of Tavannes, an experienced soldier, though young Anjou was the nominal General,
were better handled, and caught Coligny with the Huguenot
rear-guard at a disadvantage. Condé (I quote from d'Aubigné's account) flying his pennon with the device, *Doux le
péril pour Christ et le pays,* was leading his cavalry to the
rescue of Coligny when a friend's horse dashed into him and
broke his leg so badly that a splinter of the bone stuck through
his boot. He shouted out: "Here, Gentlemen of France, is
the occasion we have longed for! Come on! and remember in
what plight Louis de Bourbon goes into battle for Christ and

Country." His men were worsted, and his horse killed under him, so he surrendered, and was then shot treacherously by one of Anjou's officers who came up from behind. Coligny, however, drew off the bulk of the army in safety.

The death of his uncle made Henry of Navarre the oldest Prince of the Blood, as well as the First, and he became a person of considerably greater consequence. The day after the defeat, in recognition of his new position, Jeanne presented him to the soldiers, and he made oath, on his soul, his honor and his life, never to abandon them. He was acclaimed with enthusiasm. From that day he accompanied the army, first to the field of Moncontour, where Coligny was defeated again (October 3, 1569), and then on a long perilous retreat to the south of France, where Coligny was joined by the Huguenot chief, Montgomery, who had triumphantly cleared Béarn of Catholic invaders, and from there eastward and northward again.

The march was considered a brilliant affair and enhanced Coligny's reputation, but indeed it was a sorry story, as may be seen by the narrative of one brief stage of it. "The *Hugeneaux* were not content with assuming authority over person and property, they killed, they massacred, they ravished married women and virgins, they took all they could find, they set fire to monasteries and churches, to farms and granges, they made even the poorest laborers and their children prisoners, and in order to extort ransom, hung them up, weighted with a billet, by a cord around their heads, strung them up by the thumbs, or kindled a fire under their feet." Such was the education of Henry of Navarre at an age when most boys are still at school.

After a few months, both sides got tired of massacre and

pillage, of foreign mercenaries and of the self-seeking interference of foreign princes, and peace was again made on the
former basis, granting the Huguenots liberty of conscience and
permission to worship in those places in which they had
worshiped before the war (August, 1570).

CHAPTER VI

MARRIAGE

CHARLES IX was now twenty years old. After a sickly boyhood he developed a variable and disquieting disposition. He had times of lassitude and depression, and then wild bursts of physical energy; he loved the chase and would gallop furiously; and in Paris, at the Louvre, he would beat hot irons on his anvil like a smith, and swear, and vow that swearing was a mark of courage in a young man. Up to now he had meekly obeyed his mother; she wished him to be a bureaucrat and a politician, to make himself acquainted with the important people, to keep a list of all vacant posts and of persons deserving patronage, to give balls, to join in sports, not for friendship but from policy, to receive the high nobility at dressing and undressing; all which doings brought on reactions of intense irritation. He had taste for none of these things; on the contrary, he liked poetry and sundry other branches of literature. He used to slip away in the evening by nine or ten o'clock, saying that he was going to work on a book. Jeanne says that he really went to visit his mistress and would stay with her till the small hours of the morning. But Ronsard asserts that the King loved horses, dogs and sportsmen, and in order not to poison his youth with amours and gay living, devoted himself to the chase, and was writing a book on that subject, which would have been excellent, had he lived to finish it. And altogether Ronsard is full of his praises:

48

Charles en qui les Dieux
Tout leur mieux
Pour chef d'œuvre firent naistre,—

Charles in whom the Gods did their best to make a master-
piece.

Charles, en qui le ciel toutes graces inspire,—
Qui a le cœur plus grand que n'est grand ton Empire,
Une âme prompte et vive, un esprit généreux
De vertus, de science, et d'honneur amoureux.

Ordinarily, when a poet says that a King possesses all the
favors heaven can grant, that his heart is as large as his
kingdom, that he is sensitive, generous, and a lover of knowledge and honor, his words are ascribed to flattery; but Ronsard's tone does not change when the King dies. In his life-
time he calls him *victorieux et sage,* and after his death *en
vertus nonpareil.* The King's sister Margot also says that the
King's soul was *grande et royale;* and his confessor called him a
prince *débonnaire, piteux et plein de toute générosité.* Clouet's
picture portrays a pensive, listless, gloomy young man, as if
suspicion were whispering in one ear and doubt in the other;
but on the other hand there is a bust by Germain Pilon which
represents him, somewhat older, as a man of intelligence and
cultivation, and with the look of one who, though suspicious,
means to be master in his own house.

The King's arrival at manhood made his mother's task
very much more difficult. He allowed her to hold the rudder
of state, but now and again he would seize it and shift the
course to suit his momentary mood, and then he would run
back to the chase or to his smithy and leave her to be pilot
again. She found this no easy matter. Between the Catholic

fanatics and the Huguenot fanatics, even the Crown was in danger. On the one hand there was the Cardinal de Lorraine and his nephew, young Henri de Guise, with their excessive orthodoxy and high ambitions; on the other, Admiral Coligny, the real chief of the Huguenots, and young Henry of Navarre, First Prince of the Blood, the nominal head, already heretics and nearly ready to be rebels. Catherine had tried all the expedients she knew; she had devised a method of reconciliation, and that had failed; she had attempted a policy of balance, leaning the power of the Crown toward the side that seemed the weaker, and that had failed; and then her thoughts turned toward complete union with the Catholics and destruction of the Huguenot party. But there was doubt and danger in all these policies, and she liked to keep all doors open. At the time when she had thought the wisest plan was to adopt a purely Catholic policy, she had proposed to Philip II of Spain marriages between her children and his. Philip had refused. This rebuff obliged her to take a new tack. She now proposed Protestant marriages: Margot should marry Henry of Navarre, according to her husband's plan, and her son Henri, Duc d'Anjou, should marry Queen Elizabeth. Margot might induce Navarre to become a Catholic, and Anjou Elizabeth; but if not, this accession of Protestant strength would enable her to balance the preponderance of the Catholics and the pride of the House of Guise.

This new plan did not receive too cordial a welcome. Queen Elizabeth felt sure that Anjou would be a charming and delightful husband, but there were the Cecils and others to be consulted, and she must take time to consider. And Jeanne d'Albret, on her part, was now full of covenanting spirit, and declared herself little minded to have her son marry a Papist.

Besides, her Huguenot ministers were even more opposed than she: God had forbidden, they said, the Children of Israel to marry idolaters, and though Catholicism was not exactly idolatry still it was so corrupt that very little of the true worship of God remained in it; young Henry was no wiser than Solomon and might be won over by the blandishments of his wife to join the Roman Church; furthermore, the French court was Machiavellian and held out false promises as they would apples to children. The Pope, also, and Philip II were scandalized and protested.

There was unwillingness, too, on Margot's part. She was now nineteen years old, six months older than Navarre, and had seen enough of life to know what kind of man she wished to marry. Brantôme, who was a man of thirty-five at the time, describes her in the language of a lover: "If ever there was a perfect beauty, it is she. Her features are beautiful, their lines admirable, her eyes are clear and most agreeable . . . and this handsome face is set upon a most superb figure, her carriage and majesty of bearing is such that she seems rather a goddess from heaven than an earthly princess." He praises her courage, her determination, her generosity, her cultivation, her powers of conversation, and says that her letters put "poor Cicero's *Epistolæ familiares*" to shame. He exhausts his rhetoric upon her coiffure and her dress, and Ronsard is as flowery as Brantôme; he describes her as more beautiful than Venus, her head is divine, a miracle of nature, and he gives even more amorous attention than Brantôme to her coiffure, heaping up hair-dressing eulogies difficult to render in English,

Cheveux ondelez
Nouëz, retors, recrespez, annelez,

and then flatters her tender, delicate little ear, the dimple in her chin, and her tiny feet. Don John of Austria, the hero of Lepanto, who knew what he was talking about, said that the conquest of such a lady was worth more than a kingdom. The portrait at Chantilly, if not so eloquent, shows a white skin, black hair and deep brown eyes.

This Princess, however, so gossips said, had not set her affection on Henry of Navarre, but on Henri de Guise, who now comes forward on the French stage, fitted in mind and body for a great part, and confident that he will fill it, as his father had done before him. Guise's grandmother was a Bourbon, and he was, therefore, second cousin to Navarre; his mother was Anne d'Este, granddaughter of Louis XII. He was tall, slender and very strong, with the physical elegance of a statue by Lysippus. As la Maréchale de Retz said, "These Guises made other princes look plebeian." His body had been trained by all sorts of exercises: he could swim in all his accouterments against a heavy current, and he wrestled, jousted, fenced or wielded his broadsword with the greatest dash and dexterity. Ease was in his manner and grace in every gesture. He was "generous to profusion, affable, eloquent, and with a marvelous sweetness of manner," and he sought popularity; in later years he made a point of attending weddings, baptisms and funerals, he never spoke ill of anybody and was courteous to all. Ambition was his master trait, his *âme toute guerrière,* was *patiente de tout, hormis de ne point régner,*—his warlike spirit could not brook being second to any man. Even as a little boy he displayed these traits. When Margot was four or five and he six or seven, she told her father that she preferred another boy for "cavalier" because "he is more self-controlled, while Henri de Guise loses his temper, and always wants to be

master." In a letter which he wrote to his father at the age
of seven, he says:

Monseigneur,

I heard some fine sermons that my uncle the Cardinal
preached at Reims. He had me carry his amice before him,
and asked me if I should not like to be a canon; but I told him
that I had rather be beside you and break a lance or a sword
on some brave Spaniard or Burgundian, to find out if I have a
good arm, for I had much rather fence and break lances than
wear a frock and always be shut in an abbey.

Your very humble and obedient son
PRINCE OF JOINVILLE.

The boy, with his *biondi crini,* as an Italian says, is described as beautiful as an angel. When the father, murdered
by a Huguenot assassin, lay on his death-bed, he called this
beautiful boy to his side and gave him his last counsels: "May
God have mercy upon you, my Son, and make you an upright
man. Ah, my darling Boy, keep the love and fear of God
always in your heart and before your eyes and walk in the
strait and narrow path." If the father meant him to be loyal
to the Roman Catholic faith, well did the son obey his wishes.
Now, he was a young man of twenty-one or two, in all the
splendor of manly beauty. He had fair curly hair, a noble
forehead, blue eyes that sparkled, a smiling mouth, a delicate
mustache, a carefully pointed, close-clipped, blond beard, and
later he got, in an hour of victory, a scar from eye to ear,
that won for him, like his father, the title *le Balafre.* He was a
captivating man, *fort caressé des dames.* In later life the
Catholics came to adore him. Guy de Balzac, who lived in the

next generation but was conversant with Guise's reputation says: "It is too little to say that France was in love with him; France was mad about him." Between him and Henry of Navarre, who had a plain face, a Gascon accent and rustic manners, Margot's fancy had not hesitated; and gossip, untrustworthy always in such matters, went very far. It can hardly be doubted but that she would rather have married Guise; and the ambitious Cardinal de Lorraine, whose sister had married a King of Scotland, and his niece a King of France, wished for the match. But both the Queen Mother and Charles detested the Cardinal, and were very angry at the idea. It is said that they fell upon the poor girl and drubbed her with their own royal hands. Young Guise took the hint, and married elsewhere.

Charles IX was at this time in one of his fits of self-assertion. He disliked Philip of Spain intensely, he resented his interference, and arrogant assumption of superiority, and was ready to join almost anybody in opposition to Spain. But before bearding Philip II, he wished to have a united nation at his back, and hoped to win over the whole Huguenot party by this marriage of his sister with its titular head. Margot, though she protested that she did not want to marry a man not of her religion, was given to understand that she must. Jeanne, too, consented, for it was eminently expedient in such uncertain times that Henry should marry into the reigning family; for neither the King, nor the heir apparent, Henri of Anjou, had children, and the soothsayer, Nostradamus, had prophesied that the Valois family would die out, and then Henry of Navarre, the next of kin, a Protestant, would need all the support for his claim that he could get. So, with some misgivings, Jeanne went to discuss the matter with Catherine

and the King, leaving Harry behind, to look after a bitch
that had lately littered and some other affairs, and to make fun
of the proposed marriage in his rough Gascon peasant fashion,
saying, with a pointed reference to what gossip said of Margot
and young Guise, that *"il seroit le cocu de la cause."* On her
way she passed not very far from the Château de Montaigne
by the River Dordogne, to which Michel Eyquem had withdrawn on his thirty-eighth birthday the year before, in order to
dedicate what remained of his life to "liberty, leisure and tranquillity." Little did she suspect that her son's sword and Montaigne's pen would be the two greatest factors in the cause of
religious tolerance.

Jeanne was received by the King and his mother in friendly
fashion. Matters proceeded smoothly at first, but not for long.
Jeanne was *prompte et perilleuse,* quite ready to take offense,
and not without a good share of *Béarnais brusquerie,* and
began by asking that Margot should become a Protestant.
Catherine was irritated, and pretended to be indifferent to the
marriage even to the point of making a mock of Jeanne; at
least Jeanne thought so, and she wrote indignantly to Henry
that the Queen would never see her alone; that she would laugh,
turn the conversation to jest, assert that Jeanne had said things
that she herself had said, and deny saying things that she had
said; that they had set about her nominal Huguenots and
people facing-both-ways as spies, *armaphroidites religieux,*
until she was almost ready to burst in her efforts to keep her
temper. Of Margot she writes: "She is handsome, sensible,
and of good manners, but brought up in the most corrupt and
accursed society that ever was. I would not have you live in
it for all the world. That is why I want to see you married,
so that you and your wife can get away from this rottenness.

I had believed it was very bad, but I find it even worse. It's not the men that solicit the women, but the women that solicit the men. If you were here, you could never escape without the special grace of God." In another letter she says: "Margot has a handsome figure, but laces too tight, as to her face she helps it out so much that she vexes me, for she will spoil it," nevertheless she admits that rouge is very common at the French court. Little Catherine, Jeanne's daughter, wrote to her brother: "Monsieur, I have seen Madame [Margot] whom I thought very handsome. I wish that you could have seen her. I spoke up well for you so that she should take you into her good graces, and she promised me that she would. She was very sweet to me and gave me a nice little dog that I like ever so much."

At last, however, terms were arranged; the *dot* was agreed on, Margot should remain a Catholic, Henry should not be present at mass, the Cardinal de Bourbon should celebrate the marriage not as a priest but as a prince (whatever that meant) and not within the church but on a scaffolding outside, and so forth. Jeanne added more pearls to her own attire, as befitted the mother-in-law of a daughter of France, and wrote to her son a little maternal advice as to what his behavior should be: "Don't be afraid to speak boldly; for, remember you will establish your reputation at your first coming. Get the habit of brushing your hair up, but not *à la mode de Nérac*. Be sure that your jackets have skirts, and (according to my judgment) you should follow the latest fashion." Then, after all had been settled, Jeanne went to Paris to do the necessary shopping. While there, in the beginning of June, 1572, she fell suddenly ill and died on the ninth.

Henry, who had been delayed by sickness, learned the news

Charles IX
Portrait of the Clouet school

as he was journeying through Poitou, on his way to the French court. Suspicions of foul play were rife, nevertheless he continued on, attended by a body of eight hundred Huguenots, and entered Paris in company with Coligny, his young cousin the Prince de Condé and Monsieur de la Rochefoucauld. The autopsy was explicit that his mother's death had been natural, but the Huguenots looked upon Catherine as capable of any wickedness, royal physicians may be tampered with, and many believed that Jeanne had been poisoned. Everybody told Henry that he must be on his guard. He was young, however, and had a valiant heart; and probably was glad to get away from the austere sectaries of Béarn, and taste the pleasures of a gay court, and not particularly alarmed by his mother's account of its corruption.

In honor of the wedding there were great doings, banquets, balls, fêtes and gaieties of all sorts, and on August eighteenth the marriage service was celebrated, according to the agreement, on a scaffolding draped with cloth of gold erected in front of the chief western portal of Notre-Dame. The company was all in glorious attire; three princesses held up the bride's five yards of blue velvet train, and Cardinal de Bourbon officiated. After this ceremony the groom led the bride by a wooden gallery up the nave to the choir, where she was to hear mass, and then withdrew. At the Louvre that night there was one of those pageants that the court of Valois delighted in, gods, sea monsters, chariots, artificial rocks, musicians and poets. Ronsard, who had written the epithalamium for Henry's father, wrote verses for the son:

> *A ton chemain la paix servait de guide*
> *Et ce bon Dieu qui aux nopces preside,*
> *Pour assembler d'un lien amoureux*

La belle au beau, jeunesse à la jeunesse
La bonne au bon, le Prince à la Princesse,
Qui vit jamais un accord plus heureux?

—Peace was the guide that led you on your way,
And Hymen, who brings round the marriage day,
Brought her to you and you to her;
Youth to youth, love unto loveliness,
Good unto good, the Prince to the Princess
Who ever saw a union happier?

Ronsard did not undertake to answer his question, and probably many present entertained their doubts; however, as far as outward show went there was great happiness and content.

CHAPTER VII

SAINT BARTHOLOMEW

THE marriage had been King Charles's doing. While reciting Ronsard's verses, while riding with the hounds, while ringing blows on the anvil in the basement of the Louvre, he had meditated over the thought that this marriage between the head of the Huguenots and an orthodox daughter of France would be a step toward freeing him from daily care, from his mother's urgency, from his brother Anjou's jealousy. It was an immense annoyance, that visionaries, sourbellies, disappointed benefice-seekers, German beer drinkers, crack-brained scholars, and whatever they were, had split Europe in two with their theological differences. If the rough Teutonic peoples of northern Europe had not sufficient good sense to accept Truth, as it had been established and reestablished, time after time by divinely guided Popes and Councils, at least France, the most intelligent, sensible and right-minded of nations, might have kept out of the horrid mess. But facts must be looked in the face. Europe was split in halves, and the consequences were mightily disagreeable. Philip II, clinking his gold and silver from Mexico and Peru, and posing as the champion of orthodoxy, had become an odious bully; it was intolerable to have him telling France what to do and what not to do; he affected to be aiming at the restoration of Catholicism throughout Europe, but he really aimed at universal empire. How untoward it was that a King of France

could not hammer on his anvil, or hunt in the woods round
Fontainebleau, or talk of metaphors and rhymes with Ronsard, without being bothered by all this hurly-burly of heresy,
viciousness and folly.   At any rate France must be saved
from further civil war.   So Charles had decided to reconcile
the two factions by the marriage of his sister, a beautiful
flirtatious girl, to this rather uncouth, but promising lad, head
of the Huguenots.

An unexpected event accompanied the pursuit of this policy.
Admiral Coligny, heretic and rebel, came to court.   Coligny
was the first man, as measured by manhood, in the Kingdom;
he was endowed with rare honesty, courage, foresight, patience
and unselfishness.   The King had never met a man of so high
a character, of so much political wisdom, of so much not easily
explained charm, and turned to him with trust and expansive-
ness, as he had never turned to anybody before.   Coligny was
more than delighted.   He, too, felt that here was the opportunity to close the dreadful breach between Frenchmen and
Frenchmen, by union against a common enemy.   William of
Orange had raised the Dutch in revolt against Spain; it was a
struggle for freedom against tyranny, for manhood against
slavery, and offered a most acceptable opportunity to take advantage of Protestant allies against the overweening power
of the bully of Europe, and the Huguenots were hot to go to
help the insurgents.   If French Catholics and French Huguenots should march shoulder to shoulder against Spain, the
whole country, except a few traitorous fanatics, would cheer,
and after victory had been achieved, Holland liberated, Spain
humiliated, and France victorious, the soldiers would go back
to their homes, arm in arm, they would sit in taverns side by
side, clink their glasses, strip their sleeves and show their scars,

and then separate to go, some to the parish church, some to the Calvinist conventicle, and then when worship was over, meet again as loving friends.

It was a fine prospect. But one great political personage in the State would suffer by it. The Queen Mother was jealous of Coligny's influence; he disliked her, and distrusted her; and she knew it, for his honesty, in spite of his able statecraft, was all too frank in the ordinary dealings of life. If Coligny's plans should be realized he would be the King's director, and his first act would be to send Catherine to the Château of Chenonceaux to ply the distaff, or perhaps back, in utter humiliation, to Florence to be jeered at by the laughter-loving Florentines. No; Coligny should not be suffered to carry out his plans. Besides, Spain was vastly stronger than France in money, in men, munitions and in ships, and if Spain defeated France, Philip might oust the House of Valois and put on the throne one of his own family, or it might be, his trusty Spanish henchman, the Duke of Guise. Catherine could not understand why Charles did not see this danger; he certainly would, were it not for Coligny. That visionary man had an extraordinary way of clothing his wild imaginings in a matter-of-fact garb; he was very dangerous and must be put out of the way.

Catherine had powerful allies who were quite of her way of thinking. The House of Guise nursed a blood feud against the House of Châtillon. Nine years before, a Huguenot, one of Coligny's men, had treacherously murdered François de Guise. Coligny had denied the murder, but said he was glad of it. It would have been less insulting, so they thought, had he spoken up and acknowledged his guilt; he had lied, probably because his heretic priests had advised him to do so. Men bred upon falsehood, upon denials of divine truth, men that

were renegades to their God, followers of Judas, worse than
Turks, would ruin the Crown, the House of Guise, France itself, if they were not stopped. The Guises made up their
minds definitely; Coligny must be killed.

Others of the Queen Mother's counselors were in accord.
The ambitious Anjou, who prided himself on his soldiership,
wanted Coligny out of the way; and two able, scruple-free
Italians, Birague and Gondi, said that there was nothing else
to do. They all certainly would gain favor thereby with Philip
and with the Pope. The Queen Mother's purposes were deeper
than those of the others, for she hoped to have Coligny killed
by the Guises, and reasoned that the Huguenots would then
take vengeance, and Châtillons, Guises and all extreme fanatics
on both sides be happily removed from a world in which they
made so much trouble for the House of Valois. So plans were
laid. The Guises had in their pay the very man for the deed,
and as no time was to be lost, the hireling was at once stationed
in a room that looked out on the street that Coligny would take
on his way home from the Louvre. Four days after the
wedding, on Friday, August twenty-second, at half past ten
in the morning, Coligny left a Council meeting in the Louvre,
walked out of an east gate, taking a little street that led round
Saint-Germain-l'Auxerrois on his way to his house, met the
King coming from chapel, and returned with him to the *jeu
de paume,* where the King was to play a set with Henri de
Guise, Téligny, a son-in-law of Coligny, and a fourth. He
then walked back, reading a memorial. As he was turning
from the Rue des Poullies to enter the Rue des Fossés-Saint-
Germain, the assassin fired from his ambush, and wounded him
in the hand and arm.

The wounded man was put to bed in his house. Henry of

François de Guise
Portrait attributed to Du Moustier

Navarre, young Condé, and many Huguenot gentlemen came
to see him. Some feared a general massacre and wished to
remove him from the city, others thought flight unnecessary;
Navarre, Condé and Téligny asserted their confidence in the
King, and besides, it would be dangerous to move the patient.
The King, highly incensed, swore that he would take memora-
ble vengeance on the assassin and all his abettors. The Queen
Mother did not lose her presence of mind; she protested that
it was a great outrage and that, if they put up with it, the
assassin might attack the King himself in the Louvre. The
occasion demanded heights, and she rose to that of Lady Mac-
beth. She had to think fast: Coligny was alive, his friends
were furious, already the Huguenots were buzzing about the
Louvre like angry wasps, vowing vengeance; if she hesitated,
they would discover that she had instigated the murder, the
King's anger would turn against her, and anything might
happen, he might exile her, imprison her, or the Huguenots
might kill her, and they might kill the King, too, and the
House of Valois would go down in blood and hideous confusion. She, Anjou, Henri de Guise and the subtle-minded
Italians hastily met and talked to the point. Coligny must be
finished, and not only he, but his abettors, yes, all the Huguenots in Paris, and happily these were many, come from all
over France to witness the wedding; indeed, they must be
thorough, and kill all the Huguenots in the provinces, too, and
so save the King, save themselves, save France.

It was now Saturday, the twenty-third, and the conspirators
decided to act that night. The Queen Mother and Anjou felt
no qualms, but they needed the King's consent. That lonely, fitful, suspicious, moody young man, accustomed from babyhood to
his mother's domination, was suddenly confronted by an avowal

that not the Guises but his mother and brother had ordered the Admiral's murder, and that the only way to save his own and his mother's life, uphold the throne and prevent civil war was to exterminate the rebellious heretics. "They had great pains to make him consent," Margot says, but consent he did. Henry of Navarre and Condé were to be spared; and the King would have liked to save Téligny and La Rochefoucauld, with whom he used to play tennis, but that liking was overruled. Henri de Guise took charge of the arrangements and assigned the murderers to their posts; the *Prévôt des Marchands* was summoned, told of a Huguenot plot against the Kingdom and the King, and bidden to shut the gates and call out the city soldiery.

That night Margot, a bride of less than a week, was in her mother's room; she was sitting on a chest beside her elder sister, Claude, the Duchess of Lorraine, who was in very low spirits. When Catherine, who had been talking to some ladies, noticed Margot she bade her go to bed. Margot got up to make her curtsy, when her sister caught her by the arm and, bursting into tears, cried: "For God's sake, Margot, don't go." Catherine angrily bade the sister keep quiet. Claude protested that nothing was to be gained by sacrificing Margot, and said that if "they" discovered anything, "they" would take revenge on her. The Queen answered that, if God pleased, no ill would come to her; but, come what might, she must go to her room for fear lest something be suspected and the result be interfered with. Although Margot understood nothing of these mysterious words, the Queen bade her rudely a second time to go to bed. Claude burst into tears, and said good night, without daring to add a word. Margot went to her boudoir in alarm, said her prayers, and going to the bedchamber found her husband already in bed, and thirty or more Huguenot gentlemen about him; she got to bed, too, but there was no sleep. They all talked of the attack on the Admiral, and how the first thing in the morning they would go to the King and ask for justice against the Duc de Guise, and if the King would not grant it, they would take justice into their own hands.

In the meantime the massacre had begun. Henri de Guise sent assassins to despatch the Admiral. He followed them and waited in the street below till the body had been thrown from the window, and having identified it, went on to other murderous work. The bells were ringing, and armed men marked with white scarves and white crosses, searched for Huguenots indoors and out, and entered into the full spirit of the occasion.

Young Du Plessis-Mornay, who afterward became one of Navarre's closest and wisest advisers, was lodging in the Rue Saint Jacques at the sign of the Golden Compass. He was a very intelligent young man of three and twenty, who, after studying in Paris, had traveled for several years in Italy, Germany and the Low Countries and now had come to Paris to give Coligny the benefit of his knowledge concerning conditions in Holland and Flanders. He belonged to a family which had "abjured idolatry." Having heard talk of approaching danger, he had passed the information on to the Admiral's household, but nobody paid much attention to it. He was one of those who, on news of the Admiral's wound, had run to the spot and had accompanied the wounded man to his house. He then was full of apprehension, made his mother leave Paris that Saturday afternoon, but stayed himself. Very early on Sunday morning, about five o'clock, his servant, whom he had sent out for news of the Admiral, came running in to warn him, and he hid in a little space between the ceiling of the top story and the roof. On Monday morning the landlord besought him to leave, as there was a murdering gang next door, where they had killed a bookseller and flung his body from the window, and they were going to search the inn next. He got away in plain clothes and slipped out of the Porte Saint-Denis, but soldiers stopped him, and a furious mob of carters, quarry-men and lime-burners gathered round, and dragged him to the river. He persuaded the more reasonable of them that they would be vexed to have drowned the wrong man, and sug-gested that it would be more sensible to lock him up and in-vestigate. This they did, and in the end he escaped.

Madame de Feuquères, a widow of twenty-three, with a little girl, who had learned "the truth" from preachings in her father's house, was in Paris at the time. On Sunday morning, Saint Bartholomew's Day, her maid burst into her bedroom in terror, saying that men were being killed on every side. She slipped on a petticoat, looked out of the window, saw soldiers with white crosses on their hats, and people crowding in great confusion. Word came from her uncle, a bishop, to gather up her valuables, and that he would send for her; but the bishop having heard that his own brother, a Protestant, had been murdered in his lodgings near the Admiral's house, forgot all about his niece. However, she took her daughter, a child of three, and escaped to a friend's house, where she found half a dozen refugees already gathered. She had got away from her lodgings none too soon, for the Duc de Guise, who had hated her father, sent his servants to search for her. Soon there were forty refugees in the friend's house. The kind owner was obliged to send all over town to buy small quantities

of provisions here and there, so that he might not bring suspicion upon so many mouths; while he himself, or his wife,
stood at the door and greeted the Duc de Guise, and other
Catholic chiefs, as they passed on their way to see that the
work was proceeding well. But on alarm of a search all
scattered but two. One lady hid in the wood-pile, while
Madame de Feuquères and her maid crawled into a hollow
gable and lay there listening to the shrieks of men, women and
children who were being murdered in the streets. She was
obliged to shift her hiding-place from house to house, and
after eleven days by great good fortune was able to leave Paris
on a river boat, where two monks talked of their joy at what
had happened, and some soldiers, suspecting her, said, "Let's
drown this Huguenot." She afterward married Du Plessis-
Mornay.

Young Sully, too, was in Paris on the fatal day, but he
also escaped and lived to be the wisest counselor of King
Henry IV, and the second personage in the Kingdom—Maximilien de Béthune, chevalier, Duc de Sully, Pair de France,
Prince Souverain de Henrichemont et de Boisbelle, Marquis de
Rosny, Comte de Dourdan, Sire d'Orval, de Montrond et de
Saint-Amand, Baron d'Epineuil, de Bruières, du Châtelet, de
Villebon, de La Chapelle, de Novion et de Baugy; *conseiller du
roi en tous ses conseils,* and as much more again. He was the
second son of a Huguenot nobleman who brought him up well,
for he became a bold, sagacious, resourceful man. But two
years before this his father had said to him: "Maximilien, since
custom does not allow me to make you the principal heir of my
property, I wish in compensation to make you rich in noble
qualities, and by means of them, as has been foretold me [peo-
ple of those days believed in soothsayers] I hope that some day

you will become somebody. Prepare to endure with courage all
the difficulties that you will meet in the world, surmount them
bravely, win the esteem of men of honor and particularly of
the master in whose service I bid you live and die." So the
father took the little fellow and introduced him to young
Navarre and Jeanne d'Albret, then at Vendôme. The boy
spoke up with so much self-confidence and grace, and with so
agreeable a voice that (as he says) he made a most excellent
impression. And so it came to pass that Sully, aged thirteen,
went up to Paris to attend college and to be at Navarre's
wedding, although the father said that "if the wedding is
celebrated in Paris, the liveries will be incarnadine."

On Saint Bartholomew's Day the lad was waked by the
tocsin and cries in the street. His tutor and his valet, also
wakened by the noise, went out to see what the matter was; he
never heard of them again. His landlord, although a Huguenot, hurried off to mass and wished to take the boy with him;
but Sully refused. "I made up my mind [he says] to try to
reach the Collège de Bourgogne, where I was a student, although it was far from my lodgings. The distance made it
dangerous. I put on my student's gown and, taking a large
prayer-book under my arm, went down-stairs. As I walked
out into the street I was horrified; there were madmen running
to and fro, smashing down doors and shouting 'Kill, kill,
massacre the Huguenots.' Blood spattered before my eyes
and doubled my fear. I ran into a clump of soldiers, who
stopped me. They plied me with questions, and began to
jostle me about, when luckily they saw the prayer-book. That
served as my passport. Twice again the same thing happened,
and twice again I escaped. At last I reached the Collège de
Bourgogne; but there a greater danger awaited me. The

The Duc de Sully

Portrait by Du Moustier in the Louvre

porter refused to let me in, and I remained out in the street at the mercy of the madmen, who kept increasing in numbers. I bethought myself of asking for the Principal of the College, a good man who was very friendly to me, and by the aid of a little money, got in. The Principal took me to his room, when two inhuman priests talked of the Sicilian Vespers and tried to get me out of his hands, saying that the order was to kill every one down to babies at the breast. The Principal locked me up in a remote closet, where I stayed for three days." Finally a letter came from his father, bidding him do whatever Henry of Navarre did, even to go to mass, if necessary. And so Sully lived to fulfil his high destiny.

They were among the fortunate few that escaped, but most of the eminent Huguenots were massacred. The Marquis of Resnel was killed by a personal enemy; the son of the Baron des Audrets by an adversary in a lawsuit; Quercy wrapped his cloak round his arm, and fought as fiercely as he could; Beaudisné, Pluviaut, Berni and Soubise were murdered, stripped and dragged like dead beasts to the Palace of the Louvre, to be stared at by those within; Lavardin, hidden by his landlord, who said he was not angry enough to kill him, was murdered by a less temperate Catholic, and his body flung into the river. Brion, over eighty, in spite of his white hair, in spite of his pupil, the little Prince de Conti, who put up his baby hands to save his tutor, was stabbed to death. La Force, in bed with his two little boys, was killed together with the older boy, while the younger, covered with blood, was left for dead. Gondinel, the famous musician, Perrot, the distinguished lawyer, were murdered, flung from windows and dragged through the streets; and so on, and so on. The populace was metamorphosed into a mad mob; they stripped their victims, men and women, pulled

them out of beds, flung them from housetops, and threw them
into the Seine. Debtors murdered their creditors, whatever
their creed, others murdered those against whom they had any
grudge, and all pillaged shops and prosperous-looking unde-
fended houses. Even in the Louvre, the murderers sought
their prey. At dawn Henry of Navarre, unable to sleep, had
got up and said he would play tennis till the King was visible.
He did not go far; the palace gates were shut. He and Condé
were arrested, taken to the King's chamber and bidden choose
between the mass and death. Meanwhile, Margot, left alone,
thinking her sister's cause of alarm had passed, fell asleep, but
not for long; she was awakened by beatings and kicks at the
door and cries of "Navarre! Navarre!" Her nurse, thinking
it was Henry himself, opened the door, and a Huguenot, bleeding, and pursued by soldiers, dashed into the room, leapt on the
bed for protection, clutched Margot and rolled over with her,
both shrieking. A captain of the guards, following close,
stopped the soldiers. He escorted Margot to her sister's room.
On her way, a wounded man was overtaken and killed three
steps from her. So it went. Two or three thousand or more
were killed in Paris, and many hundreds in Meaux, Orléans,
Troyes, Rouen, Lyons and Toulouse, in almost every city in
France.

On August twenty-fifth, the Tuscan ambassador wrote to
the Grand Duke of Tuscany: "There is still no cessation of
sacking houses and murdering men all through the city and
the suburbs. The Admiral's body, it is said, will be hung up
in order to give greater gratification to the multitude, and the
Duc d'Angoulême, the King's bastard brother, who had chief
charge of this whole business, is to see to it, and Monsieur de
Guise is to assist." And the next day the mood of Paris was

expressed in an exulting pæan: "What now of Charles, of a truth Charles-le-magne, and of his most glorious mother, and of those two Cæsars, his brothers, or the Guises and other noblemen who obeyed the holy commands of our good King with so much valor and wisdom!"

Condé, who had inherited much of his father's temper, at first angrily refused to abjure, but the King called him a rebel and the son of a rebel, and swore that if he did not change his mind within three days, he would have him hanged. Condé acquiesced. Navarre, more politic, declared that he would obey the King in all things, listened to the arguments of a former Huguenot clergyman who had been very lately converted, acknowledged himself persuaded and assisted at mass under the eyes of the Queen Mother. His next step was to write the following letter. The phraseology, which is as different from his own style as black from white, suggests the cooperation of some apprehensive ex-Huguenot clergymen:

To our very Holy Father, the Pope

Paris, October 30, 1572.

Very Holy Father:

The hope I place in the paternal affection, which you always bear, as God's vicar on earth, that His children, who have strayed for a time away from our holy mother, the Catholic Church, Apostolic and Roman, and do repent, will be charitably received, has quite vanquished the doubts I otherwise should have felt concerning Your Holiness's just severity, so that, encouraged by the Very Christian King, and by the wise and prudent admonitions of the Queen, my mother-in-law, by the King's brothers, by the Cardinal de Bourbon, my uncle, and by my cousin, the Duc de Montpensier, I am at last persuaded

that Your Holiness will recognize me as one of your children
by virtue of the fact that I was baptized in the Catholic Church;
and that you will not impute to me the sectarianism which was
afterward put upon me, when, being very young, I had not
judgment to make a choice; and that you will not disdain to
open your indulgent arms and accept this confession of peni-
tence, of return to duty and obedience, which I have protested
here in the presence of the Papal legate, and receive me into
the lap of the Church of which I acknowledge you as Chief, and
consider me as a very humble, obedient and devoted son. . . .

HENRY.

He also was obliged to issue an edict reestablishing the
Catholic religion in Béarn, and then to serve in the royal army
against the Huguenots in La Rochelle.

CHAPTER VIII

THE Queen Mother had decided upon the massacre of Saint Bartholomew under the pressure of immediate danger, and now that it was done she did not know how to treat it. On August twenty-fourth, her formula for the King read: It was merely a vendetta between the House of Guise and the House of Châtillon, that the Guises having learned that the Admiral's friends meant to avenge him, caused a *sédition lamentable*. On August twenty-fifth, as the people of Paris and the more fanatical Catholics showed themselves full of approval, she changed the formula: The King, having learned that the Admiral and his friends were resolved on revenge and to attack not only his Majesty, but also the Queen Mother and the King's brother, had authorized the House of Guise to kill the Admiral and those of the faction that had joined in the conspiracy. On August twenty-seventh, as approval grew, the Queen Mother changed the formula again, the Guises were dropped out entirely and the whole credit assumed: God gave my son the means to get rid of those rebels against God and himself, and to preserve us from their cruel hands. And finally she quoted the words of Jesus: *Beatus qui non fuerit in me scandalizatus,* Blessed is he that is not offended because of me. There still was some little difficulty in adjusting the explanations to the Protestant powers; but she went on calmly, as if nothing out of the way had happened.

73

In fact, the night of Saint Bartholomew settled nothing. Coligny and many Huguenot leaders had been killed, Navarre and Condé had abjured, but an Old Testament fighting spirit had been kindled among the congregations of the south and west, and Huguenot gentlemen, ministers, sailors and soldiers, gathered together in La Rochelle and defied the King. A royal army under the Duc d'Anjou was sent to besiege the city.

Henry of Navarre had no choice but to go; and he went gaily. Pliancy was no inherited quality. From his mother he got his pertinacity, from his father his love of women, from his Uncle Condé his fiery courage, from his grandfather Henri d'Albret his brusk Béarnais manners and his robust constitution, from his grandmother Marguerite his charm; but his pliancy he learned for himself on the night of Saint Bartholomew. A contemporary says of him at this time: "The King of Navarre appeared most cheerful, and concealed his discontent so artfully that it seemed as if he felt no resentment for what had happened, making up even to those whom he knew were his enemies, so that everybody believed that his thoughts were entirely diverted from what they had made him suffer. He joked and jested over everything that took place. Indeed, ever since he was a little boy, he has made the best of everything, amusing himself poking fun at everybody without exception, and larding his conversation with raillery, and yet without ever giving offense, for he follows it up with so much familiarity, friendliness and charm, that he wipes out any ill feeling that usually attends such behavior." Nevertheless, when his soldiers took part in an assault, it happened that they shouted so loud that the garrison was put on its guard; and on several occasions he made projects of escape. Alençon, the King's youngest

brother, a hot-headed, ambitious, visionary and vicious lad of
eighteen, who was ready to marry Queen Elizabeth or do anything else, in order to get away from his mother and brothers
and become leader of something, also meditated escape. One
plan was for him, Navarre and Condé, to slip away and join the
Huguenots in Angoulême, another to board and capture the
royal fleet and sail for England. But these projects came to
nothing, for the siege was raised, and the situation changed.

The Duc d'Anjou had been elected King of Poland and
it was necessary from a political point of view that France, in
order not to hurt the susceptibilities of a respectable minority
of Polish noblemen, should deal leniently with the Huguenots.
So a peace was patched up and certain liberties granted. This
did not benefit Henry of Navarre. He was regarded by the
French court as a very valuable hostage, and kept in confinement. At the same time the young Duc d'Alençon was also held
as a hostage, for he was regarded as the likely head of a second
discontented political party, *les Politiques* as they were called.
This third party consisted of moderate men, who disliked
fanaticism and excess, and hoped for some kind of reconciliation and compromise, and of those who deemed themselves
insulted by the haughty manners of the Guises, or thought their
merits slighted by the King, or for some reason or other felt
discontented or aggrieved. Alençon, as I say, was quite ready
to be the head of anything that might gratify his vanity, and
so the two young men made all sorts of plans to escape. One
such attempt was made when the court was at Saint-Germain.
A troop of Huguenot horse promised to ride very near, and
Navarre was ready to mount and join them, when one of his
gentlemen, who is thought to have stood high in Margot's
good graces, revealed the plot; Alençon was hauled up and

made a clean breast of it. The Queen Mother wasted no time; though it was two o'clock in the morning, she had the horses hitched to her carriage and, taking Alençon and Navarre with her, drove off at a smart pace to Paris. As usual Navarre was prodigal of professions of loyalty; he vowed that, "in obedience to all laws human and divine, his life was at the King's service to preserve Crown and Kingdom;" nevertheless, he and Alençon were shut up in the Château de Vincennes. Even so, the fear of poison or dagger in the prison had more terrors than the risks of escape, and another plot was made, only to fail again. This time Charles IX himself cross-questioned the two Princes. Alençon, a mean-spirited sneak, confessed lavishly, not caring whom he betrayed; but Navarre *"n'embarassa n'y lui même ny ses amis,"* he revealed nothing, and then, when examined by an official prosecutor, conducted himself *"en accusateur plutôt qu'en accusé."* He submitted a brief on his behalf, which Margot helped him to draw up, boldly saying that he was wrongly excluded from the King's Council, and that the Guises were wrongfully preferred to the Bourbons, Princes of the Blood. Even after that, Margot, who did not lack spirit nor enterprise, planned to take one of the two Princes, disguised as a woman, away in her coach, but she could take only one, and as the Princes could not agree which should go—the rivalry was not one of chivalric self-sacrifice— this plan failed, too.

Shortly afterward Charles IX died (May 30, 1574); Henri d'Anjou, King of Poland, succeeded as Henri II, and the political situation changed again. Navarre benefited in that, in place of confinement in the Louvre, he was given much more personal liberty, put on bounds as it were. Physically this was much more comfortable, for now he had freedom of going

about as he pleased, although always under more or less surveillance; but morally, it was disadvantageous. Under imprisonment, he had chafed and been very angry; he swore that
if they did not let him out he would hack a hole through the
walls of the Louvre with his dagger, and his anger had kept
him upright and honest. At large, he played the hypocrite
and lived a life of make-believe. He felt that he was in the
hands of people who were quite ready to take his life whenever
it might be to their advantage to do so. They had murdered
thousands and thousands of innocent persons; why should they
balk at killing him? For all he could see, there were but three
things that tended to secure his safety: first, their personal
liking, for he knew he was attractive and a pleasant companion;
second, as a hostage he was of much more value living than
dead; third, both as the husband of Margot, and as First
Prince of the Blood, he was hedged about by a certain feudal
reverence. Under these circumstances all he could possibly do
to increase his chances of life was to make himself as agreeable as possible to those in whose power he was. He was
alone, he had not a single trustworthy friend at court, and he
was not yet twenty-one. The deliberate assumption of a mask
by a young man of that age, according to our conventional
ethics, is not good for his soul; but as part of his education in
kingcraft, it made an excellent discipline, and the skill that he
showed in later years in adjusting his mask to suit new circumstances or persons of uncharted disposition testifies to the
excellence of the training received at this time. So, on the outside he appeared gay, good-humored, full of banter, and nobody
seems to have suspected the condition of his heart.

But he was young, and after his close confinement his
present life had much that was cheerful. He was agile, tough,

well-made and very active, and delighted in hunting and games, and in bad weather he was always ready to romp and skylark indoors.   Moreover, after his austere Huguenot bringing-up in Béarn, it was great fun to play Don Juan and make love to the ladies in the Queen Mother's train; all life long the pursuit of women was his favorite sport.   There was no better hunting-ground than this in all Europe.   And the personages of the court were interesting; the shrewd, hypocritical, crafty Queen Mother herself, the King, an intellectual fool and pious profligate, the vicious little Alençon, the brilliant handsome Henri de Guise, and all the toadies and hangers-on.   And playing the game of adapting himself to these different persons was often exciting; and Navarre learned to play the game excellently well.   He enjoyed a sense of mental superiority; inwardly he was *secret, caché, fin,* while on the outside he was all smiles and bonhomie.

It is difficult to exaggerate the value of this Machiavellian behavior.   He made himself familiar with all sorts of people, but mostly with those from whom he hoped to get information or useful advice.   He treated the King with deference: and was profuse in protestations of loyalty.   On All Saints' Day he and Alençon accompanied the King to church to take communion together; they knelt before him, besought him to forget the past and swore by their hope of Heaven, and "by the God they were about to receive," that they would maintain their obedience to him inviolate.   Navarre never proposed to mar his fortunes by any stickling about conformity of words to feelings.   His manners to the Queen Mother were often flattering; and when Henri de Guise was accidentally wounded, he rode post-haste to see him and made a great show of kindness to the whole Guise family.   At the same time he wrote to a friend, Monsieur de Miossens:

The Duc d'Alençon

[Lyons, with the court]

Dear Cousin:

This Court is the strangest place you've ever seen. We are almost always ready to cut one another's throats. We carry daggers, wear steel shirts, and often a little cuirass under the cape. Sévérac will tell you why. The King is in as much danger as I am. He likes me more than ever. Monsieur de Guise and Monsieur de Mayenne never leave me. Lavardin, your brother, and Sainte Colombe are the heads of my Council. You can't guess how well protected I am in this Court of friends. I face everybody. The whole group that you know of wish me all possible evil, on account of Alençon's affection for me, and they have for the third time told my mistress [Madame de Sauves] not to speak to me. I am only waiting for the right moment to begin a little battle, for they say that they will kill me, and I wish to get the start of them. I have informed Sévérac very fully of all this.

> Your very good friend, cousin and master
> HENRY.

There was one respect, however, in which he played his game very badly. His relations to his wife he could not, or did not, manage well. One remembers how Jeanne had hoped that this marriage would save her boy from the *maudite et corrompue compagnie* of the court. He had married her for political advantage; she him, under compulsion. Both should have made the best of it, and she was disposed to do so, but he made no effort at all. In spite of her beauty, she seems to have been unattractive to him from the very first. He was not delicate-minded, the only reference he makes to his early married life was very coarse; but neither was she delicate-minded. Nevertheless, for a time after the massacre they got on well enough together. No doubt he was irritated because she had revealed his and Alençon's first plot to escape; but after that she had done her best to favor later plots. He knew that her motive in these attempts was love of her brother Alençon, not of himself; but she had not discriminated against him. Now that his close confinement was over, and he was with the court at Lyons, and had freedom to amuse himself, he had regained his good humor, and it seemed as if the two might come to some agreement for mutual cooperation. Margot in her understanding of this, was more mature than her husband. Both were in difficult positions. Henry must look for support to the Huguenots, but he had abjured their faith and had married a Catholic; while she, though a good Catholic, was looked upon with suspicion by the Catholics, because she had married a Huguenot, and by the Huguenots because of her morals. Moreover, Navarre was distrusted by Catherine de Médicis, who in turn was distrusted and disliked by him; while Margot and her brother Henri III hated each other. Under these circumstances Margot desired to come to an understanding with her husband as to their common interests, and to unite upon a common policy. Navarre does not seem to have been alive to the advantages of such cooperation; he was too much taken up with having a good time. So far as that went Margot had no objection, for, as she says, "knowing that she was not jealous" he used to tell her whatever he happened to be thinking about, "as freely as if she were his sister." But he paid no heed to her more serious propositions.

Margot may have looked too favorably upon her own efforts at amity and cooperation; but perhaps the fault lay with the court, which was a hothouse of backbiting, so that it was well-nigh impossible for husband to put confidence in wife, or friend in friend, or neighbor in neighbor. According to Margot, a special cause prevented the success of her hopes. Henri III detested his brother Alençon, and was suspicious of the intimacy between Alençon and Navarre, and believed that Margot had brought the two together in order to do him harm. He therefore greatly desired to effect a breach between Alençon and Navarre, and set about it with considerable ingenuity. There was a certain lady in the court, a beauty and coquette, a very Circe, according to Margot, Madame de Sauves, with whom all the men were in love, Alençon, Navarre, Henri de Guise, a certain Seigneur de Guast, and others. Now Guast was a favorite of Henri III, one of his *mignons,* and, according to Margot, a "rotter," *donné à la pourriture,* riddled with vice and villainy, who had sold his soul to the devil. At the King's behest Guast went to Madame de Sauves, and asked her to set the two Princes by the ears. Madame de Sauves accepted the task. She made them mutually jealous of her good graces, and told Navarre that Margot was jealous of his attentions to her, and for that reason was taking Alençon's part against him, et cetera; and to these lies added whatever else she could think of to breed discord between husband and wife. In all this she succeeded; for, as Margot says, "men lend a ready ear to those they love." It should be said in modification of Margot's story, that scandal busied itself outrageously with Margot's private life. But her husband was philosophic on that score; and it may be that Margot was right in laying the blame upon Guast. At any rate, the next year Guast was assassinated, or rather, as Margot expressed it, put to death *par un jugement divin.* Pierre L'Estoile also says that Guast's death was "one of the doings of an admirable and adorable divine Providence." The public, prone to think ill of persons connected with the court, believed that Margot had set divine Providence in motion.

In such an atmosphere it was very difficult for a *mariage de convenance* to hold its own, and it would have required more good-will in Margot and Henry to make theirs a success than lay at their disposal. Had they been able to work together, their lives might have been smoother. Certainly Henry suffered for much of his life from having her an enemy rather than an ally.

CHAPTER IX

GOVERNOR OF GUYENNE

THE court returned to Paris. Navarre for the time being remained attentive to Madame de Sauves; Margot was inconstant in her flirtations. Once the pair came together again while Margot was nursing him in an illness which she frankly says, *"lui venait, comme je crois d'excès qu'il avoit faits avec les femmes";* but further scandalous gossip concerning her led to another estrangement, *"de sorte que nous ne couchions plus, ni ne parlions plus ensemble,"* so that they slept apart and avoided each other. At this point Alençon succeeded in making his escape; and Navarre's mind turned toward freedom and a larger life. The only motive to keep him at court was Madame de Sauves; but, as Brantôme, who was an authority on such matters, says, "The happiness of loving can not last forever *pour beaucoup d'incommoditez, empeschemens et changemens,* there are too many hindrances and changes, and Henry's heart was *ondoyant et divers* more than most men's, and, perhaps, it beat more temperately, when not fanned by jealousy of Alençon. At any rate his thoughts turned again toward liberty, and the exercise of the gifts and qualities that he felt within him.

It is at this time that Agrippa d'Aubigné, who after Sully and Du Plessis-Mornay is the most distinguished of the Huguenots that shared the fortunes of Henry of Navarre, first became intimate with him. D'Aubigné was a gentleman from

Saintonge, not quite three years older than Henry. The two
had met as little boys in the Château of Antoinette d'Albret;
and d'Aubigné, like Henry, had been brought up a Protestant.
He was certainly a better student than his master, for at seven
he was translating *Crito*. At thirteen he was studying in Paris
under a distinguished scholar, and with him, among the other
boys, were Pierre L'Estoile, who wrote the diary that I shall
quote frequently, and two Gobelins brothers, of a family already famous for tinting wool for tapestry. D'Aubigné also
studied in Geneva, but by the age of nineteen he enlisted in the
Huguenot army, about the time that Jeanne took young Henry
of Navarre to La Rochelle. He had gone up to Paris for the
wedding, but the very day before the assault upon Coligny,
having acted as second to a friend in a duel fought in the Place
Maubert, and having wounded a policeman who tried to arrest
him, he had fled and so escaped Saint Bartholomew's Day.

One night as Navarre lay in bed, sick of a fever, his friend,
d'Aubigné, and another, overheard him repeating verses of a
psalm. This Huguenot touch gave them the courage to speak
out, and together they concocted a plan of escape. This would
not be difficult, they thought, as Navarre was permitted to go
hunting, although always attended by two of the King's gentlemen. Navarre put his talents of deception to profitable use; the
very day before the evasion he went at daybreak to see Henri
de Guise, threw himself on the Duke's bed, told him that the
Queen Mother had assured him that the Duke would be appointed Lieutenant-General of the Kingdom, invited him to
join the hunt, and embraced him warmly in public. This was
early in February, 1576. Having kicked up enough dust,
Navarre rode off to Senlis, where the hunt was to take place the
next day. The plan was to make a dash, and head for Sedan,

which at that time was held by a Huguenot commandant.
Somebody disclosed the plot to the King. The faithful
d'Aubigné discovered the disclosure, and rode at a gallop to
Senlis. Navarre's friends proposed to kill the two guardians,
but Navarre, who had a kindly disposition and also was
anxious not to offend the King unnecessarily, preferred to dis-
embarrass himself of them on ingenious pretexts, and then he
and his friends, believing that their pursuers would expect them
to make for the east, rode hard to the west. The night was
dark and bitter cold, but they pushed on as fast as possible,
reaching the Seine near Poissy. D'Aubigné and Navarre,
having crossed first, walked up and down to warm themselves
in the chill morning air, holding their horses' bridles and reciting together these verses of the psalm:

> The King shall joy in thy strength, O Lord;
>   And in thy salvation how greatly shall he rejoice!
> Thou hast given him his heart's desire,
>   And hast not withholden the request of his lips.

They rode on westward by Montfort-l'Amaury and Château-
neuf-en-Thymerais. They were in good spirits. An old
woman coming upon the King in an embarrassing situation in
her garden nearly cut his head open with a pruning-knife, but
d'Aubigné intervened. He composed an impromptu epitaph:

> Here lies our King, within this nook,
> Who died, God grant him pardon,
> By an old lady's pruning hook
> While . . . in her garden.

And so onward. That same day a gentleman guided them on
their way, and not recognizing the King of Navarre, beguiled
the time with piquant anecdotes concerning ladies of the court,

including Margot. After they had crossed the Loire the King felt safe: "Thank God," he said, "for this deliverance! They murdered my mother in Paris, they murdered the Admiral and my best friends, and but for God's protection they would have done the same to me. I shan't go back there unless they drag me." At the stops on the way, gentlemen of the religion had been coming in, and by the time Navarre had arrived at Saumur, where he felt secure, he was at the head of a goodly troop.

Navarre was still but twenty-two. Though he had left the court abruptly and without permission, he was far from being a rebel to his King; nevertheless, his situation was certainly anomalous, and it behooved him to be wary. His intention was to keep as free from partizan entanglements as possible, to look after his own little kingdom and to assert his authority as Governor of Guyenne. While he was in captivity civil war had again broken out; the union of the Huguenots with the middle-of-the-road-men, the *Politiques,* headed by Alençon, heir presumptive, had been too strong for the King, and he was obliged to make peace (May 2, 1576). He issued a new *Edict of Pacification,* in which he expressed his *très grand regret* for Saint Bartholomew, granted the Huguenots almost complete freedom of worship, rewarded the chiefs of the *Politiques* and conferred favors on Alençon.

Under these circumstances Navarre's duty was to enforce the Edict both in his own Kingdom and in Guyenne; and the practical question that confronted him was that of his religion: should he or should he not return to the Protestant fold? This he regarded from a political rather than a religious point of view. At first glance, it seems as if there could be but one answer: the Huguenots looked to him as their natural chief,

they were his strongest support, and as their loyalty to him
was based on their religion, they were the more likely to be
steadfast. On the other hand, a Catholic king of Navarre, so
close to Philip II, might have advantages over a Protestant
king; certainly a Catholic governor of Guyenne, for such he
still was, would have various advantages over a Protestant
governor; and there was the not unlikely chance that he would
become heir to the Crown of France, for Henri III had no
children, and if he should become such heir, would he not be
in a better position as a Catholic than as a Protestant; besides,
he inclined to like his Catholic followers the best, for they were
loyal to him from personal affection, whereas the Huguenots
merely because he was their party chief. However, the immediate exigencies of his position as party chief carried the
day; hesitatingly, and after a delay of three months, he became once more a Protestant (June 13, 1576). Even so, he
kept as close as possible to compromise and a *via media,* and
expressed himself most characteristically: "I have been wont
to pray to God . . . that, if my religion is true, as I believe, may it please God to confirm me in it; if it is false, may
God teach me the truth and illumine my mind to follow it, to
live and die in it, and after having expelled all errors from my
mind, may God give me strength and means to expel them from
the Kingdom and from all the world." He never shut the door
behind him.

When the old Catholic chief Montluc, who had retired from
active life, heard of Navarre's escape from court, he wrote:
"I judged that Guyenne would again have much to suffer; for
a prince, so high-born and so young, who had already given
promise of becoming some day a great captain, would easily
gain the hearts of the nobles and the peasants and keep the

others in fear." If Montluc feared that Navarre would be un-
fair to the Catholics, he was quite wrong. Henri III had
similar apprehensions, but Navarre answered a little haughtily
that "he had no other purpose than to perform his full duty, as
he had been wont to do." "Religion," he said, "is planted in
the heart by teaching and argument, it is confirmed by example, not by the sword. We Frenchmen are citizens of the same
country, and we ought to come to an agreement by gentle
means and not by deeds of cruelty. All that the civil wars have
accomplished is to fill France with blood, fire and wrongs and
to leave the people a prey to brigandage. Let every man lay
aside his wayward affections and devote himself to the service
of his King and the safety of his country."

But except for Michel de Montaigne, who had shut himself up by the River Dordogne in a tower with his books,
there was scarcely another man in France as free as himself
from religious bias. Fanaticism in one party increased that
in the other; and self-seekers sought to derive private advantage from partizan passions. And, to make matters worse
the extreme Catholics, who looked upon the King's recognition
of heresy as a compact with Hell, organized themselves into a
corporate body. Lesser leagues to combat Protestants and
Protestantism had been organized in sundry provinces, but
now, angered and outraged by the royal compromise with the
enemies of Christ, the brilliant Duke of Guise, pious, ambitious
and glorious, gathered together in one organization all these
zealots, and founded the League. Its members declared: "We
propose in the name of the Holy Trinity to establish God's
law in its entirety, to reestablish and maintain divine worship
according to the forms of the Holy Catholic Church, Apostolic
and Roman; to maintain the King, Henri III, in full authority

Henri III
From a drawing in the Bibliothèque Nationale, Paris

but without prejudice as to what may be ordered by the States-General; to restore to the provinces and to the Estates of the Realm, their rights, franchises and ancient liberties, such as they were in the time of Clovis the first Christian King. We invite all Catholics to join and to arm themselves." The articles provided that the members should fight their adversaries, and do hurt to neutrals who would not join them, and they bound themselves thereto by oath.

With the creation of the League, the situation in France assumed the general aspect that it retained during the next ten years. The unfortunate country continued to be the battle front of the contending religious forces, the main point of contact between the old order and the new, as when two ice floes meet in a stormy sea. From the north, in her sheltered island, the crafty Elizabeth looked on, helping the Protestants parsimoniously, just enough to keep the Spaniards in check. From the south, across the Pyrenees, the conscientious, red-tape-entangled Philip interfered so far as was necessary to keep the French Huguenots from aiding the Netherlands to escape from his grasp. From Germany and Switzerland, Protestant and Catholic mercenaries came to raid and rob, wherever they were offered pay. From Geneva the Protestant oligarchy sent their blessings to the Huguenots; from Rome the Pope sent his curses. Within the Kingdom Henri III twisted and turned in order, on the one hand, to free himself from the bullying arrogance of Henri de Guise and the League, and on the other, to put down the Huguenot rebels who defied his authority. This chaos of disorder smoldered with dank smoke most of the time, but now and then broke out into fitful blazes of open war only again to be reduced to the smoldering state by a new peace and by another Edict.

Henry of Navarre led, in the main, the life of a border chieftain; his task was to maintain his authority as King in Béarn and as Governor in Guyenne, to keep the peace between his Huguenot and Catholic subjects, and to avoid any appearance of open rebellion against Henri III. As for his own Kingdom, it had had harsh experiences and was disposed to be quiet and obedient. Jeanne had dispossessed the Catholic clergy, and substituted Huguenot ministers in their places; but, after she had fled to La Rochelle in 1568, Charles IX had sent down Catholic troops, which overran the country and hoisted the fleur-de-lis over castle and citadel. But that same summer (August, 1569), Montgomery, the knight who had accidentally killed Henri II in tournament, came to Jeanne's rescue with a little army of adventurers, and reestablished the Protestants. After Saint Bartholomew (1572), Henry of Navarre had been obliged to send his command to restore Catholic worship. On his escape (1576), he had put the Protestants back in power again, but with moderation and such measure of justice as was possible.

In Guyenne his difficulties were greater. His position as governor, which resembled a feudal lordship more than a modern governorship, was to say the least anomalous, especially when the Huguenots were at war with their King. And that position had been rendered still more anomalous because the King appointed a lieutenant-governor for the express purpose of thwarting the governor, of maintaining the Catholics in power, and of dispossessing Huguenots where possible. The present lieutenant-governor was Maréchal Biron, a spirited, hot-tempered soldier, who played the part his sovereign had assigned him with energy and ability.

With these difficulties to contend against, Navarre ad-

dressed himself to the task of enforcing in time of peace the
rights of Protestants under the latest Edict, and, in time of
war, of defending himself and his partizans. The task was, I
repeat, not easy. The Catholic towns, knowing that they had
royal support behind them, were often defiant; Bordeaux ab-
solutely refused to open her gates to him. In smaller places he
succeeded in establishing his authority. Sometimes, however,
it was touch and go. Sully has described one such situation.
The King of Navarre learned that the town of Eauze, which
had rebelled, refused to admit his garrison. He sent word
to his officers to conceal their weapons under their hunting
jackets, and meet him at a certain spot in the country near the
town. He approached the gates. The magistrates came out
in their red robes and delivered up the keys. He rode in with
fifteen or sixteen men. Then an old man shouted to the
portcullis keeper: *"Coupo lou rastel, que prou y a. Lou rey
y est."* (Cut the portcullis cord, the King's inside.) The
gatekeeper did so. The portcullis almost struck the rump of
Sully's horse. The rebels rang the tocsin and rushed to arms,
and some fifty came to attack; Sully could hear three or four
voices crying: "Shoot at the white plume, that's the King!"
The King turned to his followers and said: "Friends, now's the
time to show our courage and resolution; on them our safety
depends. Let every man follow me and do as I do, and don't
shoot without hitting." So saying, he pointed his pistol and
advanced boldly toward the rebels, who gave way and scattered.
Three or four times they rallied and came on in a huddle, but
were frightened off. Then a large crowd, two hundred or
more, crowded up and the King's danger was very great, for
even some of his scanty retinue had been separated from him.
He backed into the portico of a church, stood at bay, and bade

two of his men climb the tower and make signals to the soldiers outside the walls to break a gate in. Fortunately the drawbridge had not been raised, and the soldiers were soon battering at one of the gates. At the same time loyal citizens attacked the rebels in the rear. The soldiers burst in, and would have put every man to the sword, but that the King relented and spared all except four who had shot at his white plume; those he hanged.

Such a life sounds hard; but Navarre was twenty-three or four, light-hearted by nature and prone to enjoy life, and women were an unfailing source of diversion. The enumeration of the King's caprices would require a special scribe: (1) La petite Tignonville; (2) Mademoiselle de Montagu, an old flame of Montluc; (3) Arnaudine; (4) *la garce* (the best girl) of a fellow nicknamed Goliath; (5) Catherine du Luc, whom he abandoned (so it is said) and left to die of hunger or despair; (6) Anne de Cambefort, who (but all such stories are perhaps questionable) for shame flung herself from a window; (7) the wife of a charcoal burner, Estienne Saint-Vincent who afterward was ennobled, *"pour les services que nous a ci-devant faits ledit Estienne,"* (for the benefits aforesaid which Estienne has done for us) as well as many anonymous young women. The King, gay, boisterous, alternating a life of hardship with pleasure, and not delicate in his dealings with women, exposed himself carelessly to unsavory stories; and of these his adversaries circulated many. One such story was violently controverted by his partizans, and has generally been believed to be a slander, but fresh evidence gives it new credence. "In the year 1576, in one of the well-known cities of Guyenne, which I do not name for good reasons, it happened that a ball was given, which lasted late into the night; the lights were extinguished, and many highly respectable ladies, wives and maidens were shamefully used." This quotation is from a sermon preached not long afterward, and not far from the spot; nevertheless, the accusation of lights extinguished and of a subsequent orgy was so frequent a charge against the Huguenots, a charge fished up from old accusations against the early Christians, that disbelief, if it could only find confirmation in the King's character, would have strong justification.

But Navarre was nothing less than a philanderer. He was primarily a man's man, and delighted in hunting, and manly sports, in the *jeu de paume,* and riding at the ring. His early bringing-up with country boys served him in good stead, he mingled with peasants and artizans or country squires, hail-fellow-well-met, he danced at their weddings, he held their babies at the font, he was quick at repartee, he liked a joke. Everybody liked him. Many anecdotes have clustered about his Haroun-al-Raschid hunting excursions. For instance: Once, having strayed from the hunt, he came upon a peasant sitting under a tree; "What are you doing there?" the King asked. "I'm waiting to see the King go by." "If you want," said the King, "get up on the croup, and I'll take you to a place where you can see him comfortably." The peasant got up, and asked how he should know the King. "He will wear a hat, while everybody else is bareheaded." When they joined the hunt, all the gentlemen took their hats off. "Well," Henry asked, "which is the King?" "Gosh, Sir, it's either you or me."

On his journeys he often picnicked, and his books of domestic expenses show the vicissitudes of his situations and circumstances: Item, bread, 1 livre 3 sous; item, half pot of wine, 2 livres; item, herrings, 1 livre 2 sous; total 4 livres 5 sous. Or, on merrier occasions: Item, 60 doz. loaves of bread; 120 lbs. of beef; 200 lbs. of mutton; 84 lbs. of veal; 40 lbs. of pork; 32 capons; 52 chickens; 1 turkey; 6 partridges; 4 woodcock; 4 rabbits; 4 plover; 18 larks; 4 teal; 2 snipe; 1 tongue. But there was scant time for sloth. Sometimes he was journeying through Guyenne in the cause of establishing law and order. Sometimes he was hunting from the banks of the Garonne to the purple slopes of the Pyrenees, chasing deer, coursing rabbits, shooting bear, or whatever game might turn up; and then word would come that Catholics at Mont-de-Marsan, Casteljaloux, or some other town, were up in arms, or that Maréchal Biron had appeared with a troop of horse on the Lot or the Dronne, and the King must saddle and gallop away.

CHAPTER X

But picnics, hunting, Haroun-al-Raschid adventures, and pretty ladies were but beaded embroidery on the sad stuff of daily life. The Estates of Languedoc reported: "The earth is saturated with the blood of poor peasants, women and little children; towns and farmhouses are ruined and for the most part burned, and all since the *Edict of Pacification,* and not by Tartars, Turks or Muscovites, but by men born and bred in the land, who profess the religion that they call Reformed, which by their wicked and monstrous way of living they will render odious to God and to the world." In Dauphiné and Guyenne very much the same could have been said of the Catholics. The whole south was in a state of hideous confusion; and this confusion was rendered doubly dangerous by the foreign situation. The Duc d'Alençon—it is more convenient to call him so than by his newly assumed title of Duc d'Anjou—was violently desirous of becoming king of the Low Countries, and had offered his services to the Protestant rebels there; this drew down the displeasure of Spain, and also of England, which would never consent to let France be mistress of the Flemish wool towns. If Alençon continued, there was danger lest Spain, or England, or both, should invade French territory. To meet such an alarming danger, it was more imperative than ever to reconcile the contending factions and unite the kingdom. Catherine de Médicis felt

95

that here was an appropriate field for her political talents. The King agreed; so she went, carrying an olive branch in her hand. She took her daughter Margot with her. It is said that Navarre on his escape had expressed a wish for Margot, and that since then he had claimed her; perhaps he felt that the retention of his wife, as a prisoner or hostage, was an offense to his dignity, as husband and King, or that her presence as a Princess of France and a Catholic in his company, might be of political use to him. Margot herself says that her husband's friends advised him that her presence would be of advantage, and that he accordingly wrote her a very civil letter "in which he begged me to forget all that had passed between us and to believe that he loved me and wished to show his love more than he had ever done." On the other hand, common report said that she went most reluctantly. At any rate Margot served as a screen to conceal the political purpose of Catherine's journey. The Queen Mother was in her element. There was the larger matter of national union in the background, and in the foreground the desire to know what Navarre was doing, and to reconcile him with his Lieutenant-Governor, the Maréchal de Biron. This last job was difficult, for both were masterful and matters were very hot between them.

The Queen arrived in Bordeaux in September, 1578. She at once set herself to the work of reconciliation and pacification; she was very diligent and wrote long letters of what she did to the King. One wonders whether that handsome, elegant, weak and lazy young man, "always," according to the Spanish ambassador, "surrounded by ladies, one holding his hand, another toying with his ear," found time from his *mignons,* his games, and his cultivated tastes, to read all her letters. Whether he did or no, she despatched them, and we are, therefore, able to follow her itinerary and her troubles. Everywhere she found malice, suspicion and desire for vengeance; there were scores upon scores of towns and villages and strongholds occupied by Huguenots, that under the last Edict they were bound to give back to the Catholics; there were priests to be put back in their parishes, and canons in their chapterhouses; there were stolen goods to be returned; there were brigands to be put down, and poor nobles to be bribed. The first step obviously was to arrive at an understanding with Henry of Navarre. As Bordeaux had refused to admit him, the meeting was held near La Réole, a town fifty kilometers to the southeast. Here is the Queen's letter describing it:

La Réole, Guyenne,
Thursday, October 2, 1578.

Monsieur mon fils,

The gentleman I had sent to the King of Navarre came and assured me on his part that he would come to meet us to-day between Saint Macaire and La Réole, in a house that stands apart on a road, called Castéras. We got out there and he met us, accompanied by a very fine retinue of gentlemen, about one hundred and fifty, well mounted and equipped. He found us up-stairs in a reception room, and greeted us most courteously, and, I thought, very affectionately, and with no embarrassment on his part. The Vicomte de Turenne came with him and some others of note. You can imagine that we gave him a warm welcome, then after talking a little while about nothing in particular, we went down-stairs and got into my coach. He got in, too, and came here with us. On the way we were all most demonstrative and friendly. He escorted me to my room, and wished to take the Queen of Navarre to his lodgings across the street, where they will stay and sleep together. But your sister, to spare him discomfort, did not leave my house, for he was very hot, as the day is very warm, and he had been active, so he went to freshen himself up. When they came back to my room, the Cardinal de Bourbon [Henry's uncle] and the Duc de Montpensier were there, and I was looking at a despatch from Maréchal de Damville, in which he says that he has written you about the Huguenots seizing Beaucaire [in Provence]. The King of Navarre and I went on with this subject, and I explained the reason of my journey and of your great desire to enforce the peace, and that you loved him as if he were your own brother, and not merely a brother-in-law, but as his heir after Alençon. He expressed the greatest satisfaction at this, saying that your favor was the greatest happiness that could befall him, and that he was resolved to retain it by all the service in his power, *en se conformant à toutes vos bonnes et sainctes intentions.* I am in hopes that he will make his conduct square with his words, unless he is led away by some of *la religion prétendue réformée,* who I can vouch to you have plenty of malice in their hearts.

Navarre wrote of this meeting: "I have just been to meet the Queen Mother and my wife at La Réole where everything, thank God, went off to our great content." But the meeting with the Maréchal de Biron was less successful. Catherine wrote to the King: "The Maréchal de Biron arrived yesterday after dinner, as I had told him to be sure to do, at Saint Bazille. He found the King of Navarre in my room, who spoke to him more roughly than your sister and I had expected, because of what had taken place between them. The Maréchal was very angry. I assure you that I did not know what to do to straighten matters out; but the good offices of your sister and of Cardinal de Bourbon, and the great pains I took with both, succeeded in restoring their relations after a fashion." She goes on to say that she is never idle. "I speak in public and to individuals, and at table, whenever I get a good chance, so that I hope, by doing this wherever I go, that I shall curtail the evil projects that some have in mind." But soft words did not always butter parsnips: *"Monsieur mon Fils,* Would to Goodness that I had fifty or sixty thousand livres from your treasury. I could distribute them secretly to a dozen or fifteen of the principal men in Guyenne, and win them over to your side, without any one knowing about the others. That would add to the hopes I have held out to them, together and individually, as seemed best, that you would reward them with honors and gifts, as indeed you must do, if you wish to keep this great country, which is more valuable than I can tell you, both for its size and for the natural virtues of the noblesse and of the people, who are for the most part all Catholics and devoted to their religion and to you, if they are not led astray."

From La Réole the Queen Mother proceeded to Auch. She was trying to arrange for a meeting with deputies from the Huguenot churches in order to discuss the enforcement of the Edict; and in the meanwhile her company amused themselves as they went. On October twenty-second there was a fête; fiddles were playing, and the dance had begun. Margot was there and the ladies of the Queen's court. In the very middle of the dance, Navarre's first gentleman of the bedchamber came in, interrupted him and whispered in his ear, "The Catholics have seized our stronghold, La Réole. The Governor has betrayed it." Navarre made a sign to Sully,

Turenne and other intimates, and strolled out of the ballroom. He then repeated the news and added: "Tell all my men, whose lodgings you know, as quietly as you can, that within an hour I shall be on horseback outside the city gate, with my cuirass under my hunting coat, and let all that love honor, follow me." That night he rode into the little Catholic city of Fleurance, and seized it by way of retaliation.

Nevertheless, Catherine succeeded as well as anybody could have done. She made a pact with Henry of Navarre in October, and with the delegates of the Protestant churches of Languedoc in February, 1579; sometimes she smiled and cajoled, sometimes she spoke out *royalement et bien hault* even to telling the assembled ministers that she would have them hanged as rebels. Politics and religion, however, did not occupy all the time. Pau was a somber pious place, *ce petit Genève de Pau,* but Nérac was charming. There was a delightful park along the river which was traversed by paths shaded by laurel and cypress, where after mass and conventicle, Catholic and Protestant ladies and gentlemen used to meet and flirt, and then as the hours flew by on golden wings, they passed on to a series of diversions that usually ended in the evening with a ball. The banquets were sumptuous; the countryside round about supplied partridges, pigeons and quail; Bayonne supplied hams; Pau, peaches, pears or grapes according to the season; Gascony and Guyenne provided glorious wines, white and red. The ladies were young and charming; the gentlemen, even the staunchest Huguenots, d'Aubigné and Sully, were quite ready for gaiety, and there was no Puritan sinning against the freedom of youth. Sully says: "The court there was *fort douce et plaisante;* all the talk was of love and of the pastimes that attend it, every one, each with his mistress, takes part in everything." And d'Aubigné: "The court at Nérac blossomed forth in brave gentlemen and surpassing ladies, so that, at every point of nature and culture, it thought itself no whit behind the French court. Pleasure brought forth vices as heat engenders snakes. The Queen of Navarre furbished up wits and let swords rust. She taught the King, her husband, that a cavalier without love lacks a soul, and her practise was by no means secret, thinking that openness was a mark of virtue, secrecy a mark of vice. The King, sensitive in this respect, soon learned to make much of those that paid court to his wife, and she to make much of his mistresses."

Before the arrival of the Queen Mother, Henry of Navarre had been wearing old hunting clothes, shabby and out-at-elbows; now he put on silk doublets, black or white, breeches of yellow satin, shirts of Holland linen, silk stockings, velvet bonnets, and scarlet cloaks, embroidered with gold and silver. So decked out, he strolled into the many parterred garden of love. First he paid court to one of his mother-in-law's maids of honor, a Greek girl, Victoire d'Ayelle, but "that did not prevent him from showing to Margot," as she herself says, "great friendship and honor, all that I could wish." Victoire was succeeded in Henry's affections by Mademoiselle de Rebours, and she, with some interloper between, by Françoise de Montmorency, daughter of the Baron de Fosseux, and therefore called la Fosseuse, a very pretty girl. Margot, at least so the world believed, accepted the attentions of young Turenne, Henri de la Tour. As her husband showed himself as tolerant in such matters as he was in religion, the two, except for the time when la Fosseuse, *une fille malicieuse* (according to Margot), made trouble by her backbitings, were on excellent terms during the four or five years that they were in Gascony.

In spite of this gaiety at court, peace stood on a shaky pedestal. Catherine de Médicis wrote to Henri III that "Navarre is sending to you the resolutions adopted by a Huguenot assembly at Montauban, which is, in my judgment, to give color to their resumption of arms in case of your refusal to grant their demands," and also that "a real reconciliation between Biron and Navarre is most imperative, otherwise the government of the province will go to pot and fighting begin again both in Guyenne and Languedoc." The Queen Mother was right enough in her apprehensions; mutual distrust prevented each party from fulfilling its obligations, and as to Guyenne Margot says: "The King, my husband, and M. le Maréchal de Biron became such enemies that in spite of all I could do to keep them on friendly terms, I could not prevent extreme distrust and hatred between them; each complained of the other to the King, my husband asking that Biron be removed from Guyenne and Biron accusing my husband and the Huguenots of many enterprises in violation of the treaty of peace."

Tinder was there in plenty and the spark fell. According to d'Aubigné it fell in this fashion. The court at Nérac was not austere, and Henri III, forgetful of the proverb concerning those that live in glass houses, said very rude things about his brother-in-law's court and about Margot in particular. Margot, who returned her brother's antipathy to the full, determined to pay him back. She repeated to la Fosseuse these fraternal animadversions in heightened colors, how the King's tales made Alençon and Guise burst with laughter in presence of Madame de Sauves. La Fosseuse, who was young and still shy, repeated Margot's confidences to her maid Xainete, *avec laquelle le roy de Navarre familiarisoit,* and Xainete repeated

them to him. Margot also stirred up Turenne, and urged the
other ladies to rouse their lovers to action. D'Aubigné is
thought to have been wrong in ascribing so much influence to
Margot's machinations, but at any rate war was again re-
kindled, and it is known as the Lovers' War, the *Guerre des
Amoureux*.

The Huguenots had miscalculated their strength and got
the worst of it; Guyenne suffered severely; the Maréchal de
Biron, "as occasion served, went about attacking and taking all
the towns that held for the Huguenots, and putting every man
to the sword." One victory, however, the Huguenots won,
and that redounded greatly to the glory of Henry of Navarre.
He gathered together about eighteen hundred men at Montauban on the north bank of the Tarn, that charming river that
divides Guyenne and Gascony, and led them cautiously northward to within a half-league of the Catholic town of Cahors.
Sully, at that time a youth of twenty, was with them, and has
left an account of the battle. They set out on the evening of
May 28, 1589. It was very hot, and they halted in a rocky
valley, under clumps of chestnut trees, beside a spring, which
relieved their thirst; there were thunder and lightning but no
rain. The town lay in the loop of the River Lot, surrounded
on three sides by the river, and by a wall to the north. The
bridge on the south bend of the loop was the most fortified,
but Navarre surmised that on that account it would be the least
well guarded. He was now twenty-six, and this was his first
serious action as commander-in-chief. The Lot is broad at
this point, and the bridge was protected by a barbican at its
outer end, by a barricade in the center, and by the great gate of
the city on the near bank. The assailants approached late at
night under cover of the thunder. Two officers with six picked

men placed two petards close to the outer gate of the barbican, but the explosion made so small a hole that the men had to ply their axes before it was wide enough to creep in. A company of musketeers followed and carried the barricade in the center of the bridge; a petard was pushed up close to the city gate, and blew it in at the first explosion. The Commandant, Monsieur de Vezins, had a garrison of twenty-five hundred men; but as the attack was unexpected the soldiers were not at their posts. On the first alarm the bells rang, and aroused Monsieur de Vezins, who hurried forty halberdiers to the bridgehead by the time the city gate was blown in. Other soldiers of the garrison half dressed, came up, and the fight was fast and furious. Vezins was shot and his men gave way, then rallied, and the assailants in their turn fell back; the leader of the vanguard was killed, two other officers were wounded. Matters looked black for the Huguenots, when reenforcements came up, fifty gentlemen and three hundred musketeers. So reenforced the assailants advanced again, facing a storm of missiles from the roofs. They were stopped by a barricade hastily thrown up, and those around Henry of Navarre advised a retreat. "I had rather die [he cried] with my friends, doing my duty, than abandon them in dishonor." At this a rush carried the barricade, and drove the defenders back into some old college buildings, which afforded them a strong position. For two more days there was street fighting, from house to house. On the fourth day the college was carried by assault, after fire had been set to the doors; but even then there remained fourteen barricades on the main street to be carried one by one. Navarre was in the thick of the fight, his feet were wounded and bleeding. On the early morning of the fifth day, June second, the defenders made their escape as best

they could. The first thing Navarre did was to write this
letter to the wife of one of his companions:

Cahors, June 2, 1580.

Madame de Batz,

I shan't take my clothes off, though I am all blood and
powder, without sending you our good news and to tell you
that your husband is safe and well. Captain Navailles, by
whom I send this, will describe to you how we did up these
sons-of-guns. Your husband wasn't a spear's length from
my side. God led us by the hand along the narrow path of
safety, but I mourn for many of our men who fell close by us.

I remain, Madam, at your service.

HENRY.

This unsuccessful little war, *un petit feu de paille,* as
L'Estoile calls it, ended in November, by the *Paix de Fleix,*
thanks to Alençon who wished for peace at home in order to
obtain support in his enterprise to become King of the Netherlands. Everything was left very much as before, except that
Biron was recalled by Henri III, and Navarre's prestige was
so heightened by the capture of Cahors that he was now recognized as head of the Huguenot party in Dauphiné and Languedoc, as well as in Guyenne and Gascony.

CHAPTER XI

CATHERINE had gone back to Paris; she had finished her year and a quarter of travels on horseback, or muleback, and in litters, she had done all she could with wheedlings, coaxings, harangues, with smiles, promises, blandishments, with menaces and threats, and peace had been made on paper. But she conceived that the chances of peace and of Protestant submission in the south would be much greater, if she could inveigle Henry of Navarre to Paris. Many kind messages were sent to him, many friendly representations that the First Prince of the Blood, heir to the throne after Alençon, ought to be at court by the side of the King. Navarre remembered his period of captivity only too well; but butter did not melt in his mouth, and his letters dripped honey. Besides he had a very good excuse, his presence was certainly necessary to make the Protestants of the south fulfill their agreements under the Peace of Fleix. So letters were all that they got out of him:

To the King

March 1, 1581.

Monseigneur,

I thank God for your good health, and pray that He may long continue you in it. I fancy that the good time you will have had in Paris during the Carnival will have done you more good than all your medicines. We make the best of things here. But the best of all will be peace, as Monsieur de Villery will tell you; he knows how Cahors has been given back most peaceably and loyally. We shall go ahead in this way with God's help, and I beg you most humbly to believe that it will not be my fault if things do not go to your satisfaction and there is nothing in the world that I desire so much as to go and kiss your hands, and that in the meantime you will honor me with your commands and your favor. I live for nothing else.

Your very humble obedient subject and servant
HENRY.

To the Queen Mother
March, 1581.

Madam,

The greatest wish that I can frame in this world is never again to witness those evils that are past. I always tried to avoid them, and I beg you, Madam, not to make me unhappy by believing that they were of my doing.

Your very humble, obedient, subject, servant and son
HENRY.

Catherine then tried another method of luring him to Paris; she urged Margot to come, in the hope that he would follow. Margot did go; but to her journey there is a long prologue. A sixteenth-century life full of hardship and danger required more pungent pleasures than a quiet twentieth-century life that shifts from down-town and club to comfortable home. Henri de Bourbon was not refined—none of the Bourbons, one might say hastily, were refined,—and his amorous adventures play a large part in history. In our last glance at such matters, we left him paying court to la petite Fosseuse, Mademoiselle de Montmorency. That young lady had for some time behaved with great propriety, but her head was a little turned when Alençon, who had already disputed Madame de Sauves with Navarre, also made love to her. He had come to Guyenne to effect a peace between Huguenots and Catholics, in order to further his personal ambitions, and had employed his leisure in paying her his addresses. But, after peace had been made, he had gone off, as he hoped, to marry Queen Elizabeth and win a crown in the Netherlands. La Fosseuse, perhaps in order to convince Navarre that she had not really cared for Alençon, looked more kindly upon him, and soon, as Margot discovered, she was on the way to become a mother. It is a little difficult to understand the moral conventions of the time; that there were such conventions is plain enough—for everybody invokes them and passes judgment by them, Navarre, Henri III, Margot and Catherine de Médicis—but their texture and solidity are so different from Puritan or Victorian standards, as different as sixteenth-century dress is from ours, that scholars like Bishop Stubbs, for instance, rashly conclude that there were none. The Fosseuse episode and its sequel, display these conventions as well as may be.

Perhaps this little lady, believing that Margot was barren, entertained ambitious hopes that she, mother of an heir, might succeed to Margot's place. She changed her behavior to the Queen, did her bad turns, and succeeded in estranging her husband from her, and so broke up the friendly alliance between the two that had lasted all the time that Fosseuse, as Margot says, was behaving herself *"avec honneur."* Then, worried it seems about her own health, Fosseuse persuaded Henry to take her to a watering-place. He asked Margot to go, too; he said that Fosseuse suffered from indigestion, and needed the waters, and that it would not be proper for her to go there except in the Queen's company. Margot flatly refused, but sent two of her ladies-in-waiting; these ladies took pains to report to Margot whatever spiteful things Fosseuse chanced to say. When they all met again at Nérac, four or five weeks later, Fosseuse's condition was obvious, and everybody talked about it. Margot, so she says, wishing to snuff out the scandal, proposed to take the girl to a country-house and keep her there until the time when she should be delivered, while the King for propriety's sake should go off hunting somewhere else. Fosseuse, afraid perhaps to trust herself and her baby to the daughter of Catherine de Médicis, or angry at the proposal to separate her from the King, replied haughtily that she would give the lie to any slanderers, and that she knew the Queen was merely seeking a pretext to ruin her, and rushed off in a rage to tell the King. He took her side and blamed Margot. So matters continued till the time of the girl's labor arrived.

The royal couple occupied one room but separate beds; and there they were one night when the doctor came to tell the King that the pains had begun. He fearing, so Margot says, not without irony, lest the birth be discovered, and also that Fosseuse should not be properly cared for, drew aside his wife's bed-curtains and said: "My dear, I have hidden from you something that I must now confess. I beg you to forgive me, and forget whatever I have said, and go at once to help Fosseuse, who is very sick. I feel sure that you will let bygones be bygones." Margot went to the girl with her own doctor, and saw her safely delivered. "God willed [her *Memoirs* say] that she only gave birth to a daughter, and that still-born." When Navarre got home from the day's hunt, he went to see

Fosseuse, and feeling disturbed about her, returned to his wife, who had gone back to bed, and asked her to get up again and go to the girl. Margot this time refused; Henry was very angry, and the half reconciliation was wholly broken.

At this point of the episode the Queen Mother invited Margot to court. It is hard to fathom Catherine's immediate motives; did she think that Margot, bringing her lady-in-waiting, Fosseuse, would draw Henry of Navarre to court with her, keep him enmeshed in the sweets of his amours, and so remove from the Protestant provinces of the south their principal leader and standard-bearer? At any rate Margot went, taking Fosseuse. Now, it had happened that when Alençon came down to arrange the Peace of Fleix, a very handsome young man, Jacques Harlay de Champvallon, had come in his train. Margot looked and loved, with an intensity that shows itself in her letters in a strange mixture of euphuism and passion:

To Monsieur de Champvallon

Many lovers, whose unhappiness equals their passion, accuse Love of their griefs. I should have done the same, if judging by the greatness of my loss and the pain of my privation, I had listened to one side only and shut my ears to the explanations of this god, who is so often accused and so often justifies himself. He has taken possession of my intelligence and made me understand his law, and changed my opinion, so that just when I was composing a complaint against him, I suddenly thought better of it and turned completely about, and rendered thanks that he had chosen me, without my deserving but of his own goodness, as one of his blessed elect. And I remembered how the Almighty has set apart His elect, those holy fathers who are still living, in a solitary place away from men, so that far from the depraved throng, they may in perpetual contemplation await the hour of perfect joy. Such am I in this desert. . . . I live, with no diversion, in continual contemplation of my sovereign good, awaiting the hour of my beatitude. A more suitable place could not be found for me. If your perfections, sweet Heart, did not make me sure that you are a divine being to whom nothing is unknown, I would tell you that on the hardest rocks, in thousands and thousands of places, I have carved your name, your beauty and my passion. . . . If then, the Gods out of envy, should, to prevent men from being as perfect as themselves, stain your perfections with a blot of inconstancy, and you should change your love, do not think that you will have left me. I would never suffer such a reproach to fall upon you. Say, "I loved her till her death," for be sure that the hour of your fickleness will be that of my end. Lengthen, or cut short, my happiness, my love, my life, its thread is not in the hands of Atropos, but in your beautiful hands which I kiss a million times. . . . I am deaf and blind and insensible to the voices and wishes of everybody else. My soul is withdrawn into such noble meditation that it will never be diverted; and if I am allowed to follow my inclination I shall serve Love, by my thoughts and letters more devoutly and more holily than any hermit that ever withdrew from the world to give himself wholly to devotion. O my Life, why am I not always free, when I am deprived of the light of your divine presence, to be able to content my soul in the insatiable pleasure of such noble contemplation? . . . Adieu, my beautiful All; adieu, Perfect Beauty, who shall reign alone for ever in my heart. I kiss a million times your beautiful hands, bright rays of Apollo. . . .

My soul has no power of will except to love you, my heart can not bring forth a desire except to desire you. Adieu, my Life, I kiss a million times those beautiful eyes, that beautiful hair, my dear sweet hands.

Under these circumstances, although her *Memoirs* assign quite other motives, Margot wrote to her mother that she had a great desire to go to court to kiss her hand, and accepted her invitation. Her husband escorted her part way, winning favor as he went; he was gay, affable with everybody, high and low, and took care not to offend the religious susceptibilities of the Catholics; when he attended Protestant service on Sunday he went outside the walls of the town, in conformity with the last Edict. He delivered his wife to her mother and then went back to Nérac, where, indeed, he worked hard on the task of pacification.

Margot was now at court and, in accordance with her husband's wish, wrote him frequently:

March 4, 1582.

Monsieur,

The solicitude that you are pleased to show for my health, and your remembrance of me, give me all the happiness possible away from you, for in so sad an absence nothing else can please. . . . Up to now they have been at all possible pains to render us evil service and make it appear, that we mean to ruin the dukes [Guise and Mayenne], that I am trying to cause division between them, so that by pushing them down we can advance ourselves; and further, that we should be in the King's way, as he could not go on his little journeys without taking us. These petty tricks, thank goodness, are not

"Margot," Henry of Navarre's first wife

dangerous. . . . And now, to keep my letter from being too tedious, for you have bidden me act like shopkeepers who supply wares of all sorts, I will tell you the gossip. Mademoiselle de la Vernay and Mademoiselle d'Astenay, have both lost their suitors; the first is in love with his own wife, and the second devotes himself to Madame de Sauves. He went to see her at Chenonceaux and stayed there two days in hiding; but not so skilfully but that the Queen Mother found it out and pretended that he had come for our aunt's sake. Nobody contradicts her. I let you guess to what one is reduced to carry that off. . . . The day after he left, his mistress pretended to be sick and went back to Paris. She has promised to do you a good turn; Mademoiselle d'Astenay also to the best of her ability.

Next, whatever her motives, whether to remain near her lover or to fall in with her mother's policy, or in hopes to help her dear brother Alençon, she wrote with affected carelessness urging Henry to come: "The Duc de Mayenne has grown so extraordinarily fat that he is deformed; the Duc de Guise is much thinner and older. They have but small following; they get up parties frequently for tennis, ball or pall-mall, in order to draw the noblesse; but those that go twice are sure to meet with some reprimand, which shows that there is jealousy betwixt the Dukes and them. If you were here, everybody would turn to you; as for the Guises, be sure that they lack credit and means to do you an injury; and as for the King, I will pledge my life that you will receive none from him. You will win back the followers that you have lost during these long disturbances, and you will gain more new ones in a week here than in Gascony all your life long. You could expect favors

from the King, and you could do more for those of your party
by one word, being as you would be close to the King, than
all those here who are busy with solicitations can do. It is
imperative for all these reasons that you should at least come
here. I have importuned you too much; but consider that it
is my only pleasure away from you. I beg you to keep me in
the honor of your favor, and permit me to kiss very humbly
your hands."

Not much later, her letters profess the same conjugal affection:

Monsieur, It is a great pleasure to me and a supreme content
that (as Monsieur de Ségur has told you) my wish and will
to serve you now and all my life is acceptable to you; this will
increase my courage to persevere—not my affection, for that
has attained all fulness and can not go further. The King has
commanded me most expressly to write you of his wish for
you to come, assuring you that you will do much better for
your affairs in person than through others. . . .

In spite of sweet words various dislikes and animosities
began to strain and rend on all sides. Henri III disliked his
sister for herself and because she sided with Alençon against
him, he had invited her to court solely at his mother's instance
and in the hope that Navarre would come, too; Catherine for
her part, was irritated with Navarre for not coming; and both
were greatly concerned over Alençon's designs on the Netherlands and the danger of war with Spain. Navarre distrusted
the King and Catherine, and suspected that his wife wished
to play into their hands; while Margot was very much in love
and at the moment jealous:

To Monsieur de Champvallon

There is no more justice in heaven, nor fidelity on earth. . . . My grief and the very excess of my subject of complaint take from my pen the power of expressing my too just anger. . . . Triumph! Triumph in my dear love, in my too ardent love. Boast that you have been false to me; laugh over it, and make a jest of it with her—who gives me one bit of consolation, her merit is so little that it will bring you remorse for your wrong-doing. I am added to the number of women who will testify before posterity to the perfidy of your sex.

At this juncture a bad quarrel broke out in the royal family; the Queen Mother asserted her respect for the moral conventions that she upheld. She said that Fosseuse must go. Navarre was indignant and wrote to Margot to expostulate. Margot answered angrily:

To the King of Navarre, My Husband

As to *your little girl* [Navarre called Fosseuse *ma fille*] I informed you of what to my great regret I had heard and hear every day. You say, Monsieur, that it will never be a shame for me to do what pleases you. I agree, Monsieur, and believe you so reasonable that you will command nothing of me unworthy of a woman of my rank—nothing that will infringe upon my honor, in which you are deeply interested; and if you should command me to keep in my train a young woman whom you had got with child, you would find that I suffered a double shame, in the judgment of everybody, the indignity you did me and the reputation I should acquire. You

write me, Monsieur, that in order to shut the mouths of the
King, the Queen, the Queen Mother, and of all those that may
speak to me about this, I am to say that you love her and that
I love her on that account.   Such an answer would serve in
case of one of your retainers or servants, but of your mistress!
If I were born in a rank unworthy to be your wife, such an
answer would not be unfit, but being what I am, it would be
most unbecoming, and so I shall not let myself do it. . . . I
kiss your hands, Monsieur, very humbly.   M.

Margot might well have been more humble and left the
blame of the dismissal upon her mother, but at this very time
she was in a highly emotional state, either quarreling with
Champvallon, or making up.   In one of her letters to him,
she says, "If you knew the thousandth part of my troubles,
you would not find it strange that my letter, like my spirit,
should be all confusion.   Excuse its faults, and judge whether
in the midst of so many evils, I, a true martyr to love, can
still sing your glory as worthily as I should do were I free
from torment and trouble.   Adieu, my Life, I kiss a thousand
times your beautiful eyes and hair. . . . As our happiness
surpasses all felicities, so our evils are beyond all bounds.   Do
not be amazed, my Beautiful All, because I fall into such
thoughts; for indeed my soul, overcome by so many afflictions,
sinks beneath the insupportable burden of its grief, for ordinarily it confronts the horror of seeing the Heaven of your
divine presence ravished away, and of being plunged into the
Hell of tyranny from my cruel beast, who has been created
for my scourge [her brother the King, I think, rather than
her husband]. . . . I kiss a million times your loving and
lovely mouth."

'As to Fosseuse, the Queen Mother was firm. She was ready to grant considerable freedom to her ladies-in-waiting, but unmarried maidens were not permitted to have children. Fosseuse was sent back to her mother. Navarre was very angry and made matters worse by bidding his envoy, Monsieur de Frontenac, declare that if Mademoiselle de Montmorency (Fosseuse) was sent away, he would never go to court. At this both ladies, Margot and her mother, in their turn, were highly incensed. The Queen Mother wrote:

Saint-Maur-des-Fosses, June 12, 1582.

My Son,

I was never so astounded as when I was told the language that Frontenac has repeated to many people, saying that it was the message that you had ordered him to deliver to your wife. I would not have believed it, had he not, when I asked him myself, said that it was true. And he admitteed it with the utmost reluctance, for he did not know what had induced you to act so, seeing that when you left you had told him that you were saying good-by to Fosseuse, as if you never expected to see her again, and that you knew that it was reasonable that she should be sent back to her mother. That had become a matter of course, not then, but when she was such a fool as to give herself to you. You are not the first young husband who has not been circumspect in such matters, but you are the first in my experience, and the only one, after such a deed, to hold such language to your wife.

I had the honor to marry the King, my husband, and your Sovereign, whose daughter you have married, and when Madam Fleming was with child by him, what troubled him the most was that I had knowledge of it, and he approved of sending her away, and he never gave me a cold look, still less a cold speech. With Mme. de Valentinois [Diane de Poitiers] as with Madam d'Estampes, there was no scandal. He was your King and mine, and Marguerite is his daughter, who if you stop to consider does more for you than you think, who loves you and honors you, as though it had been as great an honor to marry you as if you were the son of a King of France and she your subject. Yours is not the way to treat a wife of such lineage, to insult her at the caprice of a gutter-snipe, and use language toward her, such that I can't believe you uttered it. You are too well born, of the royal house to which she belongs, not to know how to behave toward the daughter of your King, the sister of the Sovereign who rules over this Kingdom and over you, and who loves and honors you as a good woman should. You, too, must do as you ought, love her and cherish her and be glad that she gets rid of what-ever could jar upon the friendship you owe her. It was I who advised her to do this; I packed off at once that handsome beast. . . .

Vostre bonne mère
CATERINE

What could be more respectable? The moral values shine burnished and bright. Fosseuse was sent off in disgrace, and in August Harlay de Champvallon married, but as Margot had taken part in looking up a wife for him, his marriage was but a temporary interruption to their good understanding. The royal domestic sky looked as if it might become clear once more, when a still blacker cloud gathered and burst.

Among Navarre's letters there is this to his friend Mon-sieur Pailhes. Either the spelling of names at this time was not fixed, or royalty—Catherine, Margot, Navarre—disregarded it at pleasure:

Pau, September 18, 1582.

Monsieur de Pailles.

Monsieur de Brenieu goes at my command to Foix, so I wish to impart to you the good news that I have received that my wife is pregnant, and to rejoice with you at this. . . . I pray God, Monsieur de Pailles, to have you in His holy keeping.

Vostre bon maistre et afectionné amy

HENRY.

This does not read like Gascon humor. Could it be that he thought that he was to become a father? Could he be ignorant of the Champvallon scandal? Howbeit, gossip reports that a baby was born and that Henri III took it in ill part. On August 7, 1583, he commanded her to leave the court. Obliged to obey, she had not gone a dozen miles when she was overtaken by a guard of soldiers who found her in bed; they arrested two of her ladies, whom they accused of incontinence and abortion, also her esquire, her doctor, her secretary and others, ten persons in all. The prisoners were then conducted to Montargis, when the King himself cross-questioned them as to the conduct of his sister, and as to the child she was said to have had since she came to his court. Champvallon was suspected of the paternity, but he was away. The cross-questioning discovered nothing, and the King allowed her to continue her journey, but wrote to Navarre what had happened. Afterward, thinking better of it, he wrote a second letter begging Navarre not to refuse to receive back his wife, for he had now learned for sure that the accusation was false, and the Queen was quite innocent.

Navarre paid no heed to the second letter, but accepted the first, "which he knew had contained the truth," and made up his mind not to take his wife back. Irritated by this, Henri III sent an envoy with his command to Navarre to take her back: "You know [he wrote] that Kings are liable to be misled by false reports, and that the most virtuous Queens are often not free from calumny, you know what was said about the late Queen, your mother, how everybody has always spoken ill of her." Navarre read the letter and laughed, in his gay Gascon peasant fashion. "The King does me great honor by these letters; in the first he calls me cuckold, in the second the son of a b——. I am much obliged to him."

In spite of this, Navarre was very angry and despatched d'Aubigné to Henri III to resent the insult. D'Aubigné fulfilled his mission with spirit. Henri III said: "Go back to the King your master, since you dare call him such, and tell him, that if he takes the road to Paris I will lay a load on his shoulders that would bend those of the Grand Turk; go tell him that and get out yourself, he needs fellows like you." To this d'Aubigné replied: "Yes, Sire, he was nursed and bred in honor, and under a load such as that with which you threaten him. If you are just to him, he will serve your Majesty with his life, his lands, and his subjects; but his honor, Sire, he will not subject to you, nor to any King so long as he has the fragment of a sword in his hand." The King put his hand to his dagger, but turned and left the room. Queen Catherine came in, conciliatory, and said that the rascals who had insulted her daughter would be put to death. D'Aubigné answered that "one did not slaughter pigs as a sacrifice to Diana, that nobler blood was necessary for an expiation." Such, at least, is his story, and he adds that the King sent murderers on his trail, but that his friend Crillon lent him a fleet horse and enabled him to escape.

Poor Margot; she tried to defend herself. She wrote to her mother: "May it please you, Madam, that I may have some lady of rank, whose word will be believed, who can for the rest of my life testify to the condition I am in, and who after my death may be present at my autopsy so that, with a knowledge of this last imputation she may be able to inform every one of the wrong that has already been done me." Her case was hard: driven from Paris, separated from her lover, and refused admittance at her husband's court. But political considerations worked in her favor. Henri III realized that he had made a mistake to dishonor his sister publicly; so did Navarre, and insisted that concessions be made before he would wipe out that dishonor by receiving her back as his wife. Besides, Alençon had been very ill and his life seemed likely to be of short duration, and then Navarre would be heir to the crown of France. Henri III was really anxious for friendly relations, and went so far as to say that he was preparing to make war on Spain. A special envoy was sent down, reproaches were met by counter-reproaches, explanations by counter-explanations, each side wishing for peace without the sacrifice of personal dignity. The matter weighed heavily on Du Plessis-Mornay. He writes to Montaigne in envy: "You who are in tranquillity of soul, who neither stir nor are stirred for little things," and then unburdens himself. *"Gravitati ego sanè silentium opponam.* It is the sister of my King, the wife of my master. . . . I have told you and I tell you again, if I were free of this load, methinks I should jump about under my other burdens, but God wills to bend my back under a heavy load, and I trust that it will not break. *Haec tibi et tuo judicio.*" (November 25, 1583.)

The quarrel, therefore, was patched up, and Navarre took his wife back (April, 1584). Attempts were made to put a brave face on their meeting, and their letters describing it are very correct, but a witness has left a telltale passage in his memoirs: "The King and Queen arrived at Nérac about four o'clock, and walked together in the gallery of the château till evening, and I could see the princess weeping and when the two sat at table, where I saw them (it was by candle-light for it was late), I never saw a face more bathed in tears nor eyes more red with weeping. I felt great pity for her as she sat by the King her husband, who kept up an insignificant conversation with the gentlemen about him, and neither he nor any one else spoke to her. And this made me accept what Du Pin had told me, that the King had only received her because he was obliged to."

They made a sorry pair; but of the two Margot's plight deserves far the more pity. She had felt real love for Champvallon, in spite of the euphuistic phrases in which her literary vanity expressed it, and now she was far from him and without one true friend; but her husband had sought and found comfort in the society of a lady, who to the modern reader is the most sympathetic of all the many women that came into his life.

CHAPTER XII

ABOUT this time our acquaintance Du Plessis-Mornay, who escaped the massacre on Saint Bartholomew's Day, began his intimacy with Henry of Navarre. He was a highly intelligent, widely cultivated, puritanical Protestant, of the best sort, somewhat bigoted, as all the austere Huguenots were, but zealous for the public weal. In his relations with foreign princes, with the Huguenot churches, or in composing proclamations and declarations of opinions and purposes, Henry found him invaluable, not only in elaborating ideas but in suggesting them. Here, for instance is a reference to a plan for helping war-stricken Protestant victims in the northeast of France:

M. Du Plessis to M. Taffin

Nérac, December 7, 1582.

Sir:

I have lately been with the King of Navarre and while with him I remembered what an infinite number of people rendered destitute by the wars you have over there for whom there seems to be no help; so I suggested to the King of Navarre that he should bring down a good number of families to his principality of Béarn. He no sooner heard the proposal than he took it up with his whole heart, and promises to do his utmost to arrange everything for the best. In order that you

123

may be in a position to judge the scheme, the advantages would be as follows: It is the peculiar gift of God to this country that the pure word of God is preached in French and that all idolatry and superstition is forbidden and banished. If a sufficient number of Flemings were to settle, they would have permission to preach in their own tongue. Peace is profound and secure. Justice, which depends on peace, is as just and as carefully administered, I speak soberly, as in any place in the world. The country lies between France and Spain, near to the ocean in the neighborhood of Bayonne. The river is navigable for ships. Silk can easily be obtained from Spain, and wool and flax on the spot. The rivers are very suitable for dyeing. The conveniences which your people could get elsewhere would be inconveniences compared to those of Béarn. Corn and wine are plentiful and cheap; other necessities much the same. In order to attract industrious people to the country the King of Navarre would assign good farm lands to suitable settlers, while the towns are pleasantly situated and any privileges which they could properly demand would be granted. They would find everything needful for their trades and occupations and the kindness of the Prince would make up what the country lacked. I forgot to say that there is a University in Béarn, well provided with learned men in every branch of knowledge and language, where their children could be educated.

Yours, etc.

PHILIPPE DU PLESSIS-MORNAY.

The master was pleased with his servant, and the servant proud of his master, only the servant felt that the master was inclined to self-indulgence and did not use his time to the

greatest advantage.   In his zeal for efficiency, he drew up a
daily schedule for the employment of the King's day:

January 9, 1583.

Whoever considers the many graces with which God has
endowed the King of Navarre, and the times in which he
caused him to be born, will agree with me in thinking that he
is destined for great things and will be filled with impatience
at seeing him turn aside to petty ones.   Every one acknowl-
edges his vigorous body, his great courage, his incomparable
alertness of mind.   He is the stuff of which great princes are
made, and the only thing needed is that he should understand
that he is born for greatness and so rule his life that he may
serve for an example and a model.   The manner in which a
prince lives is of great importance to the government of a
State, and this is our reason for desiring that the King of
Navarre should observe a certain order in his life, for without
it no prince is respected.

A day is long if it is well arranged, and it gives plenty of
time both for serious business and for exercise and pleasure.
The King of Navarre should be dressed by eight o'clock at the
latest and should then send for his chaplain to conduct morning
prayers.   This done, he should enter his study accompanied by
those to whom he entrusts the conduct of his affairs. . . .
The rest of the time till dinner could be passed in such exercise
or amusement as the King likes except on sermon days.   At
his dinner there should be serious conversation in which his
counselors could share. . . . His afternoon should be quite
free except for the hour before supper, or such other hour as
he preferred, when he should go into his study with his council
to see what has been the result of previous decisions and to sign

necessary despatches. If there are none awaiting, the King might devise some.

If his Majesty dines at ten or eleven o'clock he could sup at six or seven, and retire to his room at nine or at the latest at ten o'clock. His time after supper is his own till the ministers arrive in his chamber to hold prayers at nine. With his time thus arranged the King of Navarre would manage everything without being bored and with ample leisure, and his servants would have the great happiness of knowing that he knew what they did and what they were worth so that their labor will be nothing but pleasure.

"Good sentences and well pronounced"—so the King thought, but having no real wife and deeming himself entitled after his strenuous exertions to ease, amusement and feminine society, he disregarded Du Plessis-Mornay's schedule for the sake of the lady, who must now be introduced.

The King of Navarre's sister, Catherine, after her mother's death, spent most of her time at Pau, in Château-Chéri, as she called it. Though she was not pretty, she was individual and attractive in her way,—when a little girl she drank asses' milk and called her little donkey her foster brother—and she drew suitors, chief among them her cousin, the Comte de Soissons, but her brother preferred to keep her dangling, in spinsterhood, before the eyes of such as might be of political service to him. Catherine had a friend, Diane d'Andouins, daughter of the Comte de Louvigny, who at the age of thirteen had married Philibert de Gramont, Comte de Guiche. It is not known how she got the romantic name Corisande. The husband had been killed in battle in 1580, leaving two children, a boy and a girl. Corisande had been brought up in the Protestant faith but had turned Catholic, and remained so. She was a year younger than the King, was rich and the possessor of several châteaux, at one of which the King was a visitor in January, 1583. Probably he had known her a little earlier than that, but not very much.

About April first of the preceding year he had left Fosseuse in Poitou with his wife and mother-in-law, and in June was still indignant at her dismissal; but he was soon paying his addresses to Madame d'Allons, and next to Madame de Sponde. Then came, as the records go, the turn of la belle Corisande, perhaps in the late autumn. The puritanical Du Plessis-Mornay, was troubled: "Sire," he wrote, "forgive one of your faithful servants for saying a word. These unconcealed amours, to which you give so much time, are not proper to the time. At this moment you should be making love to all Christendom, and most of all to France." But the King preferred less metaphysical love-making, and paid his court to Corisande; he was at her château at Hagetmau again in June, July and October, 1583. At this date Sully says that Henry was *"dans le fort de sa passion pour cette dame"* (at the peak of his passion for this lady).

This lady does not stand out from the dark of forgotten things so clearly as one would like. She had a skin of wonderful whiteness, and quick lightsome eyes, and she was intelligent and ready to understand and sympathize, but she was not beautiful. She was a good friend, and the King turned to her for advice as well as for comfort. Perhaps she nursed a hope in her heart that he might divorce Margot and marry her. She was proud of her family, and did not think her rank unequal to a crown. Moreover Margot's conduct at this time gave occasion for such a hope. Margot had been nominally recon-

ciled to her husband, but the reconciliation was hollow: "Let
no man say that marriages are made in heaven," she wrote, "the
Gods are not so unjust." Accusations of plots to poison were
passed from one to the other; what was worse, the King suspected that Margot was intriguing with the League. Margot
affected innocence: Had she known, she said, that her husband was so curious, she would have shown him all her letters.
Nevertheless, she asked his permission to leave Nérac and go
to Agen for Easter; this the King granted: "That's quite all
right, my Dear, go and pray God for me." At Agen the truth
came out. She collected a garrison and declared for the League
(May, 1585), and the Guises asked the King of Spain to
subsidize her. Certainly she was now out of the way. As to
getting rid of her entirely, that was another matter. Nobody,
according to the Catholic creed, could grant a divorce or annul
a marriage, other than the Pope; and that the Pope assuredly
would not do, except at the price of Henry's conversion and
probably of more, too.

Of all the King's mistresses, la belle Corisande is, as I
say, the most sympathetic. With his other loves you run into
the rough Gascon peasant and elementary passion for physical
beauty; but in her case, her intelligence, her moral opinions,
her taste, counted with him. The "lady" in her attracted his
better self; and she possessed individuality. At Mont-de-
Marsan every morning she used to go to mass accompanied by
a jester, a monkey, a blackamoor, a lackey, a spaniel and a page.
Perhaps this whimsicality was an added attraction in her lover's
eyes. He became infatuated, and neglected, or appeared to
neglect, public affairs on her account. The clear-eyed Montaigne, who had entertained the King a couple of days at his
château says: *Elle pouvait tout sur lui.* (She had complete

power over him.)   In September (1585) the Vicomte de
Turenne wrote to the Prince de Condé concerning despatches
that he had sent to the King: "I fear that my advice will not
be followed and that the pleasure of Madame de Guiche's company will keep the King of Navarre where he is longer than the
general good demands," and added that if he did not hear from
the King he should try to go to him.   "I find," he said, "that
pleasures and jealousies usually prevail in great affairs over
reason."

Navarre's relations with the Comtesse de Guiche play such
a part in his life that I shall quote from some of his letters, even
of a later date than the time the narrative has reached, for his
life during these years was all of a piece.   The first was written
at Mont-de-Marsan while she, I think, was at Pau fifty miles
to the south.   Hostilities had begun and a band of musketeers
had nearly waylaid him:

Mont-de-Marsan, December 7, 1585.

Ten o'clock at night

Mon Ame,

Don't be alarmed.   When this army at Nogaro [near the
way to Pau] have shown what they are going to do, I shall go
to see you, traveling on the wings of love, out beyond the range
of these miserable dwellers upon earth; first taking care with
God's help that this old fox [Maréchal de Matignon] can not
execute his design.   A man has come to me from the Lady of
the Camels [a very ill-bred reference to Margot] to ask for
tax free transportation of five hundred casks of wine for her
throat.   She produces a certified statement.   So she proclaims
herself a drunkard by document.   For fear lest she should fall
from the hump of her beasts, I have refused.   There's a gar-

goyle spout with a vengeance; the Queen of Tarvasset never did as much as that. If I were sure this would reach you, I could fill this page with good stories, but the fear I have of those at St. Sever [the waylaying party] makes me stop. I beg you to believe that I shall be faithful to the grave. On this truth I kiss your hands a million times.   H.

December 9, 1585.

Mon Ame,

The lackey who came yesterday was caught near Montgaillard [near Nogaro]. Taken to Monsieur de Pouyanne, he was asked if he had any letter. He said yes, one that you had written me. Monsieur de Pouyanne took it, opened it and gave it back to him. On Sunday there was a pretty fight near Monheurt that is worthy to be told. The governor with three cuirassiers and ten mounted musketeers, met Lieutenant de la Brunetière, Governor of Mas d'Agenois, who had twelve cuirassiers and as many musketeers all mounted. Our friend, perceiving how weak he himself was and as good as lost, called to his companions, "We must kill them or die." They charged, slew the commander and two more, put the rest to flight, took two prisoners, captured five chargers and all the horses belonging to the musketeers, and with but one man wounded. I have many despatches to write to-night. They will go to-morrow at noon, and I, too, to devour your hands. Bon jour, my Sovereign Good.

H.

Lusignan, May 25, 1586.

Dear Heart,

, ; . Do you always remember *Petiot* [her pet name for

him]? By Jove, my fidelity is a miracle. A thousand times
a day I wish that you were here in these alleys of the Lyranuse.
By Jove, that would be a desolate spot indeed where we two
would be bored together. Good-by, Sweet Heart, I kiss your
hands a thousand times. Love me more than yourself.

H.

La Rochelle, June 17, 1586.

. . . If you need a coach-horse, there is one in my troop
very like your coach-horses, a fine animal. I came last night
from Marans where I had gone to provide for its defense. Oh,
how I wished for you! It is the place most to your taste that
I have ever seen. For that reason I am trying to get it. It is
an island enclosed by wooded marshland, with canals every hundred feet for boats to get wood. The water is clear and hardly
moves. The canals are of all widths; the boats are of all sizes.
There are a thousand gardens in these uncultivated places
where you can only go by boat. The island is two leagues
roundabout. And the river flows at the foot of the castle, in
the middle of the town, which is as comfortable as Pau. There
are few houses where you don't step into your boat from the
door. The river has two arms, big enough not only for large
boats, but for ships of fifty tons burden. It is only two leagues
to the sea. It is, I should have said, a canal not a river. Big
boats go a dozen miles up the river [Sèvre Niortaise] to Niort;
there are lots of mills and farms, each in its own island; all
sorts of singing birds, all sorts of seabirds. I am sending you
some feathers. You can't believe the size, the quantity and the
low price of fish; a big carp three cents, a pike five. The trade
is great and all by boat. The land is full of excellent wheat.
One can live here most agreeably in time of peace, and with

security in war. A man can be very happy here with the lady whom he loves, and here he can mourn her absence. Oh, what a place to sing in! . . . *Mon Ame,* keep me in your good graces; believe that my fidelity is pure and spotless; there never was its like. If that brings you content; live happy. Your slave adores you violently. Sweet Heart, I kiss your hands a million times.

H.

Marans was little more than a collection of forts and fortified houses, situated on little islands, very much as the King described them. They had been held by the Prince de Condé, but after his death the enemy had seized them. On June twenty-fourth Navarre began an attack to recover them. He built bridges between various islands, and then proceeded to attack, island by island, fort by fort. He ordered up two galleys on the main canal that flanked the first island, effected a landing and advanced his mantelets against the counterscarp. The fort surrendered. Then he threw a bridge across from this island to another, in spite of the depth of the canals and of the cannonade from the other forts, and so on; "the King was always at the head of his men in order to see with his own eyes what should be done." When all was ready for an assault, his troops knelt down. Some one in the garrison was heard to shout, "They are praying to God, they will beat us as they did before." And so they did. In four days the two main islands, Marans and Charron, with all the fortified houses were taken, and Navarre was acknowledged to have "shown as much courtesy and kindness in sparing French blood, as he showed prudence, valor and diligence" during the fighting. And yet in the very midst of it, he found time to scribble a love-letter to Corisande.

Montguyon, June 25, 1586.

How delighted I am that you are going to Pau! Oh, my dear Mistress, what would I not pay to be able to be there! Such content is beyond price. I send you copies of the letters that the Queen of England wrote to the King and the Queen Mother, about their Peace with the League [July 7, 1585]. You will find brave language and a pleasant style [Elizabeth spoke of her grief, vexation and anger]. Dear Heart, I can't write more, for I must to horse. Good-by, my love, I kiss your hands a million times.

H.

P. S. I have two little tame wild boars and two little fawns. Send me word if you want them.

March 6, 1588.

My Lady,

I have received your letter, in which you say that you are not indifferent to me, but that you have no sense of security with a man so fickle as I. It gives me great pleasure to know the first; but you are all wrong to entertain any doubts of me. When did you know me do anything fickle? I mean toward you. You were suspicious and turned about; and you thought that I was turning. I have always remained steadfast in the love and allegiance that I swore to you. God is my witness. . . . Yesterday the Maréchal [de Matignon] and the Grand-prieur [brother and successor to Duc de Joyeuse] came up to offer battle, knowing full well that I had dismissed all my troops. It was at the top of the vineyard toward Agen. They were five hundred horse and near three thousand foot. After spending five hours in getting into order, which was disorderly enough, they advanced with the purpose of driving us into the ditches of the city. They ought to have succeeded, for they brought up all their infantry. We received them at the wall of the farthest vineyard, and retired slowly, skirmishing, to within five hundred paces of the city, where our main body was, some three hundred musketeers. We then conducted them back to the spot where they had first assailed us. It was the liveliest skirmish that I have ever seen, and with the least loss; only three soldiers wounded, and as to two of them but a scratch. Two of their men were killed (we have their bodies) and others that they carried out of sight, and a good many wounded. *Mon Ame,* keep me in your favor, that is what I want most in the world. To seal this truth, I kiss your hands a million times.

H.

Nérac, Midnight, March 8, 1588.

The Lord knows what sorrow I have to leave here without going to kiss your hands. Dear Heart, I swear, I am sick in consequence. The Devil is let loose. You should pity me; it's a wonder that I do not succumb under the burden. If I were not a Huguenot, I should turn Turk. My wits are put to the most violent proof. I can't help but becoming soon either an idiot, or a capable man. This year will be my touchstone. . . . All the Gehennas that a soul has room for are practising on me; all of them together. Be sorry for me, *Mon Ame,* and do not add your own brand of torment. That I apprehend most of all. I am going on Friday to Clairac. I shall remember your advice to hold my tongue. Believe that nothing but lack of love in you can change my resolution to be yours for ever; not always a slave, but a very true servant. My all, love me. Your favor is my soul's stay in the push of afflictions. Do not refuse me this support. Good night, *Mon Ame;* I kiss your feet a million times.

H.

His monitors, Du Plessis-Mornay, d'Aubigné, Turenne, were unnecessarily concerned lest he should neglect public affairs for his lady-love. He was very much in love, but he was more ambitious still, and his activity and energy were amazing. As his letters show, year in, year out, he was leading his men, here, there and everywhere, raiding, attacking, rushing to defend, or reconnoitering or skirmishing; going without food for twenty-four hours; dragging his horse down the winding stair of a turret just in time to escape by the castle's postern gate; gathering his friends for a foray: "Put wings to your best horse; I've told Montespan to founder his. Why? I'll tell you at Nérac. Come, run, fly! It's the command of your master and the prayer of your friend, Henry;" or again, "Go to the rendezvous with your men, just as soon as you get this, and if you pick up any news of the enemy, let me know at once"; or, laughing at danger, when Mayenne was writing to the King that he could not escape, "Monsieur de Mayenne isn't such a bad fellow as to prevent me from going where I like in Guyenne. . . . They have surrounded me like a wild boar, and think to take me in the toils; but I shall slip through, or crawl out on my belly;" and so on, giving pet names to his friends, *Grand damné!* (Old Rascal); *Monfaulcher,* (Reaper in allusion to prowess on battle-field); *Crapaud* (Toad); *Petit Enfant, Petit fou* (You little Lunatic); or writing affectionate notes, "I'm passing by your house tomorrow, I mean to stop and sample your wine bin."

But if he did once or twice sacrifice chances and gains for

love, so much the better. Wariness had been so necessary to him that it had become a second nature; usually one meets it in him at every turn; but as to his conduct after his victory at Coutras (to which I shall come later) and at Castels, perhaps it is fair to agree with d'Aubigné and gratefully admit that a boyish pride to show his conquests to his lady overrode all other thoughts.

CHAPTER XIII

On June 10, 1584, not two months after Margot's return to Nérac, the Duc d'Alençon died and Henry of Navarre became heir presumptive to the throne of France. Both the King and Navarre had disliked Alençon; and Navarre had said of him: "He has little courage, he is mean and a double-dealer, his body is ill-made, he has little attraction in his bearing, and little skill at any game; I can not think that he will ever accomplish much." Now he wrote:

June, 1584.

Monseigneur,

The sad news that I have received by Your Majesty's letters of the death of the Duc d'Alençon has brought me sorrow that is most due. I recognize my inestimable loss, and I feel your Majesty's no less, for I am sensitive to the quick in all that concerns you. Nevertheless, that steadfastness, which it is your Majesty's habit to oppose to grief, ought to enable you to surmount this. Your Majesty, I am sure, will do so, and bow beneath the will of God, under which we all must bow. . . .

Henry.

With poor Alençon out of the way, the three Henrys occupy the foreground of the stage; all three destined to die at

137

the hands of assassins. Did they think of their boyhood days where they sat together on the benches of the Collège de Navarre? Or, of that twenty-fourth of August when Henry of Valois gave the order to Henry of Guise to murder the wounded Coligny in his bed, and Henry of Navarre heard the shrieks and groans of his friends as they waked from their sleep in the palace of their royal host to be cut down, hacked and stabbed to death? Or, of those days when during the fêtes in honor of Henry of Valois's election to the throne of Poland, Henry of Navarre and Henry of Guise *"couchoyent, mangeoyent et faisoyent ensemble leurs mascarades, balets et carrousels"* (slept, dined, danced and tilted together)?

Henri de Valois, like his brothers, lacked the poise and stability usual to normal human beings. His boyish love of distinction that had won him renown in the early battles with the Huguenot rebels, and had caused his mother to think him a great soldier, had faded away; in its place he desired to pose as a patron of culture. He was handsome, intelligent, and of good presence, and ambitious to emulate his grandfather, François I, and his relations, the Medici. He patronized two savants, Bernard Palissy and Henry Estienne, though both were Huguenots; he converted the Academy of Poetry, that Charles IX had founded, into an Academy of Philosophy, and endeavored to make up for the deficiencies of boyhood by studying Latin. It is said of him that he was "an intellectual with a dislike for action." But intellectual interests by no means occupied all his time. Latin grammar did not prevent him from less academic interests; and, whether due to grammar or to women, his disregard of his royal duties lost him all good opinion in the minds of men. Epigrams rained upon him. One ran:

The King in his palace studies his grammar,
Until he—fine fellow—can decline "amo, ama,"
"I love, she loves," and so on, all through,
Till by constant declining he declines too.

He was frivolous in his amusements, in his religion, in all his habits. At balls he tricked himself out in millinery, till his dress was like a woman's, open at the neck with a necklace of pearls; and again, in a pious fit he would lay his finery aside and go from oratory to oratory, or walk through the streets in midnight processions of monks and priests. But at times, like his brother Charles IX, he had fits of energy. He was told that Guise referred to him slightingly as a monk; he mounted his horse, galloped about at a furious pace and shouted out: "Go ask the Duc de Guise if that is the way a monk rides." He and his wife, Louise of Lorraine, would make visits to Chartres, in order to pray to the statue of *Notre-Dame-de-Sous-Terre* to grant them a child; and sometimes they would drive through Paris, or in the country round about, looking for lap-dogs, and enter private houses, or convents, and take dogs they liked from their unwilling owners.

But more than all such practises, the King's band of favorites brought him into general disrepute and contempt. At this time, L'Estoile says, the word *mignons* came into vogue to designate the King's favorites. They were a troop of debauched young men, who carried foppery to an Oriental height; they frizzled their hair, painted their faces, covered themselves with scents, "gamed, blasphemed, jumped, danced, vaulted, quarreled, frequented brothels, followed the King about, saying or doing anything to please him, and snapped their fingers at God and righteousness." The two principal favorites—men of better stuff than the others—Arques and

Epernon, were the most costly. When the *premier mignon* Arques was married to the King's sister-in-law, he was created Duc de Joyeuse and peer of France; and at the fêtes that celebrated the wedding, where day after day the ladies and gentlemen of the court wore fresh garments of cloth of gold or silver, ornamented with *passemons, guipures, recaneures* and *embroderies,* heavy with gold and silver and precious stones, one million two hundred thousand crowns were spent, and, at a time, as L'Estoile says, when the people were "eaten and gnawed to the bone" by taxation.

Henri III heaped upon Joyeuse and Epernon honors and offices, hoping to raise them to an estate of power, where they would balance the Guises; the lesser *mignons* received less and did nothing but swagger about, gamble, make love and stir up broils. They were well hated. One of them, Saint-Megrin, who was believed to be paying court to the Duchesse de Guise, was set upon by a band of men, as he was leaving the palace of the Louvre one evening, and murdered. Report said that the Duc de Mayenne had led the assassins. Navarre's comment was: "I am obliged to my cousin, the Duc de Guise, in that he did not permit a *mignon de couchette* like Saint-Megrin, to make him cuckold. That's the proper way to deal with these little court gallants who come dangling about to make love to princesses!" In such society the King's reputation sank low; every wit made a butt of him: "Henri, by the grace of his mother, doubtful King of France, and imaginary King of Poland, Janitor of the Louvre, Sacristan of Saint-Germain-de-l'Auxerrois and all the churches in Paris, Son-in-law to his wife's hairdresser, Haberdasher to the palace, Guardian of the Old Beggars' Home, Conscript Father of the White Penitents, Protector of good-for-nothings."

Jean Louis de Nogaret de la Valette, Duc d'Epernon, Pair et Amiral de France, nome 1581

Jean Louis, Duc d'Epernon
From the portrait in the Bibliothèque Nationale

The brilliant Henri de Guise despised the King; and he did not content himself with sneers. After the Edict of 1576, which had granted to the Huguenots full liberty of worship, he had founded the League in order to give to Catholic resentment a corporate body, and create an instrument by which he should be able to dominate the King, and, it might be, win the Kingdom. The King's attempt to foil him by the assumption of the captaincy of the League, and then by the dissolution of all leagues, had had little effect; the League indeed fell for a time into abeyance, for later Edicts had reduced the privileges of the Huguenots to small dimensions, but now that a Huguenot had become heir to the throne, Guise's organization raised its head with a start. France, as a whole, was profoundly Catholic, the great majority of her people did not believe that a heretic could be the lawful king, clearly he could not be anointed at Reims; and the Guises proposed to make the most of this sentiment.

Henri de Guise was a staunch Catholic at heart, but his ambitions were stauncher. He chafed at not being the first man in the Kingdom. Though but thirty-five, care had aged him beyond his years and he had grown thin, but his lean cheeks and premature wrinkles served to set off the more brilliantly the great scar that ran from eye to ear. In his early youth he had been impetuous to folly, at the battle of Jarnac, at Saint-Yrieix and at Moncontour, but in his defense of Poitiers he had won a renown comparable to his father's for the defense of Metz, and at Dormans, where he got his scar, he had defeated invading German mercenaries. Both his impetuous folly and his prudent skill had won him admiration, and now this big, handsome, brilliant, bold, abstemious man had become the hope of his party and the favorite of Paris.

A dukedom was too narrow for his thoughts. He had intrigued with the Pope, devising projects to invade England with Spanish troops, dethrone Elizabeth, and save Mary Stuart; and now he cast his eyes upon the Crown of France.

The Duke was so good a Catholic that he rated his duty to his religion higher than patriotism; and he had, under pressure of great pecuniary need for his ambitious plans, accepted a pension from Philip of Spain, and in return he shared with Philip his knowledge of important matters that took place in France. But Guise also believed that his purposes, religious and political, were for the best interests of France. It was usual to turn to foreign potentates for help; Coligny had done so, and the practise lasted for a hundred years up to the time of the Great Condé. Guise felt, as most Frenchmen, that heresy deprived an heir of his inheritance. And now, after the death of Alençon, he was confronted not only with the duty of excluding a heretic from the Crown of France but also with the possibility of wearing that crown himself; did not his family boast that they were descended from Charlemagne? In December, 1584, therefore, Henri de Guise, his brothers, the Duc de Mayenne and the Cardinal de Guise, his cousins, the Dukes of Aumale and Elbœuf, entered into a pact with the King of Spain to exclude Bourbon heretics from the throne of France, to declare Navarre's uncle, the Cardinal de Bourbon the lawful successor, to maintain a Holy League for the defense and preservation of the Catholic religion, Apostolic and Roman, and to extirpate all heresy from France and the Netherlands. Philip promised a subsidy of six hundred thousand crowns a year. Henri de Guise was actuated by love of his religion and by ambition, but he probably did not forget that Navarre had pushed him aside when he wished to marry

Margot, and that they had been rivals for the affections of Madame de Sauves; besides, his vendetta with the Huguenots for the assassination of his father, had not been wiped out by the death of Coligny. Religion, revenge, ambition and jealousy worked on that haughty spirit. As yet he did not venture to proclaim his highest hopes, and therefore put forward the Cardinal de Bourbon as a stalking-horse.

By the side of the big handsome ambitious Duke of Guise, Henri de Valois made a pitiful figure. Between the rebellious League to the right and the rebellious Huguenots to the left, he did not know what to do, and he had no counselors worth their salt. Some months earlier when he knew that his brother was dying and that the strenuous Catholics were stirring uneasily, he had turned toward Navarre, and sent the Duc d'Epernon to invite him to come to court, and say that if Navarre would but attend mass, he would acknowledge him before the nation as his heir and treat him accordingly. Navarre undoubtedly had made up his own mind what to do, but he called his chief counselors together and asked their advice; they were pleased to be consulted and if skilfully chosen, were sure to contradict one another, and so leave Henry free to follow his own wishes. The Catholics encouraged him to go, bade him accept the national religion, if only *"à la bouche et à l'extérieur,"* for then he would have the power of France behind him; the choice, they said, lay between a crown and psalm-singing, which did he prefer? The Protestants asserted that he ought not to abandon his religion, and asked how could he trust the King, had he forgotten Saint Bartholomew? Others, less partizan, said that to their thinking, if Navarre turned Catholic, his reputation for constancy and sincerity would suffer, Protestants would forsake him and Catholics distrust him, he would be certain to lose his present position as party chief, and for most uncertain advantage. Navarre agreed with the last opinion; he did not wish to be thought to shift his religion for the chance of grasping the Crown; and supposing he should, and that the King acknowledged him as heir presumptive, would the League accept him? He believed, he said, that there should be tolerance, freedom of conscience and freedom of worship, that, for his own part, he was ready to be instructed, and if a religious council would discuss all the points at issue and discover a way of agreement, he would lend a ready ear to their conclusions. And so saying, he had declined the King's invitation.

Henri III did not acknowledge Navarre as his heir, but continued to be friendly toward him. He was but thirty-two and might have children yet; so he went on with his debauches and his pentitential processions, and dances with his *mignons* in the Louvre. Loyalty dwindled to most pitiful proportions. And then the League, confident in the King's weakness, launched its "Declaration of the causes that had moved Monseigneur the Cardinal de Bourbon, and the Catholic Peers, Princes, Gentlemen, cities, and towns of the Kingdom of France, to oppose by every means those who are trying to subvert the Catholic religion of the State." The Declaration also attacked the King's *mignons,* and their evil influences, and various other grievances; it pledged the League to reestablish by force the Catholic religion, to restore the Noblesse to rights, to ease the people of burdens, to defend the privileges of the Parliament, and to hold meetings of the States-General every three years.

The King answered by a royal manifesto (April, 1585). And to the King's answer, Guise retorted by hiring Swiss and

German mercenaries. Catholic lords took up arms in Normandy, Brittany and Picardy; Mayenne occupied Dijon, Mâcon and Auxonne. Almost all the north and center of France, and the large cities, declared for the League, while the west and south held for the King. Royalists were in office in Paris, but the Parisians were very restive and uncertain. For a month or two the King made a show of resistance; and then, for he was utterly incapable of meeting a crisis, he gave way and yielded to every point of the League's demands (July, 1585). Henry of Navarre said afterward, that when he heard this news "apprehension of the evils that he foresaw for his country turned half his mustache white." He wrote to the King:

July 10, 1585.

Monseigneur,

. . . I hear that you have made peace without me and against me, that you have joined your enemies to ruin your servitors, your most faithful subjects and those that have the honor to be your nearest of kin. And what is more you have bestowed your soldiers, your authority and your money, to strengthen those that have taken up arms against you, to give them ampler means to impose their law upon you. To me this is hard, almost unendurable. Still, Monseigneur, I can not abandon the hope that I have always had in your Majesty's goodness, justice and love toward your servants, your subjects and your Kingdom. I await a declaration of your will, to which I shall try to conform so long as my life shall last.

Your very humble, obedient subject and servant

HENRY,

He issued a manifesto in which he deplored civil war and
the misery brought upon the French people and offered to meet
Henri de Guise in mortal combat, they two alone, or two to
two, ten to ten, or twenty to twenty, in spite of their different
rank, *honneur certes, veu la disproportion et inegalité de leurs
personnes et degrez.* It was a useless protest. In obedience to
the League, Henri III issued the Edict which forbade all exercise of the Reformed religion, ordered all ministers to leave
the country at once, and their congregations to become Catholic, or else also to leave within six months; he also handed
over many fortified towns to the chiefs of the League and
made large grants of money. Navarre wrote again to the
King:

Bergerac, July 21, 1585.

Monseigneur,

When the authors of these new disturbances first gave in-
dication of their enmity toward your Majesty and the State,
you were pleased to write me your opinion, that you had very
justly made, concerning their purposes; that you were well
aware, whatever pretext they put forward, that they were acting against your person and your crown, that they wished to
benefit themselves at your expense, and aimed at the total ruin
of the State. Those were the words in your letter. . . .

And now, Monseigneur, when I hear that your Majesty has
made a treaty with the very men who rose up against you, upon
terms by which your Edicts are quashed, your loyal subjects
banished, the conspirators not only armed, but armed with your
forces and your authority, against your very loyal subjects and

against myself, I leave it to your Majesty to judge of my confusion and despair. . . .

Your very humble, obedient and faithful subject and servant,

HENRY.

To the King's ambassadors he spoke out roundly: The King was ill advised to surrender to the caprice of men who were really his enemies, and as for himself it would be neither right nor honorable to abandon his religion from motives of fear or of personal advantage; he valued his soul's health more than all the crowns of the world, but he was ready to be instructed and to change, if he was not on the right road, ready to submit to the decision of a council; that it was unreasonable to ask the Huguenots to give up their strongholds, their cities of refuge, and that the Reformed religion was too strongly rooted in France for this new Edict extorted from his Majesty to uproot it in a moment.

At the same time Navarre did what he could to strengthen himself. With the aid of his accomplished counselor, Du Plessis-Mornay, he appealed to the Parliament of Paris, to the Sorbonne, wrote more expostulations to the King and the Queen Mother, and complained to the Swiss, to the Duke of Saxony and the King of Sweden, of this attack on their religion and so on. He also made up his disagreements with his cousin, Condé, and with Damville, son of old Anne de Montmorency, Governor of Languedoc, so that all should work together for their common safety.

The Catholics also made preparations. On September 9, 1585, Pope Gregory XIII launched his bull; he declared Henry of Navarre deposed as a relapsed heretic and released his subjects from their duty of allegiance. Navarre answered by a counter-proclamation to the clergy of the realm: "God caused me to be born a Christian Prince; I desire the establishment, the increase and the peace of the Christian religion; we believe in the same God, the same Jesus Christ, we acknowledge the same Gospel: If we disagree about the interpretation of certain texts, I believe that the peaceful course that I propose would bring us together; I believe that the war which you encourage so hotly is unworthy of Christians, unworthy between Christians, especially among those who profess to expound the Gospel; since you like war so much, since you prefer battle to discussion, I wash my hands of it all; the blood that is shed be on your heads."

Proclamations and counter-proclamations led speedily to actual war, the Huguenots and the Moderate Catholics of the south defended themselves against the League and the King. Nothing decisive occurred. Henri III gave but half-hearted support to his generals; he was reluctant to let the Guises strengthen themselves with a victory, for in his heart, though a stout Catholic, he dreaded them more than he did the Huguenots; he really did not know what to do and virtually left public business to the vigilance of the Queen Mother, and concerned himself "to an alarming extent" with his devotions.

CHAPTER XIV

THE situation was chaotic. Catholicism and Protestantism were in grapple for domination in Europe. Elizabeth of England, wishing to break the Spanish hold upon the Netherlands, but unwilling that France should control them, grudgingly subsidized Dutch rebels, German Protestants and French Huguenots, according as money would go farthest, and at the same time did her best in every way to keep France and Spain at odds, and France divided against herself. Philip hated Protestantism as a heresy and as a form of rebellion, and he was afraid lest Protestantism in France should enable the Netherlands to cast off the Spanish yoke. France wished to obtain suzerainty over the Netherlands, but was afraid to challenge Philip openly; and Henri III, although he had given in to the League, both feared and hated it, and thwarted it in underhand fashion whenever he could, in the vague hope that he should hold the balance of power by setting the Huguenots and the League against each other. With this in mind, he still nursed hopes that Navarre might be converted, or, if not, then persuaded to lay down his arms and come to court; and this time he asked his mother to undertake the mission, which she gladly did.

In such troubled waters as these, the Queen Mother delighted to fish. She was now sixty-six years old, rich in unrivaled political experience, and as confident as ever in her activities and talents of persuasion.

For several months Navarre eluded an interview, but the two finally met at the castle of Saint-Brice near Cognac in December, 1586. The Queen was suspicious and prudent; she requested Henry not to bring more than fifty gentlemen of his suite with him to the meeting, and when they met in the great hall of the castle, she put her arms round him and playfully tickled him. Henry understood the meaning of her act; he undid the buttons of his doublet and said, "Madam, you may see that I wear no armor when I pay my respects to a lady." She smiled one of her wan Medicean smiles, and they talked, according to report, as follows:

She: Well, my son, are we going to accomplish something?

He: Ma'am, that does not depend upon me, but it is just what I desire.

She: You must then say what it is that you desire.

He: Your Majesty's wishes are mine.

She: Let us not bandy compliments; tell me what your demands are.

He: Ma'am, I demand nothing; I have merely come to receive your commands.

She: Oh, make a suggestion.

He: Ma'am, I have none to make.

She: Do you wish to ruin the Kingdom? Have you forgotten that next to the King, you are the person most interested?

He: Ma'am, you and he have not given much consideration to that fact, having put eight armies in the field to cause my ruin.

She: What armies, my son? You deceive yourself. Do you suppose that if the King had wished to destroy you he could not have done so? Not power, but the will, to destroy you was absent.

He: Excuse me, Ma'am, my undoing does not lie in the hands of men; it is neither in the King's power, nor in yours.

She: Are you ignorant of the extent of the King's power?

He: I know very well, Ma'am, what he can do and what he can't.

She: Indeed! And don't you wish to obey your King?

He: I have always wanted to, and to testify my desire, I have often begged him to honor me with his command to place myself under his authority against the leaders of the League, who have taken up arms against his Edicts and the public peace.

She: Don't deceive yourself, my son, they are not leagued against the Kingdom, they are all Frenchmen and the truest Catholics in France, but they are afraid of the Huguenots, and to speak frankly to you, the King is quite aware of their purposes and approves them. But drop that, speak about yourself, and ask just what you want, and the King will grant it.

He: I ask for nothing, Ma'am, but if you wish to ask me for something, I will propose it to my friends, for I have promised not to do anything without consulting them.

She: Very well, my son, since you put it in that way. I will say no more than that the King loves and honors you and wishes to have you by his side and treat you like a brother.

He: I thank you very kindly, Ma'am, and I warrant you that I shall never fail in my duty toward him.

She: Is that all you have to say?

He: Isn't that a great deal?

She: Then you mean to continue to cause misery and ruin the Kingdom?

He: Me! Ma'am! I know very well that the Kingdom will never be so utterly ruined but that there will still be some little corner in it left for me.

She: Don't you mean to obey the King? Aren't you afraid that he will be angry with you?

He: I must admit the truth, Ma'am; I have not obeyed the King for eighteen months.

She: Don't say that, my son.

He: I must, for the King, who should be a father to me, instead of treating me like his son, has hunted me like a wolf, and you, Ma'am, have joined in like a she-lion.

She: What, haven't I always behaved toward you like a mother?

He: Yes, Ma'am, when I was a little boy, but during the last six years you are much changed.

She: My son, the King and I desire nothing but your good.

He: Excuse me, Ma'am, my experience is just the opposite.

She: Well, no matter about that. Do you want all the trouble I have been taking for the last six months to go for nothing after having kept me dancing about?

He: It wasn't my fault, Ma'am, but yours. I have not been keeping you from sleeping in your own bed, whereas for the last eighteen months, you have been keeping me from mine.

She: Must I always live in turmoil, I who ask for nothing but rest?

Henri, Duc de Guise, called "le Balafré"

Portrait in the Louvre

He: Ma'am, this turmoil is your delight and daily food, if you were quiet you would not live long.

She: How, how! You used to be polite and reasonable, and now anger flashes from your eyes, and out of your mouth.

He: Yes, I am changed from what I used to be by your unkind behavior and the long series of obstacles that you have put in my way.

She: Well, well! As long as you can't act of yourself, let us make a temporary truce, during which you can confer with your pastors and associates, in order to effect a lasting peace.

He: Very good, Ma'am, I will do so.

These conferences dawdled along for a month or two and came to nothing. The difficulties of the triangular situation—King, League, Huguenots—and their mutual distrust made accommodation impossible. War followed; and in this warfare of raids, forays, defenses, surprises and privations, Navarre was incomparable. He was in the trenches beside his men with pick and shovel, sleeping where he could on the grass or in an ox-cart, not once in his bed for two weeks at a time, so tired that he could not sit his horse, and always in the forefront of danger; once while an envoy was shouting in his ear, in order to be heard above the din of battle, a cannon ball took the man's head off. He won the devotion of his soldiers and a great reputation for valor, discretion and good-fellowship. To oppose him Henri III sent the elegant young Duc de Joyeuse, perfumed like a milliner.

The two armies met at the passage of the River Dronne which flows into the Dordogne, not far from Bordeaux. The

Royalist cavaliers, in gilded armor, were as *gaillard* as if they were on a parade, each man vowing to do more valorous deeds than the other, and to take no prisoners except Navarre himself. The battle was fought on October 20, 1587. The two armies were of about the same strength, four to five thousand foot, and near fifteen hundred horse each, though in this arm the Royalists seem to have had two or three hundred more. Navarre drew up his army in the form of a crescent, on a small plain to the east of the town of Coutras, in the corner between the Rivers Dronne and Isle; he had his back to the town, with a little brook on one hand and a park and bushy field on the other, where, in a ditch along a road, he stationed a line of musketeers. The artillery was placed on a little eminence to the left. The cavalry was drawn up in three squadrons and musketeers were stationed in the gaps between the squadrons. The Duc de Joyeuse all clinquant, his armor inlaid with enamel and silver, gave evidence that his talents were more suited to the boudoir than to the battle-field; he stationed his artillery in a spot which did not command the Huguenot position, and was obliged to move it at a time when it should have been firing vigorously; he massed his infantry on his two wings in the open, wholly unprotected; he armed his heavy cavalry with long spears, which required the riders to leave a considerable space between them in order to give the spears play; all which tactics, as it turned out, were wrongly planned.

The King assumed command of one of the squadrons of horse; Condé and Turenne commanded the other two. He said to his cousins, Condé and Soissons: "Remember your Bourbon blood! God's wounds! I will show you that I am the eldest son of the House." Condé answered: "And we will show ourselves worthy younger brothers." And, indeed, that day the armor of all three was dinted and hacked. "You see," Henry continued, "they are arraying themselves against our House. It would not be quite right for this gay dancer and the *mignons* of the court, to carry away our three heads, which God has preserved so far that they may save the heads of our friends, likewise the State. This is our common quarrel and we shall share the honor." Then addressing his soldiers he said: "My friends, here is a quarry better than any yet; here is a young bridegroom with his marriage portion in his coffers, and the pick of the courtiers with him. The meanest among you shall ride a charger and eat out of silver dishes. They are ours. Nevertheless, let us remember that the event is in the hands of God. He knows and favors the justice of our arms. Pray Him to help us. This is our hardest fight. Victory will glorify God, benefit the King, honor us, and save France." Brantôme says that he wore his famous white plume; d'Aubigné that he put on a plain morion and gray armor like his men.

The Huguenot cannon blazed away. Prayer was said, and the army chaunted the psalm:

This is the day which the Lord hath made;
We will rejoice and be glad in it.
Save now, we beseech thee, O Lord,
O Lord, we beseech thee, send now prosperity.

The Royalist cavalry charged, and in some places broke through; there was cross-fire from the Huguenot infantry ensconced on the right, charges, counter-charges, confusion. Condé was unhorsed, Turenne's steed killed under him. Navarre was in the thick of the fight. Two cavaliers bore down on him, making signs for him to surrender. His squire,

Frontenac, struck one on the head, and the King, who had just fired his pistol at a third, grasped the second round the waist, crying: "Surrender yourself, Philistine!"; a fourth smote the King's helmet with the fragment of a lance, but a gentleman of the bedchamber, Augustin de Constant, beat off this assailant. One of his squires, Rives, was struck down in front of him, at which another, Fons-le-bon, jumped into Rives's place. The King kept his captive. The heavy musket fire from the Huguenot right threw the enemy's left into confusion. The Duc de Joyeuse fell, his men lost courage, turned and fled, the rout was complete, three hundred Catholic gentlemen were slain, several of great note, including the Duke and his brother, and many hundreds of the common soldiers. D'Aubigné says that the victors lost but five gentlemen and twenty soldiers. It was a great victory, the first that the Huguenots had won on a battle-field in twenty-five years of civil war. The eulogy upon the King that Du Plessis-Mornay had written in 1583 had been fully justified: "In the person of the King of Navarre, every one remarks his vigor of body, his quickness of intelligence, and his great courage, that are all but incomparable. That is the stuff of which the greatest princes are made."

In his victory Navarre behaved with magnanimity. He gave honor to the dead, although report said that the *"archi-mignon"* Joyeuse had once cut the throats of five hundred Huguenot captives, he looked to the wounds of his prisoners, and sent many home without ransom. He wrote to the King: "Sire, Monseigneur, and Brother, I have beaten your enemies and mine. *Vive Dieu!*" and to Monsieur de Matignon—perhaps from the White Horse Tavern, where Du Plessis-Mornay put up (the house still exists): "Dear Cousin. . . . I feel very badly that I could not make a difference between loyal Frenchmen and partizans of the League, but at least those that are in my hands will bear witness to the courtesy that they have received from me and my officers, who took them prisoner. Believe me that I regret deeply the blood that has been spilt, and it will not be my fault if it is not staunched. But everybody knows that I am guiltless. . . . Henry."

He said that he was ready to make peace, on the basis of the Edict of 1577, which had granted but a very moderate liberty of worship to the Protestants. And then he disgusted his friends.

A force of German and Swiss mercenaries, hired to aid the Protestant cause with money contributed by Queen Elizabeth and the King of Denmark, had gone through Lorraine and marched into Burgundy, intending, if they could, to cross the Loire and effect a function with Navarre's army. Henri III, having sent Joyeuse to Gascony, had himself taken command of the forces guarding the Loire, and despatched Guise against the invading mercenaries; probably in his heart he hoped that Joyeuse and Navarre would hold each other in check and that Guise would be beaten. Things turned out otherwise. After the defeat of Joyeuse, Guise attacked and beat the Germans at Vimory (October 26, 1587) and at Auneau (November 24). The Swiss came to terms with Henri III and withdrew. But why did Navarre not push on after the victory at Coutras and join the Germans and Swiss—as the Huguenots all expected him to do, and then, with united forces, crush the League and force the King to grant complete liberty of worship? Some say, that Navarre did not wish to come at the head of an army and confront his sovereign face to face; others, that his forces consisted of random volunteers, who refused to stay together any longer, the gentlemen being impatient to get back to their estates, the common soldiers to their fields and cattle. But d'Aubigné says: "There was great discontent among all the Huguenot captains, when the King of Navarre, giving but one day to reckoning up the gains of victory, and neglecting what he could have done, either to capture the cities of Saintonge and Poitou, or to go to meet the foreign army that was approaching the Loire, as many wished, tossed all such advice to the winds and offered up his victory to love; he traversed all Gascony in order to carry twenty-two battle flags to the Comtesse de Guiche, then at Béarn," and ironically adds: "I will not reckon up the churches and mills that constitute the fruits of the great victory."

CHAPTER XV

THE DAY OF THE BARRICADES

FROM this time on Henry of Navarre had need of all his wariness. Another death strengthened his position as chief of the Huguenot party and added to his responsibility. On March 5, 1588, his cousin, the Prince de Condé, died from poison. The two men had scarcely been friends; for a long time there had been jealousy and rivalry between them. Their characters were different; Navarre always looked before he leapt, whereas Condé leapt upon the first impulse, without looking. At Coutras, Condé had commanded one of the squadrons of horse under his cousin and had fought gallantly, but he was vastly annoyed when Navarre, instead of following up the victory, galloped over to lay the trophies before the Comtesse de Guiche. On the other hand, some two years before, Condé had pushed himself forward in Navarre's place, much to Navarre's annoyance, to go to the relief of a castle, which the Leaguers were besieging, and had been beaten; and Navarre and his friends had laughed. And although Navarre was of the elder branch of the Bourbons and was therefore indisputably entitled to precedence, Condé's reckless spirit commended him to the more bellicose Huguenots, and some thought him the better leader, the first to fight and the last to retreat. It may have been jealousy, therefore, that made Navarre think meanly of Condé's military abilities. But all rivalry was now forgotten, and Navarre not only regretted Condé's death, but he felt that his own life was in danger. He wrote to Corisande:

March 10, 1588.

One of the worst misfortunes that I could dread has befallen me, the sudden death of Monsieur le Prince. On Thursday the poor Prince rode at the ring, dined, and was perfectly well, at midnight a violent fit of vomiting came on him, and lasted until morning. All Friday he stayed in bed. In the evening he dined, slept well, and on Saturday morning got up, had his meals at table and played chess. He stood up, and began to walk up and down the room, chatting. All of a sudden he exclaimed, "Give me a chair. I feel very weak." He had hardly sat down, when he lost speech, and suddenly died. The marks of poison made themselves apparent at once. . . . I am likely to have much trouble. Pray God for me. If I am to escape, He must keep me. I remain your faithful slave to the grave, to which perhaps I am nearer than I think. Good night, my Soul, I kiss your hands a million times.

H.

Sainte Foy, March 13, 1588.

Remember what I have often told you. I am never wrong in my judgments. A wicked woman is a dangerous beast. All these poisoners are papists. . . . *Mon Ame,* I am well in body but sad at heart. Love me and let me see that you do.

H.

Taillebourg, March 17, 1588.

The papists . . . are canonizing this fine deed and the man that did it, and advise all good Catholics to take example by so Christian a feat. And you belong to that religion! Dear Heart, now you have a fine chance to show your piety and

virtue. Don't wait, but fling that smock to the nettles. I must
to horse and therefore stop.

H.

La Rochelle, March 21, 1588.

Since I came here I have been continuously on horseback.
I have had but one hour's sleep. As to the death of Monsieur
le Prince, more and more wickedness is being discovered, and
in the quarter that you can guess from my last letter. My
soul, do not forget me, and never doubt my constancy. Let
me hear from you often. Good-by, dear Heart. Your slave
kisses your hands a million times.

H.

The Prince, it is believed, was poisoned by his wife; but
the memory of the spirit behind Saint Bartholomew was fresh
in Henry's mind. In 1585 he had arrested his wife's
secretary on the charge of trying to poison him; perhaps he
believed the charge, perhaps it was in revenge for Margot's
accusation that Madame de Guiche wished to poison her;
recently, almost at this very time, a man was arrested who
confessed that he was one of twenty-four sworn to kill him.
So strong was his fear of poison that the Florentine Ambassador wrote home that the King of Navarre "who is accustomed
to go about and eat freely with everybody, has completely
changed his mode of life." Nevertheless, Condé's death had
removed a rival and left Navarre undisputed head of the party;
and new circumstances roused him out of this depression.

During the progress of the war the League had been organizing and enrolling new adherents; from Paris, head and front
of the popular movement, emissaries had gone to the cities

round about, Chartres, Orléans, Blois and Tours, spreading their propaganda, and Guise's victories over the German mercenaries had made him more of a hero than ever. In Paris, the Leaguers grew so bold that the King became frightened, ordered up his Swiss troops to the neighborhood and forbade Guise to enter the city. Guise disobeyed. Philip of Spain had at last completed his slow preparations, and in May the Invincible Armada was ready to sail; and, as it was important that Henri III should have his hands so well occupied at home that he could give no aid to England, Philip ordered Guise to provide him with such occupation. Guise, therefore, rode into Paris on May ninth. The people (as L'Estoile says) "poisoned and besotted by their love of him," waved their hats, cheered, kissed the flaps of his cloak, and shouted "Vive Guise!" "Long live the pillar of the Church!"; while he, hat in hand, bowed and smiled back. He went directly to the palace occupied by the Queen Mother, which stood where the *bourse* stands now. She sent word to the Louvre of the Duke's arrival. But Henry had already been told. "By God," he cried, "he shall die for this," and then sat silent for a while with his head in his hands.

The Queen Mother and the Duke followed soon after her messenger. Some say that they drove together in her carriage, others that she went in her litter and he on foot. They entered the palace together, he walking magnificent beside her, in white satin doublet and black mantle, with a green feather in his hat. The Queen Mother was in anxiety as to what might happen and, revolving in her mind how she could mitigate the King's wrath at the Duke's disobedience and forestall a breach between the two that could not be healed, made the Duke a suggestion. As she expected, the King broke into reproaches. The Duke replied: "I came at the request of the Queen Mother." And Catherine, standing by, declared that it was so. The King was probably not deceived, but the French usage of deference from son to mother prevented him from contradicting her. The first danger was over and the Duke soon took his leave; but a rash deed had been imminent. Rumor busied itself with the interview: a Corsican colonel had offered to take off the Duke's head; a priest had quoted Holy Writ, "I will smite the shepherd and the sheep shall be scattered"; members of the King's Gascon body-guard, the Forty-Five, had been hidden in ambush, and so forth. Paris was excited and credulity pricked up its ears. At any rate, when the Duke was seen to come safely out of the palace, he was greeted with a frenzy of delight; as he passed along, flowers were thrown at his feet, people thronged about to touch the hem of his cloak, they held out rosaries to be blessed, they cried, "Hosanna to the Son of David!"

For a day or two the agitation of the city was kept under control. The Queen Mother's enjoyment of excitement rose above her sense of danger, and she smiled, made suggestions and showed her pretty hands. On the night of the eleventh, in violation of the city's privileges, the King ordered his Switzers and his regiment of French Guards to come within the walls. The troops took their stations in various parts of the city. There was the momentary quiet before the storm. The historian De Thou says: "I remember that some time in the morning, before the streets were barricaded, I was in great suspense as to what was going to happen and very anxious to find out how the two parties stood. For that purpose I left my house, oblivious of the danger that I ran, and went on foot to the Louvre. I found it deserted in doleful silence, a sure sign of consternation within.　Sick at heart, I walked away from there, and went by the Hôtel de Guise.　The Duke was pacing up and down, and as I passed I whispered into my companion's ear, that if I was not mistaken this day would give the final blow to the King and to royal authority, and that I thought I perceived a gay confidence in the eyes of the Duke and his people."

The calm did not continue for long.　As soon as the citizens discovered that the troops had orders not to shoot, they fell to building barricades; students, clerks, artizans, carters, hauled beams, paving-stones, carts, all movable things, and dug entrenchments, until the soldiers were shut up in narrow spaces, barricaded in on all sides.　The Queen Mother went to ask Guise to interfere; he said curtly that such authority resided in the city magistrates, he had none.　After they had built these defense and offense works, the citizens became more and more emboldened; the violent among them urged their comrades to take *"ce bougre de roi"* in his palace, others wished to attack the soldiers.　The state of things was very much what it had been in the time of Charles V, then Dauphin, when Etienne Marcel was asserting his ideas of democracy, and what it was again to be during the Revolution when Robespierre, Danton and Marat were asserting theirs.　The Queen Mother went to and fro; she had lost her calm and was reported to be in tears, but against all the King's counselors she maintained that he should not leave Paris.　Guise had at first refused to interfere, but now he acceded to the Queen's request to save the soldiers, who were so compassed about that they could not get out, and were in great danger from the furious mob.　He walked about the streets, his cane in his hand, and solicited his fellow citizens to let them go.　The Switzers had already been

Henry of Navarre as a young man
Portrait by Clouet

roughly handled. But at the Duke's remonstrances, all the soldiers were let out, and hat in hand and muskets reversed they slunk away.

On the thirteenth the Queen Mother again went to Guise begging him to calm the people; he again replied curtly: "They are like excited bulls, it is hard to hold them in." He also refused to go to the Louvre "to put himself at the mercy of his enemies." While they were still talking, word was brought that the King had escaped. Guise turned to the Queen and exclaimed, "While you bear me in hand, the King has gone to do me harm." The Queen denied all knowledge of the matter, but the news was true. Henri III had slipped out of the Louvre by a postern gate, which led into the Tuileries gardens, where his stables were; he, and all his suite that could get horses, mounted in hot haste and rode for Chartres. And Henri de Guise, *Roi par la grace du Diable,* as the Huguenots put it, remained master of Paris.

When Henry of Navarre heard the news, he was lying on his couch; he remained thinking for a few minutes, then he got up and said merrily: "They haven't got the Béarnais yet." But he fully appreciated the seriousness of the situation; he wrote to his friend, Monsieur d'Aubeterre:

La Rochelle, June, 1588.

Dear Cousin:

You will have heard the very bad news of what has happened in Paris. It will have the most dangerous consequences for many a hundred years. Monsieur de Guise has seized the city, taken the keys of all the gates and forts, and has compelled the King to seek refuge at Chartres. From there the King has sent orders to the Catholic princes, the nobility and the cities to remain true to their allegiance; he proposes to go to Angers. I thought I ought not to fail to give you this news by the bearer, and grieve with you over the miserable state to which the Kingdom has been reduced by the unfortunate ambition of its enemies. You can imagine how badly I feel to see matters in such a pass. We foresaw all this clearly enough, and there was plenty of time to make head against it, and there still is, provided that the King is faithfully served by his loyal subjects, and they do their duty. Now's the time to tell who are good Frenchmen. For my part I wish to do all I can.

> Your very affectionate cousin and faithful friend
> HENRY.

To Monsieur de Saint-Genyès

June 25 [?], 1588.

Monsieur:

We do not know yet what the results will be of this affair in Paris; they are trying to patch things up, and make the King drink down the insult. We shall soon see what will happen; in the meantime we mustn't go to sleep. Adieu, Monsieur de Saint Genyès.

> Your very affectionate master and good friend
> HENRY.

The League and the King did patch matters up. The King, though bitterly outraged, did not have the necessary stability of character to hold out, and he did not know where to turn for help. The Queen Mother urged reconciliation; and the Duc de Guise and the city of Paris, though they spoke as masters, protested humble obedience. With sullen anger in his heart, Henri III accepted their dictation, and issued the *Edict of Catholic Union.* He promised to expel all heresy from the Kingdom, never to make peace with heretics, never to admit a successor who was a heretic or who upheld heretics, he declared that those who refused to accept the Edict were traitors, he forgave the barricades and all offenses, he created the Duc de Guise Lieutenant-General, and accepted the Cardinal de Bourbon, Henry's uncle, as heir presumptive.

Navarre's vain hopes that the *Day of the Barricades* would bring the King to his side did not interfere with his border warfare. He won a little victory near Nantes on August twelfth, and in October he laid siege to the town of Beauvoir-sur-Mer, on the coast southwest of Nantes. By good luck he had the narrowest escape from capture on a reconnoitering party; and a little later the town surrendered. The first thing he did next day was to write the good news to la belle Corisande:

Beauvoir-sur-Mer, October 21, 1588.

To Madame de Guiche.

God has done for us even more than I expected. . . . At the first blast of the trumpet they began to parley . . . at ten o'clock they surrendered, and by God's grace I am within the walls. . . . Dear Heart, I am a better man than you thought. Your last letter renewed your old punctuality in writing, that had seemed lost to me. I read your letter every night. If I love it, how much must I love her from whom it comes. I never longed to see you as much as I do now. If the enemy does not press us, I shall take a month off. Send Licerace to me; give out that he is going to Paris. There are always a thousand things that one can't write. Tell me the truth. What did Castile do before you quarreled with him? Oh, *Mon âme,* you really belong to me. . . . I have a petition to make; forget all quarrels with any of my friends. That is one of the first changes that I wish to see in you. Do not fear or believe that anything can shake my love, I love you more than ever. Good night, dear Heart. I go to bed with a lighter heart than in twenty days. I kiss your beautiful eyes a million times.

H.

Besides these little successes in Poitou, Henry was encouraged by the disaster which Philip II had suffered in the destruction of the Invincible Armada (July-August, 1588). He saw in it, or professed to see in it, the hand of God, and wrote to the Protestant Duke of Saxony, not without the help, perhaps, of Du Plessis-Mornay, a magniloquent Latin epistle, in which he said: *"Et absque animo nostro, absque manu nostra, potens fuit, eritque æternum, Deus suos servare, alienos perdere. Docuit hoc nudius tertius insignis illa, et Ecclesiæ Dei semper memoranda, classis Hispanicæ clades."* (Without our planning, without our deed, God has been able, and will be for everlasting, to save His own and to destroy enemies. Proof of this has come but the day before yesterday, portentous, and by the Church of God never to be forgotten, the destruction of the Spanish fleet.)

CHAPTER XVI

THE STATES-GENERAL AT BLOIS, 1588

ÁBOUT this time the States-General, which the King had convoked in the vague hope of obtaining support from it, met at Blois. The elections had been strongly orthodox, for the Huguenots had abstained from voting, and the Three Orders were solidly agreed that they would not tolerate heresy. Henry of Navarre submitted for their consideration, a pacific memorial, which he had drawn up with the help of Du Plessis-Mornay: As to our religion, he said, he had been brought up in that established by his predecessors in his Kingdom; and he believed that it led to salvation; he thought that it would be wrong in them to require him to give it up, and unworthy in him to do so. They all worshiped the same Trinity and prayed to the same God through Jesus Christ, they had the same Bible. Devout men, he continued, have long grieved over the abuses in the Church; everywhere in Europe men have protested against these abuses; whole kingdoms have protested. So great a concurrence of opinion shows that there is something in the protest. Reformers have sealed their belief with their blood. The matter deserves to be discussed and decided. For his part, he was quite ready to listen to an ecclesiastical council, whether national or ecumenical, lawfully brought together, quite ready to learn all that was possible concerning his salvation.

His conciliatory attitude, however, was in vain; the Estates declared him deprived of all rights as Prince of the Blood; and

it must have seemed to many that his star had set. Even his
cousins, the Counts of Soissons and Conti, who had fought
beside him at Coutras, left him. But the League had over-
reached itself. It had overthrown the Salic law of succession
that lay at the foundation of the constitution of the monarchy,
in complete disregard of the heir's professed willingness to
abide by the decision of a national Council. Such radical action
made many people realize that a faction had usurped the
sovereign power, and gave a new principle of cohesion to the
various groups that supported Henry of Navarre. Those
groups were of many minds: there were Catholics who detested the Guises, others who detested the King's *mignons,*
others that thought the Salic law should be upheld, and there
were Huguenots, too, of all sorts—gallant, braggart cavaliers,
like d'Aubigné; there were cautious, far-sighted negotiators,
like Du Plessis-Mornay, who regarded politics as a game of
chess; there were dogmatic Calvinists hot for no compromise
with corruption; and so forth. All united in opposition to the
high-handed arrogance of the League.

At this same time, the Huguenots held an assembly at La
Rochelle, and Navarre sought to make the most of this opportunity to consolidate the opposition to the League. He opened
the session of the assembly with a speech that was intended
not only for the representatives of the Huguenot churches
there present, but for the ears of moderate Catholics all over
France. He first dwelt upon the need of securing God's help
by suppressing misbehavior, swearing, blasphemy, rape and
robbery, upon the need of helping the destitute; he emphasized
the immense advantages of indissoluble union; he urged upon
them the problem of ways and means, representing that the
provinces least troubled by the enemy should contribute all they

could spare to those provinces where the fighting was. He said that he would expose his life, and that though he intended to be parsimonious of the public money, he would be liberal of his own, all the more so because his hands were clean of loot, and this he spoke, so he said, to the shame of those that might behave otherwise. He referred to his suggestion to the States-General of an ecclesiastical Council, and to his readiness to receive instruction. But the stress of the speech was upon the duress laid upon the King. D'Aubigné quotes this portion: "Gentlemen," Navarre said, "it is very easy for me to urge you to maintain the cause of God, for that cause, by His blessing, is also ours. And, as to the respect which we owe to our King, I am sure that it lies deep in your hearts. In truth, his Majesty is a captive in the hands of the enemies of the Kingdom, and has need for the time being of your patient tolerance. There are few, or none, among you who do not know that we must attribute the edicts against us, not to the King's will, but to his captivity."

The Assembly thanked him formally for his care of the churches and of the public weal, and promised to devote their lives and substance to the cause; they agreed to his demand for a Council, but they rejected any suggestion that he should be ready to abandon his creed. As a body they behaved respectfully; but there was much murmuring, and individuals expressed many criticisms of him very frankly. Some of his household complained that they had been left in intolerable poverty; officers said that other officers had been allowed to die of want; others found fault because he gave too many gifts to his Catholic followers, and because he spent too much money on his mistresses; others blamed his conduct after the battle of Coutras and his failure to support the German allies, who, in consequence, had been defeated by the Duc de Guise; others asserted that he deprived victorious soldiers of ransoms by taking their captives from them and letting these captives go free, and that in other ways, too, he curried favor with the enemy; and sundry moralists were very severe on his random amours. Henry learned of all this, through spies whom he employed to pick up such information, and at the close of the session he took great pains to conciliate all who had spoken ill of him. But he wrote to Corisande: "To tell you the truth, if there were another such assembly, I should go mad. But all is over and satisfactorily, thank God. I am off to Saint-Jean to meet Monsieur de Nevers."

Henri III had already despatched the Duc de Nevers with an army to Poitou; and Navarre, with the States-General damning him at Blois, and the Huguenot moralists condemning him at La Rochelle, had to meet danger in the field.

There were, also, various important affairs awaiting decision, such as the King of Scotland's demand for the hand of his sister Catherine. Private matters, also, weighed upon him; one of his little babies died, one whose birth perhaps had furnished the Calvinistic ministers with a text for criticism. He sought comfort of Corisande, in spite of the fact that by this time she must have begun to doubt the eternal constancy that he still so often vowed to her:

La Rochelle, November 30, 1588.

Dear Heart,

. . . I feel very badly for the loss of my little fellow. What, then, do you think I would have suffered had it been legitimate? He was just beginning to talk. [This illegitimate baby was not hers.] . . . what I said to you about not being ill-disposed to anybody, is for your sake as well as mine. I speak to you about this as you are my very own. My Soul, I feel an extraordinary desire to see you. There is a man here with letters from the King of Scotland to my sister. He is urging me more than ever to consent to the marriage. He offers to come himself to my help with six thousand men at his expense. He is sure that he will become King of England. Try cautiously to make her like him, tell her the condition we are in, how great a prince he is and how good. I shall not write direct to her about it. Talk to her in rather a casual way about the matter; that it is time for her to marry, and that there is no other party but him. As for our relation [the Comte de Soissons], he is no good. Adieu, my Heart, I kiss you a hundred million times.

H.

La Rochelle, December 22, 1588.

Dear Heart,

I am off to Saint Jean to gather our forces together, in order to pay a visit to Monsieur de Nevers, and perhaps cause him some displeasure. You shall soon hear of it. All is in God's hands; He has always blessed my labors. I am very well, thank Goodness, having nothing on my mind but a violent desire to see you. I don't know when I shall be so fortunate. If the occasion shows itself, I shall take it by the forelock. I shall not beseech you to love me; you have done so when you had less reason to do so. There are two things that I shall never doubt; your love and your faithfulness. I would pay dear for three hours' talk with you. Good night, *mon âme;* I wish that I were by the corner of your hearth, to heat your soup. I kiss you a million times.   H.

Meanwhile the States-General continued in active session; they declared the *Edict of Catholic Union* to be the fundamental law of the realm. The King at first attempted to assert his own will; and then, as usual, he had yielded and solemnly took again his former oath, that he would put down heresy. He had hated the Duc de Guise as author of the *Barricades,* and now he hated him still more as the cause of the arrogance of the States-General; but even so, when the Estates refused him supplies, he was forced to ask the Duc de Guise to use his influence with them. He sounded the depths of humiliation; pouring out promises of all sorts with the asseveration, "May God damn me to the bottomless pit, if I contravene them." Stories got about that the Duc de Guise meant to take him to Paris, and men recalled how the last of the Merovingians had been tonsured, cowled, hooded, and forced into a monastery by the Mayor of his palace; next, it was reported that Guise's sister, the Duchesse de Montpensier, had said that with her scissors she would cut the tonsure. The King's hatred of the Guises became so manifest that the States-General made him swear, by the host on the altar, reconciliation and friendship, that he forgot and forgave.

In spite of the King's oath many of Guise's friends urged him to be on his guard. Admirers in Paris sent him a steel corselet covered with white taffeta, and begged him to wear it. Guise laughed: "If I had the heart of a hare," he said, "I should have run away long ago." His friends persisted in expressing their apprehensions. "The King is too big a coward," he said, "besides, I don't know a man in the world who, hand to hand, in single combat, shall not feel half the fear." Afterward men felt the ineluctable hand of destiny. L'Estoile noted in his journal: "Great God, whose judgments are other than the judgments of men, walked in of sudden upon the stage."

The Duke was always attended by a large retinue that followed him everywhere except into the royal chamber; any attack upon his person would require careful prearrangement. On December twenty-first, he had an interview with the King. Some report that hot words were said, others that there was a prodigal show of courtesy, that the Duke kept unbonneting, while the King continued to bid him cover his head. At any rate, after the Duke had gone, the King manifested great resentment. The next evening Henri III announced his purpose to go to a country house in the neighborhood and bade the Duke rise betimes to attend an early meeting of the Council. When the Duke sat down to supper that night (so it was reported in Paris) he found under his napkin a note on which was written, "Have a care, an evil turn is impending"; he wrote underneath, "They would not dare," and tossed the paper on the floor.

In the Château at Blois, the second story of what is called the François Premier wing, was not arranged at that time quite in the same way that it is to-day. After mounting the gorgeous Renaissance stairway in the court, visitors then found the *Salle du Conseil* to the left and the *Salle des Gardes* to the right, both with windows on the court. These rooms were separated from those on the outer side of the château by the great wall, seven feet thick, which François Premier had left when he had enlarged the edifice. The outer rooms that were then added included a bedchamber, with one room opening out to the left, and a *cabinet neuf* opening out to the right, and beyond the *cabinet neuf* an oratory. A narrow passage led through the wall from the *Salle du Conseil* into the bedroom; and another from the bedroom into the *cabinet vieux,* which was side by side with the *Salle du Conseil* and also faced upon the court, but the former door between the *Salle du Conseil* and the *cabinet vieux,* had been stopped up, so that the *cabinet vieux* could only be reached from the King's bedchamber.

On the morning of December twenty-third by five o'clock, while it was still dark, the King's Gascon body-guard, *les Quarante-cinq,* assembled quietly in the hall below; they were taken up to the second story, and hidden in the room to the left of the King's bedchamber, and in corridors and stairways close at hand. Two priests came and were sent to the oratory where they robed themselves to say mass. The Duke left his rooms in the east wing of the castle bright and early (others say that he lodged outside), and went first to pay his respects to the Queen Mother in her apartments on the floor below that which I have described. The Queen had been "taking medicine" and was not visible. The Duke then went up to the *Salle du Conseil;* some members of the Council were already there, others, including the Cardinal de Guise, drifted in a little afterward. Somebody inquired why the meeting was held so early, and was told that the King was about to drive away for a few days' visit. The Duke had passed the earlier part of the night with Madame de Sauves and had gone to his own room at three o'clock and after so short a sleep had not got up in time for breakfast; he bade his secretary go fetch him some raisins. The secretary did not return, for the simple reason that he had been prevented. The King's *valet de chambre* gave the Duke some plums. The Duke then stood with his back to the great fireplace and, feeling cold, bade the servant put wood on.

The King in the meantime was walking up and down in his chamber in nervous agitation. He reminded his Gascons that the Duke was big and strong, and bade the two priests in

En ceste figure henry de vallois faict assassiner trahitrement monsieur le duc
de guise: puis le montre a monsieur le cardinal son frere.

Assassination of the Duc de Guise, at Blois

From a contemporary drawing in the Bibliothèque Nationale

the oratory pray for the success of a project that he entertained for the good of his Kingdom. About eight o'clock all was ready. A secretary stepped into the *Salle du Conseil* to say that the King wished to speak to the Duc de Guise in the *cabinet vieux,* which was then, as I have said, only accessible through the bedchamber. When the secretary entered, the members of the Council were seated around a table, discussing business. At the summons the Duke put some of the plums in his comfit-box, scattered the rest on the table, saying: "For those gentlemen that wish them," gathered up the folds of his cloak, and with comfit-box and handkerchief in his left hand, and his cap in his right, he bowed, "Adieu, Messieurs," pushed open the door and went through the narrow passage into the King's bedchamber.

After he had passed through, the door was shut behind him. Several of the *Quarante-cinq* got up at his entrance and saluted. He turned to the left to go round into the *cabinet vieux.* They followed him, as if out of respect. Guise walked to the passage that led from the King's bedchamber through the massive wall into the *cabinet vieux,* and lifted the portière. The passage through the old wall was narrow and low; and as he stooped to enter he saw more guards at the farther end. He turned and cast a searching glance at those following him. So lordly and dangerous was his look that, for an instant, the murderers fell back, then they leapt upon him. Some grasped his arms and caught his sword in its scabbard, one seized him by the back, while the rest struck at him with their daggers. The Duke shouted for help—*"Ha! mes amis!"*—so loud that the sound penetrated even into the *Salle du Conseil,* and heaving his great frame, he shook off four of his assailants, struck one in the face with his comfit-box and tried to draw his sword. Lucky for them that he could not. As it was he hurled one and another against the walls with his hands *"fortes et généreuses,"* and dragged them to and fro about the room, while they stabbed and stabbed him. So he fell, murmuring, *"Mon Dieu! miséricorde!"* Then the King, who was in the *cabinet neuf,* lifting the portière, peeked into the chamber and cried: "Finish him, finish him!"

There was a ring on the dead man's finger, a heart set in diamonds, given him by a lady that once loved him; this was afterward sent to Henry of Navarre by the courier that carried the news. Did Navarre wonder then if Margot in her wild girlhood had ever worn it? Henri III looked at his dead enemy and said: *"Mon Dieu,* how big he is, he seems even bigger dead that alive." The next day the Cardinal de Guise was murdered also, and the story went abroad that the bodies of these two famous men were burned and their ashes thrown into the Loire.

CHAPTER XVII

THE END OF THE VALOIS

So THE great Duke died. Henri III went down-stairs to his mother's room. She, having taken medicine, was still in bed. "Good morning, Madam," he said, "excuse me. Monsieur de Guise is dead. His vaunting is ended. I had him killed, forestalling his purpose to kill me. . . . I mean to be King, no longer a caitiff slave as I have been from May thirteenth up to this hour, at which I begin once more to be King and master." He reckoned without his host. The League leapt up in horror and fury. Paris renounced its allegiance; the Sorbonne declared all oaths of loyalty dissolved; the Parliament vowed it would shed its last drop of blood to punish the murderers. All the world was aghast; Estienne Pasquier wrote to a friend: "We are like a bird on a branch, waiting for what may happen."

Henri III was more helpless than before. And then his most faithful counselor failed him; his old mother, who of all her children loved him alone, came to the end of her cajoleries and entreaties, of her promises and lies, of her smiles, flatteries, threats and browbeatings. She was old and ill, and now the future looked black with danger to her idolized son, the last of her ten children (for Margot was dead to her), the last of the House of Valois. She got out of bed to pay a visit to old Cardinal de Bourbon, the make-believe heir presumptive, who had been arrested with other chiefs of the League. "Madam," said he, "if you had not tricked us, and enticed us here with sweet words, with warranty of safety, the two Guises would not have been dead, nor I a prisoner." The thrust went home, her fever grew worse and she died. Her body was buried next to the ashes of her husband in the abbey church of Saint-Denis. On February fourth, Regnault de Beaune, Archbishop of Bourges, a very eloquent preacher, delivered her funeral oration; he said: "Christians! Ye who behold this pitiful spectacle of sorrow common to the human race and mourn the loss of so great a Queen, Mother of so many Kings and Queens, so noble, so virtuous, so good and still so useful and necessary to our King her son and to all the realm, lift up your eyes to heaven. . . . Humble your hearts before God, you who are true Frenchmen, recognize that you have lost a Queen, the greatest in virtue, the noblest in birth and breed, the most excellent in honor, the most chaste among women, the most wise in administration, the sweetest in conversation, the most affable and benign to all who approached her, the most humble and loving toward her children, the most obedient to her husband, the most devout toward God, the kindest to the poor, that ever reigned in France."

The King felt his loneliness and mourned for her; and while he mourned, his Kingdom fell away. The League elected the Duc de Mayenne, brother to Guise, Lieutenant-General of France; it set up a government, and adopted a great seal. Most of the cities joined it. The political change was so sudden and complete that the King did not know what to do, he helplessly held out his right hand to Mayenne, asking for a reconciliation, and his left to Henry of Navarre. Up to the murder, the League and the King's party, the Royalists, were acting together against the Huguenots; now the League and the Royalists were at war. To the pious Huguenots this change

seemed like the act of God. Du Plessis-Mornay was greatly
excited and keenly alive to its immense significance; he wrote
at once to the King, and could not restrain himself from giving
him unasked-for advice:

December 26, 1588.

Sire,

We must praise God. His judgments are great. And it is
no small grace that He has done you, to avenge you upon your
enemies, without staining your hands. Our Church must make
public recognition that this is the handiwork of God, but with
due moderation, rather in humility than in rejoicing. I do
not think that, great as the change in affairs is, you ought
therefor to change your policy either at home or abroad. . . .
Henri III, will continue to make war on the Huguenots because he will not wish it thought that he has been acting under
the orders of the Guises; but he can do little, as Mayenne and
the League will keep him busy. And yet I think it useful
that your Majesty should inform the King not directly but
indirectly, by the Duc d'Epernon, of your joy to have him
delivered from so great an enemy, and that you hope that he
will now be able to enter into actual possession of his Kingdom and to give his subjects peace, after so much misery. . . .
We must sleep for a night over this great event, in order to
calm first impulses. . . .

Your humble, obedient, etc.

Du Plessis-Mornay.

Du Plessis-Mornay also wrote to Théodore de Bèze, the
Calvinist theologian: "Monsieur, God deals great blows when
he will. This is one of them, and it is the more portentous as

not hoped for on the one hand, nor feared on the other. . . .
So many blessings frighten me. Let us pray to Him for grace
to render worthy thanks.

Yours, etc.
Du Plessis-Mornay.

To Monsieur des Reaux

December 30, 1588.

Dear Sir,

While we have been acting here, the King has acted at
Blois, or rather God has by the King's hand. Never were men
cast down, and men raised up, so greatly by one death. Never
were more plans changed, nor more years undone in a morning. I think that the King of Navarre has great cause to praise
God, since without his participation God has taken away his
enemies, and he has soiled neither hand nor conscience. And
at this very time our Prince has taken the town of Niort without loss (under the eyes of Monsieur de Nevers), and seven
pieces of artillery; that is, in one night he had undone all that
Nevers' army had accomplished, and you know what benefits
will accrue. Our poor petards always get the better of their
cannon. I fear lest God overwhelm us with His mercies so
great are they above our hopes, so much above all the gratitude
we can show; but our Prince is moderate and above all relies
on himself. . . .

Yours, etc.,
Du Plessis-Mornay.

To Navarre the news of Guise's death could not but be
welcome. His worst adversary was gone; and murder had rent

asunder the alliance so dangerous to him, between Leaguers and Royalists: it had annulled the Catholic Union. References in his letters show what great importance he attached to the Duke's death, thinking that the chief obstacle to peace had been removed. He alludes to it in the most pious terms, as the act of Providence: "But while we adore the *admirable judgments* of God, and hope that He will continue His work . . . " Again: "God has made it plain that He can do all things; the *sample* of the work that He has lately done, gives us good cause for hope as to the whole." Again: "You have already seen the *marvelous* works of God," and "Such an act of His *handiwork.*" In his letter to Madame de Guiche he speaks with less piety:

January 1, 1589.

The King is making a success of it. He has had Cardinal de Guise strangled in prison, he has had President Neuilly and the *Prévôt des Marchands* [two Leaguers] hanged, also the secretary of the late Monsieur de Guise and two more. The Queen Mother said to him: "My Son, grant me a boon." "That will depend, Madam." "It is to spare Monsieur de Nemours and the Prince de Joinville [sons to the late Duke], they will do you good service some day." "With pleasure, Madam, you shall have their bodies, but I will keep their heads." He has sent to Lyons to catch the Duc de Mayenne. Nobody knows what luck he has had. There is fighting at Orléans, and even nearer, at Poitiers, not twenty miles from where I shall be to-morrow. I am sorry for you, if you are having such weather as there is here, it has not thawed for ten days. I am waiting to hear that they have given orders to strangle the late Queen of Navarre. That, together with the death of her mother, will make me sing the canticle; now Lord, let the soul of Thy servant depart in peace. This is too long a letter for a soldier. Good night, my Soul, I kiss you a hundred million times. Love me as much as you have cause to. It is New Year's Day.

H.

The Huguenot prospects looked brighter than they had ever done. Henri III, pressed by the League, would be forced to turn to Henry of Navarre for help. All that was needed was to be patient and prudent, to smooth the way for reconciliation, and to abstain from aggression. Then Du Plessis-Mornay was frightened, so much hung on the thread of a single life. Henry caught a cold from exposure to the inclemency of the weather, which developed into a fever and pleurisy, and he became so ill that he took to pious talk and psalm-singing.

To Madame de Guiche

[Château de la Mothe-Freslon,] January [10], 1589.

Yesterday I could not send any letter on account of my illness; but I am getting over that, thank God. You shall soon hear news of me, as good as the capture of Niort. If you wish for the truth, that lady who came, was a great bore; she must have bothered you importunately. I can't write yet. Well, Sweet Heart, I have seen the Heavens wide open; but I was not virtuous enough to enter in. God has more work for me to do. Twice in twenty-four hours I was all but wrapped in a shroud. You would have pitied me. If the crisis had not come till two hours later, the worms would have had a grand banquet of me. This minute news comes from Blois. Twenty-five hundred men, led by Saint Pol, started from Paris to the relief of Orléans. The King's troops have cut them to pieces; so they think the King will take Orléans within twelve days. Monsieur de Mayenne does not budge. I stop, because I don't feel well. *Bon jour, Mon âme.*

H.

A few days later he was able to travel by litter, and within two weeks was out hunting. And on March fourth, desiring to take full advantage of the changed political situation, with the aid of Du Plessis-Mornay, he launched his policy of reconciliation. He issued a proclamation to the Three Estates of the Realm, in which he pictured the miseries of the country and urged union and concord:

Gentlemen:

When I remember that for four years I have been the argument of the tragedies in France, the talk of our neighbors, the subject of civil war, and therefore of a world of miseries; when I consider that on a possible event, as far from the thoughts of the French people as from my wishes, this Kingdom has been subjected to infinite calamities; that, on the empty fear of my succession to the Crown, usurpation has been planned and put into practise; when, with these eyes that God gave me to look to the welfare of my country, I am forced to see it on fire, its cities in flames. . . . I should be the most heartless of all heartless men. [And so on, to the questions, To what are we coming? and, What can we do?] I know that you have ordered your deputies [to the States-General] at Blois in your instructions to them to insist as a general maxim that there should be but one religion in a kingdom, and that

piety, which is the foundation of a state, can not exist where
God is worshiped in divers ways. That is so: I admit it, and
to my great regret I see many people who complain about it,
but few who try to help it. I have always offered to submit
to reason and I do now. I and all of my religion will accept
what a free Council shall decide. That is the true path; and
it has always been followed. We will submit to condemnation
by such a body. But, that submission can be forced from us
by sword strokes, I believe before God, is impossible. In fact,
the event has proved it. I need not linger over this point, for
I have long discussed it. I have often been called on to change
my religion, but now, with a dagger at my throat, even if I
had no respect for my conscience, my honor would prevent me.

What would the most zealous partizans of the Catholic religion say, if they should see me after having lived for thirty
years in one creed, suddenly change it for the hope of a Kingdom? What would those who have seen that I am a brave
man say, if I forsook out of fear the religion in which I have
served God since the day of my birth? If after being bred
and brought up in one profession of faith, then, all of a
sudden, without listening or offering a word, I should shift
to another? No, gentlemen, that is not the way of the King
of Navarre were there thirty crowns to win. . . . Teach me;
I am not obstinate. . . . If you will show me a truth different
from that which I believe, I will accept it; and I do not think
that there is a man of my party who will not go with me. . . .

Is it not pitiful that there is no man, great or lowly, in this
Kingdom, who does not see the evil, does not cry out against
fighting, does not denounce it as the mortal illness of the State
and that nevertheless up to now not one has opened his mouth
to point out the remedy? That, in all the States-General at

Blois, not one man dares pronounce this sacred word *Peace,*
the word on which the welfare of the Kingdom depends? . . .
We have all done, and all suffered, enough evil.   For four
years we have been drunk, senseless, mad! is that not enough?
What will happen to the State, what to the noblesse, what to
the cities, what to the proud citizens, what to the peasants,
what to the clergy?   Confusion, disorder, wretchedness everywhere, that is the fruit of war.   And what is the remedy?
None other than Peace, peace which shall reestablish order in
the heart of this Kingdom. . . . I call upon all to join me,
who have this holy wish for peace, whatever their rank or condition, in the hope that, if God shall bless my purpose, I shall
show courage, and that, at the end, I shall have rendered obedience to my King, done my duty to my country, won for myself
rest and content and general liberty for honest men.

The Manifesto was ably drawn; Navarre pledged his honor
never to deny the Catholics liberty of conscience and of worship,
and protested his devotion to the King.   But to the King he
made a direct appeal.   He sent Du Plessis-Mornay to Tours to
confer with him.   That unfortunate monarch had but five
faithful cities, Blois, Beaugency, Amboise, Tours and Saumur,
and he was pitifully alone; the League was in the field, the
Catholic population estranged, the Pope had issued an ex-
communication, Philip of Spain was angry, his partizans were
few, his counselors of small account.   Du Plessis-Mornay
arrived in an opportune time; terms were discussed and on
April third, an agreement between the two Henrys was signed.
The chance afforded by the situation was so clear that Sully,
who had been on his estate at Rosny at the time of the
murder, took it upon himself to go to Blois and see what he

could effect toward a reconciliation. He, too, had an interview with the King, and then went on to see Navarre. Henry of Navarre listened attentively, "scratched his head and asked Sully several times, in an anxious manner, if the King was acting sincerely," but he said nothing of Du Plessis-Mornay's mission; and when Sully, thinking that he had effected the concord, found that Du Plessis-Mornay was to receive the governorship of Saumur as a reward for it, he was greatly chagrined. No doubt had not d'Aubigné been serving with Henry of Navarre, satisfied perhaps at being the first man to enter the town of Niort in the assault, he would have taken, or claimed to have taken, a part in the reconciliation also.

On the last day of April, the two Henrys met at Plessis-lès Tours. Navarre with his army encamped on the north side of the river, and when an invitation came to visit the King, some of his officers deemed it very imprudent in him to cross over and put himself in the King's power. Nothing they could say affected him. He wore his usual old doublet, frayed on the shoulders and at the sides by his cuirass, and a scarlet cloak, and in his gray hat a great white plume. He was accompanied by his guard, and by some lords and gentlemen. The park, where the two Kings met, near the castle, was crowded with people. There followed a great plenty of salutations and embracings, and as the royal couple pushed their way through the crowd, they were greeted with delighted cheers. The reconciliation came none too soon; a week later, Mayenne's troopers were so close to the town that Henri III, who had gone incautiously outside the walls to ride, was nearly captured, and in the battle that followed the Royalist army was getting the worst of it when Navarre's forces came up to their rescue. It was a triumphant moment for Navarre, and as usual he turned

for sympathy to Madame de Guiche. The letter is unusually
interesting, as there are interpolations added by her.

Blois, May 18, 1589.

Dear Heart:

I write from Blois, where five months ago I was condemned
as a heretic, and unworthy to succeed to the crown, and now
I am its chief pillar. Behold the works of God toward those
that have always trusted in Him. Could anything seem so
final as an enactment of the States-General? But I appealed
to the Almighty, [note, in Corisande's handwriting, *"So have
others"*] and He has reviewed the case, quashed the decrees
of men and reestablished me in my rights, and I believe that
it will be at the expense of my enemies. [Note, *"So much the
better for you,"* also in her handwriting.] They that trust in
God and serve Him are never confounded. [Note: *"That's a
reason why you should think about it."*] I am very well,
thank God, and I swear to you that I neither love nor honor
anything in the world as I do you [Note: *"There is nothing
to show it."*] and I shall remain [Note: *"un"*]faithful until
the grave. I am going to Beaugency where I think you shall
soon have news of me. I am getting ready to have my sister
come before long. Make up your mind to come with her.
[Note: *"Yes, when you shall have given me the house that you
have promised me near Paris, so that I may get ready to take
possession of it and to thank you suitably."*] The King has
spoken to me of the Lady of Auvergne [i. e., Margot confined
in the Château of Usson] ; I think that I shall make her take
a bad jump. *Bon jour, mon cœur.*

He that is bound to you by an indissoluble knot.

H.

Beaugency, May 21.

If the King uses diligence, as I hope he will do, we shall soon see the spires of Notre-Dame de Paris. God grant that we shall do something this week as brilliant as last. *Mon cœur,* love me always like your own, for I love you like my own [Note by Corisande: *Vous n'estes à moy, ni moy à vous.*— You are not mine, nor I yours.] This truth I seal with kisses on your hands. *Adieu, mon âme.*

H.

Poor Corisande, with her blackamoor, her spaniel, her monkey, her parrots, her fawns, her two little wild boars, her coach horses and her page! These comments made on the margin of the King's letter by the hand that had been actually or metaphorically kissed so many millions of times, show that the fires of love were dying down. Perhaps she had heard of Esther Ymbert de Boislambert, the daughter of one of the municipal officers at La Rochelle, and of Madame Martine, as well as of uncanonical babies. At any rate the lady seems not to have yielded to despair, *"ni moy à vous,"* for the King had already reproached her for lack of zeal in letter-writing.

Pluviers [near Tours], June 24, 1589.

Verily, I hesitate to write to you, for your letters show that mine do not give you much pleasure. God blesses my labors more and more; yesterday we took Pluviers, and I think Estampes will soon follow. . . . Whatever you may do to me, I shall neither love nor honor anything but you in the whole world. I seal this with a million kisses on your hand.

H.

Figure de l'admirable & diuine refolution de F. Iacques Clement Iacobin, de fon atrince à S. Cloupres Paris, accedzaux Gardes, & addreffe au Roy, de vint lequel fa gne vaillant luy donne va coup de couteau, dont à cette occafion eft fouflain tué, & fon corps porté mort deuant le Roy, ayant efté mis bleffé au lic, aprez le decedz duquel fuit l'edict F. Clement mort, martyrifé, turé à quatre thraeaulx, puis bruflé.

Assassination of Henri III by Jacques Clement

From a contemporary drawing in the Bibliothèque Nationale

[July 14, Pontoise].

Mon Cœur, I am furious when I see that you doubt me, and
out of spleen I shall not try to take your doubts away. You
are wrong. I swear that I have never loved you more than I
do now. I had rather die than fail in one thing that I have
promised you. Believe me; be sure of my constancy—a million kisses, etc.

H.

As Navarre's letters show, the two Henrys with their
combined forces had been advancing toward Paris. The citizens
were still furious over the murder of their two favorites, they
had broken the statues of the King, and were cursing the whole
race of Valois. The allies drew near, but hesitated about an
attack, old officers asserted that a siege would be long, and
might well be unsuccessful; however, Navarre maintained
"that audacity begets hope, and hope strength, and strength
victory, and that it would be tantalizing to come close enough
to kiss this beautiful city and then not put an arm around her
waist." So the royal army advanced near the walls and began
a blockade (July thirtieth). Henri III was lodged at Saint
Cloud in the house of Gondi, a protégé of Catherine de
Médicis, while Navarre had his quarters at Meudon. All the
roads into Paris were secured; it was merely a question of time,
and hunger would force the city to surrender.

On August first Henry of Navarre was in the Faubourg
Saint-Germain intending to make an assault upon the walls by
the *Pré-aux-clercs,* which lies on the left bank of the river. It
was eleven o'clock in the morning. A gentleman galloped up
and whispered a few words in his ear; Navarre turned to Sully
and said, "My friend, the King has been wounded by a knife

thrust in his belly. Let us go see what it is. Come with me."
He then rode off to Saint Cloud, and found the King in bed.
Doctors were about him, and he did not seem to be in danger.
A Jacobin monk, who had done the deed, had been killed by
the guards, and his body flung out the window into the court.
When Navarre entered, the King stretched out his hand;
Navarre kissed it. His Majesty said: "Brother, you see how
our enemies have treated me, you must take care that they do
not do the same to you." Navarre stammered out that the
wound was not dangerous, that the King would soon be on
horseback and able to punish those who were guilty. The
King continued: "Brother, it is for you to possess the inheritance that God has given you, and that I have worked to preserve for you; that is what has brought me to this plight. I
do not repent of it, since justice, of which I have always been
the guardian, requires that you should succeed me in this
Kingdom. You will have many obstacles, if you do not make
up your mind to change your religion. I expect you to do so,
as much for the salvation of your soul as for your temporal
advantage."

Navarre showed great grief and great respect, and again
murmured a few words to the effect that the King was not so
ill as to think himself near his end. Then the King, raising his
voice, addressed the whole room, telling them that he wished
them to hear his last injunctions. He said that he had been
obliged to proceed to extremities because rebellious subjects
had wished to usurp the Crown to the prejudice of the lawful
heir: "Now I beg you as my friends, and order you as your
King, to recognize my brother here after my death, and to
show the same affection and fidelity to him that you have to
me, and for my satisfaction to take the oath to him in my

presence." Navarre wept a little, and all the gentlemen burst
into tears, and with sighs and sobs, swore fidelity to the King
of Navarre, and told the King that they would obey his commands at every point. The King then gave some minor orders,
and seemed tired. He died at three o'clock on the following
night.

In Paris there was great enthusiasm; the League invited
Iacques Clement's mother to come, and greeted her with
chaunts: "Blessed is the womb that bore thee, and the breasts
that gave thee suck."

CHAPTER XVIII

ARQUES AND IVRY

For the moment the gates between Navarre and the Crown seemed thrown wide open: Henri de Valois was dead, and he was the lawful heir; Henri de Guise was dead, and no man of equal talents left to bar the way; Mayenne was cooped up in Paris with famine, and his adherents were falling off. And yet within twenty-four hours the gates swung to again. But yesterday, the dying King proclaimed him his heir, and Navarre had received promises of allegiance from all. To-day the King lay stark and stiff; priests with beads and candles were kneeling about the bed, and as they muttered paternosters, murmurs of discontent were heard, hats were pulled down on the forehead, or thrown on the floor, fists were clenched, there were whisperings and hands shaken in accord, there were vows and promises, and all as clear as if said aloud: Better death a thousand times than a heretic King. The old centrifugal forces burst out. The Catholics wished to be loyal, but they could not bring themselves to accept a heretic; and they differed among themselves, for some were more tolerant than others, but all were firm on the fundamental question; while the Huguenots, on their part, were very suspicious and wished Navarre to make no concessions. Again the question of religion came to the fore. What effect would Henry's conversion have on the Leaguers, on the *Politiques,* on the Huguenots? And there were the foreign powers: Would Elizabeth of England help a Catholic King against the League? What would the German Protestants do? Would Philip of Spain accept any such conversion? Navarre sat on the anxious seat. If he turned Catholic he might lose the Huguenots; if he remained a Huguenot he would never be acknowledged by the Catholics.

It was a trying time. Paris had been so nearly within his grasp; could he but have captured Mayenne, he might have broken the League. But now it was no longer the beleaguered garrison that was falling away, it was the besieging army. Some agreement must be reached. A group of Catholic lords offered an ultimatum; on August fourth Henry IV accepted it, and together they issued a document called the *Declaration*. Henry promised to maintain the Catholic religion, Apostolic and Roman, without alteration; he would appoint only Catholics to office, except in the Huguenot towns; he would convoke an ecclesiastical Council within six months, hearken to instruction and accept its conclusions; and in consideration thereof the Catholic lords acknowledged him as their King. As usual, compromise was unable to affect the extremists; the sterner Huguenots went off in discontent, and the League utterly rejected a heretic King. The siege of Paris was raised of necessity, for half of the besieging army went away: Huguenot lords, because they were dissatisfied, Catholic lords bent on private ambitions, gentlemen and other volunteers, eager to get home, German and Swiss mercenaries because there was no money to pay them, until out of forty thousand men not twenty thousand remained.

As Navarre could not reduce the capital to obedience, he addressed himself to the task of subduing the hostile provinces. He divided his army into three parts; of these he sent one into

Picardy, another into Champagne, and the third he himself led into Normandy, to Dieppe. This town was important, as enabling him to receive supplies from England, and was held by a friend. He arrived there on August twenty-sixth, and was immediately welcomed. It was on such occasions that he was most charming, full of *bonhomie* and *camaraderie:* "No ceremony, my Friends," he cried. "Give me your fellowship, good bread, good wine and merry faces;" and described himself gaily as a King without a Kingdom, a husband without a wife and a general without an army. The army of the League, in double his numbers, followed him up; Mayenne vowed he would make the Béarnais surrender, or jump into the sea. Fortunately much needed supplies came from England: powder and shot, food, wine, beer, sheets and shoes; and Henry did not let himself be cooped up in the city, but moved out and erected fortifications at Arques, a little town a few miles up the river of the same name, where another stream joins it. From here he wrote to the Comtesse de Guiche:

Trenches at Arques, September 9, 1589.

My heart:

It's a wonder that I survive the work I have to do, but God is merciful and blesses my labors. In spite of a great many people, I am well and my affairs prosper. The enemy is double as strong as I am at present. I am pretty close to Dieppe, waiting for them in a camp that I am fortifying. I shall see them to-morrow, and I hope, by God's help, that if they attack they will find it a bad bargain. This messenger goes by sea. The wind and business compel me to stop. I kiss you a million times.

H.

For nearly three weeks there was a series of marches and counter-marches, of skirmishes and combats. Sully says that at this time the King's countenance was calm and serene, with an air of *sang froid* and of *sage ardeur,* that conferred upon him something heroic, beyond ordinary humanity. The main battle took place on September twenty-first. Early that morning a patrol captured an officer of the enemy, who said that the King could not resist the attack, because Mayenne's army outnumbered his three to one. "You don't see all our forces, Monsieur de Belin," the King replied. "You have not included in your reckoning God and our righteous cause. They are on my side." And besides God and the righteous cause, there was Henry's reputation won at Cahors and Coutras. The fight was hard; the King, as ever, in the thick of it. In the end the enemy was driven back with considerable loss. On the following days there was further fighting, and then the arrival of Huguenot levies and of reenforcements from England induced Mayenne to retreat. He took his way through Picardy toward Laon. Long afterward, d'Aubigné, who thought the King's victory an act of special Providence, asked Mayenne to explain it. Mayenne replied, *"C'est la vertu de la vieille phalange huguenote, et de gens qui, de pére en fils, sont apprivoisez à la mort."* It was the valor of the old Huguenot phalanx, of men who from father to son had been trained to die.

Henry, elated by success, hoped that his prestige might frighten the citizens of Paris into surrender, and marched on the city. His troops carried the outer fortifications on the southern bank of the river, but he could not prevent Mayenne from entering the city by the north. Further attack was useless; so he withdrew and conducted a series of little campaigns in Touraine, Maine and Normandy during the winter. At this time he is still writing affectionate letters to the Comtesse de Guiche:

Lisieux, Normandy, January 16, 1590.

My Heart,

You have not deigned to write me by Byçose [a messenger]. Do you think that this coldness becomes you? I leave that to your judgment. I am very glad to know that things go well with you. God keep you so, and continue his blessings to me, as he is doing. I have taken this place without firing a shot. There is little or no sickness in my army, which is increasing daily. I never was so well, and never loved you more than I do now. My soul, I kiss you a million times.

H.

From Lisieux he marched southeastward and laid siege to Dreux, on the River Eure, some fifty miles west of Paris. Mayenne came up to the relief of the town and on March twelfth crossed the river near Ivry. The King's troops had been scattered, but he gathered them together that same day at Nonancourt a dozen miles to the southwest. Here Henry made his plans for the order of battle, went to church himself, and sent his officers and soldiers to their respective Catholic or Protestant places of worship. The next day he marched northward and took a position near Saint-André. That night he had but two hours' sleep, for after he had stationed the guards he went about visiting the sentinels. D'Aubigné says that one of the King's remarkable qualities was that he left nothing to chance. The next day they advanced against the enemy who were drawn up to the west of the River Eure in the plain now marked by the obélisque of Ivry. The King

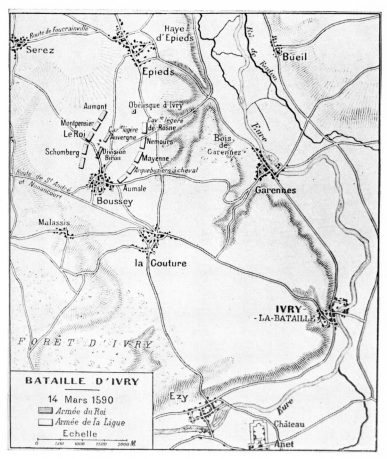

Plan of the Battle of Ivry

From Maxime Petit's *Histoire de France*

wore a hat with a white plume, fastened by a clasp of an
amethyst and pearls, which two years before had cost a hundred crowns. His order of battle was somewhat like that at
Coutras: three squadron of horse, with musketeers and pikemen between the squadrons and on both flanks as well, and a
regiment of cavalry as a reserve. He had six thousand to
seven thousand infantry and twenty-five hundred horse. The
enemy numbered from eight thousand to ten thousand infantry
and five thousand horse, including Walloon musketeers and
pikemen sent by Philip II and commanded by Count Egmont.
The army of the League had crossed the little river, that is
scarcely twelve yards broad, hard by the villages of Garenne
and Epieds to the north of Ivry, mounted the low bluffs to the
west, and had taken position across the plain of Ivry, where,
as Mayenne believed, the superior members of his cavalry
would have the advantage. The plain is broad and flat, and
slopes but slightly, and it offered an excellent place for a trial
of strength and the best man to win.

At the beginning of the day the advantage lay with the
Leaguers. Sully was wounded and dragged himself off under
a pear tree and thought the battle lost. The Walloon lancers
had broken the Royalist light horse at the King's left and driven
them in; but the reserves coming up pushed back the Walloons.
The Royalist artillery played with good effect. There were
charges, confusion, reformings and counter-charges. Mayenne
then led his cavalry and mounted musketeers against the royal
center. The King was ready for them. "Comrades," he cried,
"God is on our side! There are His enemies and ours! Here
is your King! At them! If the colors fall, rally round
my white plume, you shall find it on the road to honor and
victory!" He dashed into a disorderly mass of Mayenne's

cavalry two horses' length ahead of his men. His standard-bearer lost control of his horse and was carried to one side; so the troopers followed the white plume. Nobody knew what happened. The enemy's ranks scattered in disorder, and Henry, with only fifteen or twenty men, rode furiously, chasing fourscore helter-skelter. He slew seven men with his own hand and captured a standard. Sully, after a rest, had crawled out from under the pear tree and had managed to hoist himself on a little horse and riding forth met seven mounted Leaguers carrying the white flag with the black crosses of Lorraine, who, to his amazement, begged him to save their lives. The victory was complete; the German mercenaries were cut to pieces, the Swiss surrendered. Mayenne, however, escaped with the bulk of his French cavalry and infantry across the Eure. That night the King issued a circular letter to announce his victory:

Camp at Rosny, March 14, 1590.

It has pleased God to grant me what I have most desired, to be able to come hand to hand with the enemy, for I was full of confidence, that being there, He would show me grace and give me victory, as has happened to-day. We met the enemy between ten and eleven o'clock this morning. We went toward them, for they did not leave their positions until the charge; and so the battle began, in which God has shown that His protection is always on the side of the right. In less than an hour, after they had spent their spleen in two or three charges, all their cavalry turned to seek safety, abandoning their infantry, which was there in great numbers. When the Swiss saw this, they begged for mercy, colonels, captains, privates, all surrendered with their flags. The lansquenets and the French had no opportunity to take the same resolution, for they had already been cut to pieces, some twelve hundred of each; those that were left ran away in the woods to the mercy of the peasants. Of their cavalry, between nine hundred and a thousand were killed, and four or five hundred taken prisoners, not including those drowned in crossing the Eure (which they did at Ivry in order to escape) of whom there was a great number. The best mounted got off by flight, with all their baggage lost and in great disorder. I followed them up until near Mantes. Their colors are in my hands, the standard-bearer is a prisoner, also twelve or fifteen other standards of the cavalry, twice as many belonging to the infantry and all their artillery. An immense number of gentlemen are prisoners, a great many are dead, some of high rank, whom I have not had time to identify. I know that Count Egmont, who was in command of all their Flemish forces, was killed. Prisoners say that their army consisted of four thousand horse, and from twelve to thirteen thousand foot, of whom I don't believe one quarter escaped. As to our numbers, we had perhaps two thousand horse and eight thousand foot. . . .

It was God's miracle. He first granted me the purpose to attack, and then the grace to bring the battle to a victorious conclusion. To Him alone belongs the glory; as to the share which, with His permission, may belong to men, it is due to the princes, the officers of the Crown, to the gentlemen and captains, to all the nobility who were present. They dashed in with such ardor, and bore themselves so triumphantly, that none of their predecessors left to them such examples of courage as they by their deeds this day will leave to their posterity. I am mightily contented with them and I think they also are with me; for they have seen that I do not send them anywhere without first opening the way myself. Please give this news to all my other faithful friends.

HENRY.

It was indeed a charming victory, and the King had good right to be pleased with himself. The next day but one he was coursing rabbits near Mantes. The Duc de Mayenne and other leaders of the League were apprehensive lest Henry should march directly on Paris and take the city unprepared. But the King had learned that Paris was not easy to take. The walls were too strong to permit of carrying them by assault, and a siege required long, slow, thorough preparations. To begin with, he occupied all the highroads that led into the city, and secured the rivers, so that supplies could not go in by land or water, then he placed his artillery on the heights of Montmartre, and finally encamped his troops in the villages round about.

The city of Paris is said to have contained at that time three hundred thousand souls. It had been strongly fortified by Charles V, and his fortifications had been extended by François I. On the south bank of the Seine the walls began at the Tour de Nesle, about where the Institut now stands, and made a half-circle round the Latin Quarter eastward to the river again at a point, a little above the Ile de la Cité, on which Notre-Dame stands. The Pré-aux-Clercs and the Abbey of Saint-Germain-des-Prés were outside, near the Tour de Nesle. On the south side, in the middle of the half-circle, came the Porte Saint-Jacques, through which the Rue Saint-Jacques ran north, dividing Paris into two halves, east and west. On the north side of the river the space enclosed was twice as large; the walls started at the river bank a little above the islands, passed the Bastille,

The Battle of Ivry

From the painting by Steuben in the Musée de Versailles

then the Porte du Temple, and on by the Porte Saint-Martin, which was the northern outlet for the continuation of the Rue Saint-Jacques, then to the Porte Saint-Denis, the Porte Mont-martre, to the Porte Saint-Honoré, where the Rue Saint-Honoré passed on into the Faubourg Saint-Honoré, and so on, separat-ing the Tuileries Gardens from the Louvre, to the river again. The faubourgs outside the walls had also been fortified. With so large a circuit, it was difficult to maintain an effective blockade.

Mayenne had gone to Flanders for help, and left his brother, the young Duc de Nemours, as commandant. This young man showed energy and capacity in bringing in troops and provisions and in organizing the train-bands. A month passed, then a second; food ran low, and the defenders asked permission to send out three thousand useless mouths. This the King granted. When Queen Elizabeth, who grudged every crown that she gave to the Protestant cause, heard of it, she wrote a tart letter in which she rated him soundly for such sentimental weakness. The King answered good-humoredly, if a little lamely, in his defense. In fact his action had not been dictated by sentiment but by policy; he was desirous that no unnecessary suffering should erect more of a barrier than was inevitable between his subjects and himself. He never acted from pure sentiment. He loved his mistresses, but when passion cooled, he showed little regard for their feelings. He loved his sister Catherine, but he interfered ruthlessly to pre-vent her from marrying the Comte de Soissons, to whom she had plighted her troth. And at this very time, while granting favors to the Parisians (for he not only let useless mouths pass out, but he allowed hampers of food to pass in), he wrote to his officers at Bayonne, where he feared an uprising, "to

let conjecture take the place of proof." He could be stern
enough on occasions. When he heard that the Comte de
Soissons had secretly gone to Pau to marry his sister, he wrote
to the President of the City Council there: "Monsieur de
Ravignan, I am displeased by the way my cousin the Comte de
Soissons has made his journey. I have nothing to say to you,
except that if anything happens contrary to my will, with your
countenance or consent, you shall answer for it with your head.
Henry." And when he found among the prisoners at Ivry
German mercenaries, who had got into his trenches at Arques,
by pretending that they had come as friends, he put them all
to the sword. Moreover, by this leniency the King may have
entertained a design to lull the garrison into security, for three
days later his troops made a fierce attack all around the city
and captured the faubourgs.

After three months of siege, the garrison sent out envoys,
the Cardinal de Gondi and the Archbishop of Lyons, to ask that
the surrender of Paris might wait for the general peace that
must before long be made between Henry and the League.
The King replied: *"J'aime ma ville de Paris.* She is my eldest
daughter and I am jealous of her. I wish to show her more
good, more kindness and mercy, than she asks. But I wish her
to be grateful to *me* for it, and not to the Duc de Mayenne or
to the King of Spain. If they were to make the peace, Paris
would be grateful to them, and she would consider them her
liberators and not me." The Cardinal de Gondi replied that,
if Paris surrendered before a general peace, the King of Spain
and the Duc de Mayenne might come and win it back. The
King flashed up: "By God," he said, "if they come with all
their allies, we will beat them well, we'll show them that French
gentlemen know how to defend themselves." Then, remember-

ing how his pious Huguenot tutor had taught him not to swear, he added: "I have sworn, contrary to my custom. But I repeat: By the living God, we will not put up with such an insult." The gentlemen about him applauded, and said that his words justified the oath. The King then offered to grant the envoys a week, but they must give hostages and agree that, if Mayenne should not succor them within that time, they would surrender.

The Cardinal and the Archbishop replied that they would communicate the terms to Mayenne, but they proceeded slowly, and it was full two weeks before they came back to decline the offer. The embassy seems to have been a trick to gain time. In the meantime Mayenne and Alexander Farnese, the King of Spain's very able general, had joined forces and were marching to the relief of Paris.

The King's leading officers were of different opinions as to whether he should wait in his positions before Paris for the enemy to come, or go to meet them. He decided upon the latter course, and on August twenty-ninth broke up camp. Farnese, who was a master in the art of war, tricked the King with the expectation of a battle, slipped by, took possession of positions that broke the blockade, provisioned the city, and then withdrew in triumph to Flanders. The baffled King, his spirits in his boots, let his nobles scatter to their homes, and retained only a small mobile army of horse and foot to meet emergencies.

CHAPTER XIX

GABRIELLE D'ESTRÉES

DURING the campaign, although the King had been very busy with his soldiers, his officers and his correspondence, with guns, powder and forage, he had found leisure not to forget the other sex. In Normandy he had made the acquaintance of a lovely lady, la Comtesse de la Roche-Guyon, a widow, and had promptly fallen in love with her. His wooing had been going on during the winter, but it did not interfere with affectionate expressions in his letters to the far-away Corisande: "Jan. 8, 1590. *Mon Ame.* I love nothing but you, and if you give me no cause to change, I shall die in that determination. . . . Adieu, *Mon Cœur,* I kiss you a million times." "Jan. 16. *Mon Ame.* I kiss you a million times." "Jan. 29. *Bon soir Mon Ame.* I kiss you a million times." "April 5. *Mon Ame,* we have won a victory. . . . May God give me as great a victory over your heart! That will be everlastingly more precious to me. *Bon soir, Mon Ame.* I kiss your white hands a million times." "May, 14. *Mon Ame.* . . . I kiss your hands, your mouth, your eyes, a million times." Four days later comes this letter to Antoinette Guercheville, Madame de la Roche-Guyon:

Saint-Denis, May 28, 1590.

After having hovered so long about the desired pot, the point must be coming near at which Antoinette will confess her

206

love for Henry. Lady mine, my body begins to enjoy health,
but my soul can not depart from affliction until you have taken
this leap. Since you have the warrant of my words, what
difficulty prevents you from making up your mind, what
hinders it from making me happy? My fidelity deserves to have
you push aside all obstacles. Do so then, my Heart, and let's
make a wager as to which will show the truest, the faithfullest
love. If I speak too familiarly, and my words offend you, tell
me, and forgive me at the same time . . . my All, love me,
for I shall adore you to the grave. On this truth I kiss your
white hands a million times.

H.

Within a few weeks this Lothario, in whose heart were
many mansions, wrote again to Corisande: "July 15, 1590.
Mon Ame. I love nothing in the world as I love you; that I
am sure you will never doubt. I kiss a million times those
lovely eyes that shall be dearer to me all my life long than anything in all the world." The next month, just after he had decided to break up his camp before Paris and march out to meet
Farnese and Mayenne, he wrote again to Madame de la Roche-
Guyon:

August 31, 1590.

My Lady,

I write this line on the eve of battle. The issue is in the
hand of God, who has already ordered what shall happen, according as is expedient for His glory and the salvation of my
people. If I lose it, you will never see me again, for I am not
the man to run away, or give ground. I can assure you that if
I die, my next to last thought will be of you and my last of
God, to whom I commend us both. Written this last day of

August, 1590, by the hand of him who kisses yours and is your servant.

HENRY.

But even the King's emotional suggestion of his approaching death did not shake the resolution of this virtuous lady; she remained impregnable, even her lover's proposals of marriage did not budge her.   Tom Moore says:

> When we are far from the lips we love,
> We've but to make love to the lips that are near.

With this dictum the King was in entire accord.   While he was encamped before Paris, from May to August, and during the time of his correspondence with these two absent ladies, he made love to a pretty young novice, Claude de Beauvillier; and, it is said that after the siege she accompanied him, still wearing her nun's gown, on the hasty stages of his campaign. Also, there came into his life during the siege another young nun, Catherine de Verdun.   Both ladies were soon made abbesses.   And about this time he met Gabrielle d'Estrées.   This girl, the Charmante Gabrielle of history, was the daughter of Antoine Comte d'Estrées, and of his wife Françoise Babou, a lady of some notoriety.   Gabrielle d'Estrées had been seen and admired at the court of Henri III; at that time she could not have been more than fifteen.   One of the court minions, the Duc de Bellegarde, was very attentive to her.   Henri III approved of their intimacy, and as they were a handsome couple, made them often dance together at the court balls.   She is said to have been beautiful, with a very fair skin, sparkling blue eyes, dark eyebrows and golden hair, and when dressed in white satin, worthy to attract a monarch's eye.   Legend says that she attracted and held many others. But the balls at the Louvre had ended with *les Barricades,* and Gabrielle had been lost in the seclusion of the Château de Cœuvres, near Soissons, until Bellegarde unexpectedly found her again. The fool boasted of her beauty to the King. The King came, saw and was conquered. Nevertheless, the lady for some time continued to prefer the handsome Bellegarde.

At this point a black cloud of disreputable intrigue rises high in the sky. Nothing is very clear; but, under the circumstances, suspicion has a good foothold. The girl's family were out of luck. Her father had been governor of La Fère, in the Ile-de-France, near Laon, but had been driven out by the League in 1588; her uncle François de Sourdis, husband of her mother's sister Isabeau, had been governor of Chartres, but he too, had been driven out; and, third, her aunt's old lover, Cheverny, who had been chancellor under Henri III, had not only been turned out of office in the end of 1588, but also driven from the governorship of the country round Chartres. The only asset left to the family was the beauty of Gabrielle, age seventeen. During that summer of wooing (1590), Henry IV reinstated Cheverny as chancellor. He next rejected the advice of his military advisers, who urged him to attack the important city of Rouen, which was then ill-prepared for defense, and marched against Chartres, where he met with stout resistance and consumed much time. After the town was captured, Uncle François de Sourdis was reinstated as governor, and quasi ex-uncle Cheverny as governor of the country district. During the progress of the siege, the young lady surrendered to the King's attentions. Gossip ascribed the credit of this intrigue to Isabeau de Sourdis, *fine s'il en fut jamais* (as cunning a woman as ever was),

Chartres fell in April, 1591, and military opinion again urged the King to besiege Rouen; Queen Elizabeth promised to aid such an operation with the English fleet and four thousand men; but Gabrielle asked him to attack Noyon, which is not far from La Fère, where her father had been, governor, and to Noyon he went. There he learned that Queen Elizabeth was as good as her word, and was going to Portsmouth herself to superintend the expedition. In a wayward pattern Destiny wove the great threads of European history with the lesser threads of human passion. England, Holland, the German Protestant States, Denmark and the Huguenots were striving with Spain, Austria, the Papacy, the League and the Jesuits to make the new order prevail over the old, the principle of individual freedom over that of corporate responsibility, the spirit of nationalism over that of European Christendom; and of the two great Protestant champions, one was fighting at Noyon for the beautiful eyes of a seventeen-year-old-girl, and the other was doubting whether or not she would gratify the ambition of her brilliant young favorite, Essex, with command of an expeditionary force.

Henry wrote Elizabeth a warm letter of thanks, he asked if he might not cross the channel to kiss her hands, spend two hours in her company, so that once in his life he might see her to whom he was devoted body and soul, to whom he would consecrate all he had, and whom he loved and revered more than anything in the world. On the same day, for, as I say, the threads of European policy and of private passion twisted and twined together, he wrote to Sully, at Mantes: "I am writing to my mistress; see that I get her answer, and assure her that I shall adore her always." When he had taken Noyon, he appointed her father governor of the town, and her brother bishop.

Essex, in the meantime, had landed at Dieppe and proceeded to Compiègne to pay his respects to the King. He was magnificent; before him rode six squires, dressed in orange velvet all embroidered with gold, and handsomely mounted, a dozen dragoons and six trumpeters; Essex's own bonnet was of orange velvet covered with jewels, and his saddle, bridle, and the horse's caparisons, were ornamented to match. All this made a deep impression on the poor and shabby French soldiers. One wishes that Essex and Gabrielle had met.

The King did not sit down before Rouen until the end of November, 1591. In the meantime the Leaguers had strengthened the city's defenses and laid in a good supply of food and ammunition. The siege was slow, December passed. The English army dwindled by death and desertion to a thousand men. January, 1592, came, and with it came the diabolically clever Alexander Farnese. Again the King was confronted with the problem of whether he should stay in his position before the town, or go to meet the enemy. After some debate, he divided his forces, and with inferior numbers attempted to harass and check Farnese till some reenforcements, that he was hoping for, should come up. Again Farnese showed his better generalship; he contrived to throw twelve hundred men as well as supplies into the beleaguered city, and again with consummate skill eluded the King and retreated to Flanders.

In this miserable way the war dragged on—little battles, sieges, skirmishes, harryings, raids, pillage, murder, theft, rape, and all the incidents that attend the clash of two militant religions. Lesdiguières commanded for the King in Dauphiné, Montmorency in Languedoc, Matignon in Guyenne, La Vallette in Provence, the Comte de la Voulte in the Limousin, and outmatched their adversaries in ability; but the League, strong in the possession of Paris and other cities, had a far greater hold upon the mass of the people, and the war was at a deadlock. The whole country, unless it were a few soldiers by profession or habit who did not wish to say farewell to their occupation, was sick and tired of these horrors, and men more than ever asked themselves for some way out. The extreme Huguenots were considering whether it would not be better for them to reestablish their former covenanting, republican, partizan government and have a Huguenot state; and the League, now that its candidate, old Cardinal Bourbon, was dead, was looking about for a new pretender, but owing to the conflicting ambitions of Mayenne and of King Philip, had reached no conclusion. Some of the Catholic Royalists turned to thoughts of some Bourbon who was a Catholic; for instance, the King's own cousin, Charles, Cardinal de Vendôme, might doff his frock and strengthen his title by marrying the Infanta of Spain, a granddaughter of Henri II, or, there was the Cardinal's young half-brother, the Comte de Soissons, who might marry the King's sister, Catherine. And so on. It was becoming very clear that the country would not tolerate a heretic king. At his accession, the King had promised to convoke an Ecclesiastical Council within six months and receive instruction, but the years 1590, 1591 and 1592 had come and gone and now in 1593 he had done no more than repeat his willingness. His excuse was the civil wars, but the answer to that was that an Ecclesiastical Council would stop the civil wars.

Henry's hope, apparently, had been to win a smashing victory in the field, and frighten Paris into submission, but since Ivry Farnese had been too clever, and Mayenne too prudent to give him that chance, and now there was but one door to

Gabrielle d'Estrées, Duchesse de Beaufort
Portrait by Benjamin Foulon

the throne. His intimate counselors, both Catholics and Huguenots, urged him to be converted. The Marquis d'O, a Catholic,
spoke for his party; "Sire," said he, "you must not diddle
daddle any longer. Within a week there will be an elected
King of France, with the League, the Pope, the King of Spain,
the Emperor, the Duke of Savoy, and all your other enemies
as well, on your hands. You will have to withstand all that
with a pitiful handful of Huguenots, if you do not make a
handsome and quick decision to hear mass." Sully, a stout
Huguenot, was equally urgent: "There are two ways before
you, that of force with its multitudinous dangers and acts of
violence, its battles and bloodshed, the other is to accommodate
yourself in the matter of religion to the opinion of the great
majority of your subjects, follow that and in this world you
will not have many difficulties, as to the other I say nothing."

It seems that there was a still more persuasive counselor.
D'Aubigné says: "The last instrument of his conversion, which
accomplished more than all the others, was Gabrielle, Marquise de Monceaux, soon to be Duchesse de Beaufort." The
King was very much in love and very jealous, for the handsome Bellegarde had been hovering about and, so gossip said,
had given the King ample cause for jealousy; to prevent her
marrying him, the King had married her to the Sieur de
Liancourt, an empty ceremony. Now, he was ready to do
anything that she should ask, as the tenor of his letters to her
shows:

February 4, 1593.

Mon Bel Ange,

If I were only free every hour to importune you to remember your slave, I believe that the end of every letter would be
the beginning of another, and I should be conversing with you

by letter uninterruptedly. . . . But my affairs, or rather my importunities, are more numerous than at Chartres. . . . Souvray is making a great banquet for me to-day; all the ladies will be there. I dress only in black, as I am widowered of all that can cause me joy. Never was fidelity seen like mine; be proud of it. . . . As soon as I have seen my sister, I will send you La Varrenne, who will tell you the day of my coming, which I hurry on, as a man does, who is deep, deep, in love and absent from his goddess. Believe me, my dear Sovereign, and accept forty or a hundred *baise-mains,* as heartily as I gave them yesterday. . . . February 9, 1593. *Mon Bel Ange.* You shall have news of me every day. Let me have yours, particularly of your health. I never left you sadder nor more loyal. Hold it for sure that my love can not receive alteration by any means whatever, except a rival. I am, and shall be to the grave, your faithful slave. I kiss your hands a million times. . . . February 10. I don't know what magic you have used, but I have borne all other absences more patiently than this; it seems a hundred years since I left you. You need not urge me to come back. Not an artery, not a muscle, in my body but shouts aloud the pleasure of seeing you, and the sorrow of your absence. Believe me, my dear Sovereign, that love never shook me so violently as now. . . . Good-by, my Sovereign. I kiss your lovely hands a million times. . . . February 17. I am so unfortunate as to continue to have no news of you, so I send La Fon in hot haste, for I fear something may have happened to you. Send him quickly back, *Mes Chères Amours,* I beseech you. . . . I have sent you a messenger every single day. My love renders me as jealous of my devoirs as of your favor, which is all my riches. Believe, *Mon Bel Ange,* that I value it more than the glory of a

dozen victories. Be proud of conquering me, who never
wholly loved any one but you. I kiss your feet a million
times. . . . April 15, 1593. Ah, how wretched I was last
evening, to find no more her that had made the evening before
so sweet. A thousand joys lingered in my memory. . . .
Certes, *Mes Belles Amours,* you are admirable; but why should
I praise? I tell you that regret at leaving you has so clutched
my heart that all night I thought I should die, and I am still
miserable. I kiss your hands a million times. . . . April
16, 1593. Meulan. . . . Don't fail, *Mes Chères Amours,* to
come the day you promised. The longer I go, the less I can
bear your absence. You have charmed me more than ever I
was. . . . Indeed I adore you with extreme passion and
fidelity. *Bon jour, chère Maîtresse,* I kiss your feet million
times. . . . April 19, Mantes. . . . Jesus! I shall see you
the day after to-morrow. *Quelle joye!* . . . I kiss your
beautiful eyes a million times. April 20, Mantes. *Mes Belles
Amours,* to-morrow I shall kiss your hands . . . if you are
a day late, I shall die. . . . Never has your absence caused
me so much sorrow. To pass the month of April away from
my mistress, is not life. April 21. I had no news of you yesterday; I don't know what has happened. . . . It is noon,
and I have none yet. How far this is from your assurance
that I should see you to-day! When will you learn to value
your troth? I swear I hate you and I will not kiss your lovely
mouth, even if you beg me. H.

Gabrielle had been in love with Bellegarde. They were
separated partly by the jealousy and power of the King, and
partly by her ambition. This royal infatuation kindled high
hopes in her heart. At the beginning of their liaison she had

surrounded herself with Huguenot servants, and affected to trust no one else, but when she became aware of her power over the King she turned about. It was no longer for her interest to be a Huguenot, but a Catholic. Only as a Catholic could she hope to marry the King. But for that three steps were necessary: first, the annulment of her marriage to Liancourt; second, the King's conversion; and third, annulment of the King's marriage to Margot. The first step was easy, for that lay wholly in the King's power, and in due course the marriage was annulled; but although she became free the King was still bound, for Margot though a wayward was a lawful wife, and a whole synod of Calvinists could not untie that knot, only the Pope was great enough, only he could annul that royal marriage, and he would do so only to an obedient and orthodox son. The King must return to the religion of the State. And so it came to pass that the threads of personal passion, interweaving with the great European political pattern, contributed this colored patch to the general design.

CHAPTER XX

THE CONVERSION

FORTUNATELY for the King's party, there were also serious differences of opinion among their enemies. Some were staunchly national, some ready to accept Spanish domination; some were ultramontane, others were partizans of Gallican liberties; and in Paris there was a fanatical faction, similar to the Jacobins of 1793. Disintegration was threatening them; the only hope of preserving union was by the speedy election of a king. For this purpose Mayenne summoned the States-General to Paris; it met in January, 1593.

There was no dearth of claimants. Philip II, who had supplied men and money, who had saved Paris and Rouen, wished the crown for his daughter the Infanta, child of his French wife, Elizabeth; and there were many to assent, by way of compromise, if she would marry a French prince, for instance, the young Duc de Guise, son to the murdered Henri. The Bourbon princes were willing to have their claims fully considered. Mayenne wished the crown for himself; he had brought, he said, the fruit to maturity, and it would not be fair that another should pick it. And if Sully is right, the Princes of the Blood, the Dukes of Mercœur, Guise and Nemours, were desirous virtually to dismember France and procure independent principalities for themselves. There was, indeed, a large number of men of lesser importance, who resented foreign domination, and were ready to accept Henry IV if he would become a Catholic; but among these there were also

217

divisions, some thought that Henry must be received into the Church before he was acknowledged King, others that the reception might accompany, or come after, the acknowledgment. Rift crossed rift; division intersected division.

Mayenne was nearly as much afraid of Philip as of Henry, and wished to curry favor with the moderate, anti-Spanish Catholics, so he took a venturesome step. He invited the Catholic Royalists in the King's camp to a conference. If worst came to worst, he thought, and the conference should agree upon Henry, on condition that he became a Catholic, such an agreement would check Philip's pretentions, and come to nothing, for the Pope would not accept Henry's professed conversion. Mayenne's invitation was accepted, and, in spite of bitter opposition by the violent Leaguers, a joint conference of Catholics from both camps was held at Suresnes, a village on the Seine just beyond the Bois de Boulogne.

The impoverished and destitute citizens of the poorer quarters in Paris knelt down before the envoys of the League as they set out for Suresnes, but the Jesuits denounced the conference as a covenant with Hell, a compact with Sin, and the stricter Huguenots were also troubled in spirit. Du Plessis-Mornay went apart and meditated on the one hundred first Psalm, which he interpreted to apply to a Protestant King:

> I will behave myself wisely in a perfect way. . . .
> I will walk within my house with a perfect heart.
> I will set no wicked thing before mine eyes:
> I hate the work of them that turn aside; . . .
> He that worketh deceit shall not dwell within my house.

The first meeting of the conference was held on April twenty-ninth. But already before this, Henry had made up his mind. The great mass of the people was against him, it was impossible for him to take Paris, and among his friends, as Sully says, petty motives were rampant *vanité, désir de la faveur, bas intérêts, vil artifice, jalousie, fourberie* and *trahison.* When, therefore, the conference at Suresnes had been agreed on, he felt that the time to make his decision public had arrived. It is characteristic of him that he hoped in consideration of his conversion to obtain not only the Crown of France, but incidental advantages as well, to procure, for instance, certain concessions from the Duke of Lorraine, and also a loan of men and money from the Grand Duke of Tuscany:

> To the Grand Duke
> > Mantes, April 26, 1593.
>
> Mon Cousin. . . .
>
> I wish to confirm what I communicated to you by Cardinal Gondi concerning my conversion, and I also have been wishing and do wish to promise you, as I am doing, on the faith and word of a King, by these presents written and signed by my hand, to make a public declaration and confession of the Catholic Religion, according to the canons of the Church (as my predecessors, the Kings of France, have done) within two months after my cousin the Duke of Lorraine shall have come to terms with me in a just agreement. [But he affixes a rider to this promise, for he asks the Grand Duke to send him four thousand Switzers and two hundred thousand crowns] since I am only waiting for this to put my promise aforesaid into effect.
>
> > HENRY.

On May fifth, at Suresnes, the conference agreed that the civil war was terrible and that they must put an end to it;

but how? The Archbishop of Bourges, for the Royalists, maintained that the duty of all was to obey the King, while the Archbishop of Lyons on behalf of the League, maintained that that duty only applied to a Catholic King. The result was that it became evident that if the King would turn his religious coat, he would be acknowledged by all the moderate Catholics. In Paris, in the meantime, the States-General became busy with the election of a King. In order to forestall any such action, Henry IV, without waiting further, announced his intention of conversion. First, out of deference to his family, he wrote to his cousin, the Prince de Conti:

Mantes, May 10, 1593.

. . . The election, for which the League is working seems to incline toward the King of Spain, as there is no subject powerful enough to make them secure. I have come to the conclusion that I can find no better remedy than to summon a number of prelates about me, to take up the matter of my instruction; this will also serve to satisfy the general wish of such of my Catholic subjects as recognize me.

HENRY.

Accordingly, on May seventeenth, the Archbishop of Bourges announced to the conference that the King had decided to "receive instruction and return to the bosom of the ancient religion which the prejudice of his religion had made him abandon." The King made a similar statement to those about him. He denounced his enemies *les François Espagnoles,* the Hispanified Frenchmen, "whose hearts are infected with Spanish poison," and reiterated that he had always intended to hearken to instruction on the religious matters that divided his

people, and now he was free to do so, and that for his own
part he had but one desire, "to embrace and follow the true
path to salvation." He also wrote letters to various people,
ecclesiastics and laymen, inviting some ecclesiastics to join the
committee of instruction and the others to a meeting of notables, at the same time giving to each person such a statement
of proposed action on his part as he judged most likely to accord with that person's sympathies:

To the Bishop of Chartres

Mantes, May 18, 1593.

Monsieur de Chartres.

  . . . I have decided—in order, if possible, to leave no
scruples to these people in rendering me obedience, on account
of my religion—to receive instruction as soon as may be
concerning the differences which cause the schism in the
Church. I have always declared I would not refuse to do this;
and I should not have delayed so long before attending to it,
had it not been for the notorious obstacles that have hindered
me. And although the present state of my affairs could still
justly excuse me, I do not wish to postpone my instruction.
Therefore, I have been advised to summon a number of
Catholic prelates and doctors by whose good instructions I
shall be able (with peace and satisfaction to my conscience) to
be enlightened concerning the difficulties which keep us apart
in the exercise of religion. And as I desire my advisers to be
men of learning, piety and honor, with no purpose other than
God's glory (I myself will come in absolute sincerity), and as
you are one of those of whom I have a good opinion, I beg
you to come here on July fifteenth. I am asking some others
of the clergy to come at the same time. . . .

HENRY.

To Master Benigne Ocquidam
Councillor of the Parliament of Burgundy

Mantes, May 20, 1593.

My trustworthy Friend:

. . . I have summoned here a number of Catholic prelates and doctors for the fifteenth of July next, as I am quite
disposed to receive and follow whatever their good instruction
shall teach me belongs to piety and religion. . . . I wanted
to give you notice of this. . . .

HENRY.

To the Reformed Churches

Mantes, May 25, 1593.

My dear good Friends. . . . It has been decided to hold a
general assembly of princes, prelates, officers of the Crown,
gentlemen and others of our subjects, of both religions, on July
twentieth next, at Mantes, to assist us with their advice and
counsel on matters that shall be submitted to them for the
safety of the State, and the good of my subjects.

HENRY.

To another he writes that he has convoked a general assembly
of his principal subjects of both religions at Mantes, on July
twentieth, "in order to look for and decide upon means of a
general peace and to break the designs and conspiracies of my
enemies."

Very different feelings greeted the King's announcement;
the poor people of Paris, and the moderates, both those who
had joined the King and those who had joined the League,
were overjoyed, but the men of deeper convictions, both Huguenots and Catholics, regarded the conversion as a mere act of

political expediency, a shame and a blasphemy. The Protestant clergy said: "We are greatly displeased, Sire, to see you torn by violence from the bosom of óur churches. Do not, may it please you, permit such a scandal to happen." The King replied: "If I were to follow your advice, in a little while there would be neither King nor Kingdom in France. I wish to give peace to my subjects, and rest to my soul. Take counsel among you as to what you need for your security. I shall always be ready to satisfy you." Du Plessis-Mornay was one of those who did not approve. He wrote to his friend, Monsieur de Morlas: "*O Mores! imo O Amores* [for he, too attributed the King's action to Gabrielle] and yet, in my tears, I wish to hope, I wish to believe, though he can forget God, that God, nevertheless will not forget him. . . . The resolution to turn about was taken upon human considerations, without hearkening to Holy Writ, for the bishops were only invited in order to give form and ceremony to this pretended conversion. In fact one of the principal among them, writing to the Bishop of Chartres, said that there was no need to brush up his theology; and the King, himself, when the prelates came to instruct him, said that he was not in need of very much instruction, as he had made up his mind as to what he must do."

Du Plessis-Mornay was invited to the assembly of notables on July twentieth, but he refused for he believed the whole affair to be a mere sham. Nevertheless, he wrote to the King that if he wished a serious religious conference to enlighten himself and his people, he would face all dangers with a front of bronze, and would attend with a dozen ministers, capable of making God's truth shine out in the face of falsehood, but he humbly besought his Majesty, if he was already resolved on conversion and entered into a conference only for formality's sake, not to lay such a crime on his conscience; because, if, after an argument in which it was impossible for truth to be vanquished, he should yield to idolatry, he would cause quite as great a scandal to the Christian Church, as if he had yielded or fallen without any such argument, and, all the more because he would have seen the religion that he professed triumphantly vindicated.

The King did not like to distress this loyal friend, or run the risk of losing his services; and, later, explained to him why he had done it. He had been, he said, on the edge of a precipice through the intrigues of his own partizans, and that conversion was his only means of escape; and, moreover, he had not received from those of his religion the support he had needed from them; but his heart would always remain unchanged toward the religion and those that professed it, and he hoped that God would have mercy on him. The King, also, seemed to Du Plessis-Mornay "imbued with the opinion, [and this mitigated his wrong-doing] that the difference of religion was so great only because of the animosity of preachers, and that he hoped some day, by means of his authority, to compose it." D'Aubigné agreed with Du Plessis-Mornay that the conversion was purely political. Sully, as we know, had counseled it; but Sully was cynical in politics, he said his idea of proper conduct was this: "Receive everybody cordially, promise little, seem to wish to come to a conclusion, lay the blame for delay on obstacles, work hard to remove those obstacles; in my opinion, almost all doubtful political matters should be dealt with in that manner." To him the conversion was simply a political matter.

On the other hand, the extreme Leaguers were very angry with what they considered a sham and a trick. In Paris the preachers, especially the Jesuit Fathers, were violent. On May twenty-third the first Sunday after the news came out, the Curé of one church called the King "a devil, a wolf, a heretic, a villainous relapse, an excommunicate, a rogue and a bastard." At the church of Saint-André, Father Boucher, who preached in the presence of the Duc de Mayenne and his mother, the Duchesse de Nemours, declaimed against any peace or truce; he said that they must have a King, but a King of pure gold, that the people of Paris were fools to let the moderate party brave them to their faces, and added, with an impolite reference to Mayenne's girth (Henry IV called him "the fat Duke") that they who governed them had plenty of body but little mind. At the church of Saint-Jean, a Cordelier, known as *Feu Ardent* "vomited one million insults against the King, he said that some day a thunderbolt would strike him, or that he would burst, as his belly was all rotten." At Saint-Germain, the Curé denounced the conversion; and at another church, the preacher, Génébrard, tore the King's reputation to tatters, uttering the vilest slanders. On the next Sunday Father Boucher was still more virulent; he larded his vocabulary with all the billingsgate of *le Petit Pont,* called the King *"vilain, voleur, sacrilége, noir pendard, larron vérolé, putier, violateur de vierges et nonnains,* a rascally thief, a black sacrilegious gallowsbird, a pocky rake, a ravisher of maids and nuns." But a few priests who belonged to the moderate party were more Christian. The Curé of Saint-Merri preached that they ought to welcome the conversion of a heretic, and the Curé of Saint-Sulpice called down curses on all who hindered the work of peace.

Did the King have any twinges of conscience? He belonged to a generation that firmly believed in an anthropomor-

phic God and in supernatural powers, in witchcraft, in sooth-
saying and necromancy; and he often ascribes the mishaps of
his enemies, and his own victories and escapes, to the direct
intervention of God, and not merely in public utterances but
also in private letters. He writes to Corisande or Gabrielle
that the *Grand Maître* has conducted his affairs, that *la justice
de Dieu* has won him a victory, that God has done this or that
for him, *vraiment, Dieu m'a bien aidé,* et cetera. He certainly
was not an atheist, nor an agnostic. He had learned to think
that the men of strongest convictions on both sides, Calvinist
ministers and Jesuit Fathers, were all unreasonable, and that
more Christian charity would diminish the theological differences between them; and what he said to Du Plessis-Mornay
was probably true, he believed that he would be able to effect
a compromise by means of his authority. A year later somebody referred in his hearing to a man who had belonged "to
the religion which the King once held." "What do you mean,"
the King asked, "what religion are you talking of that I once
held? I never knew and do not know but one Catholic religion;
I am not a Jew." Sully says that he told him that he had
adopted the Catholic religion, as *la plus sûre.*

At any rate, the King prepared for the ceremony of instruction. His thoughts, however, were not wholly given to
considering the verities or errors of transubstantiation, of
Purgatory, of papal authority, or the correct number of sacra-
ments. On June sixteenth, he wrote to Gabrielle that "his love
had never been greater nor his passion more violent," and on
June twenty-third that "he kissed her feet a million times,"
on June twenty-sixth "her hands a million times," and on
July twelfth at Saint-Denis, three days before his instruction,
"Indeed, *Mes Chères Amours,* you should rather fear lest I

love you too much than too little," and he sends a further mil‑
lion kisses. And just before his conversion he wrote her the
famous letter:

Saint-Denis, July 23, 1593.

I arrived yesterday afternoon, and was nagged by sky-
pilots (*Dieu-gardes*) till I went to bed. We think that the
further truce will go through and that it will be signed to-day.
But for my part, in regard to the League, I follow doubting
Thomas. I am to begin to converse with the bishops this
morning. . . . On Sunday *Je ferai le saut périlleux* [I shall
take the perilous leap]. At this time of writing I have a hundred importunate fellows on my back, who will make me hate
Saint-Denis as you do Mantes.

Bon jour, mon Cœur, come early to-morrow, for it seems a
year since I saw you. I kiss a thousand times my Angel's
beautiful hands and the lips of my dear Mistress.

He scribbled his letter bright and early, and then conferred
with four learned bishops from six in the morning till one
o'clock. He asked three questions: Is it an obligation of
Christian duty to pray to all the saints? To which the bishops
answered: Every one need have only his own patron saint,
nevertheless one must invoke all the saints according to the
litany. Second: How about auricular confession? to which
the King thought there should be certain limitations. Answer:
An upright man accuses himself, but the confessor ought to
inquire as to anything held back. Third: As to papal authority? Answer: The Pope has absolute authority in matters
spiritual, but as to matters temporal he has no power to interfere with the liberty of kings or kingdoms. As to the Real
Presence, the King said that he had no doubt of it. He

learned that the errors, which as he had been taught to think
had crept into the Catholic Church, were errors of usage and
practise and not of doctrine. Thereupon he declared himself
ready, and begged to be received back into the Church and
allowed to attend mass. So it was done. On July 25, 1593,
in the abbey church of Saint-Denis, in the presence of the
Archbishop of Bourges, attended by several bishops and a
number of Royalist priests, the King dressed in a doublet of
white satin embroidered with gold, stockings of the same, a
black cloak and black hat with a black plume, made oath to live
and die in the Catholic religion. Before the ceremony he took
an affectionate farewell of his Huguenot friends, he put his
arm around one minister's neck and kissed him two or three
times, and he bade the others pray for him, love him always,
said that he should love them and remember them and that he
should never permit any wrong or violence to their religion.

As soon as the ceremony was over, the King became his
own pleasant spirited self. He noticed the presence of a
Huguenot gentleman at mass, and asked him if he was not a
Huguenot and had not always attended the Protestant service.
"Yes, Sire." "Then why are you assisting at mass to-day?"
"Because you are attending, Sire." "Ah," answered the King,
"I understand the reason: you would like to win a crown."

The ceremony was followed by the issuance of a circular
letter announcing the King's abjuration:

Saint-Denis, Sunday, July 25, 1593.
To my Friends and Liegemen,

In pursuance of the promise that we made on our accession
to this Crown by the death of the late King whom God absolve,
and after the convocation made by us of prelates and doctors

of our Kingdom for the sake of receiving instruction, so much desired by us and so often prevented by the artifices of our enemies, at last, thank God, we have conferred with the aforesaid prelates and doctors, assembled for that purpose in this city, on the points concerning which we desired to be enlightened; and after the grace that it has pleased God to confer upon us by the inspiration of His Holy Spirit, which we have dearly sought after with all our heart for our salvation's sake, and satisfied by the proofs that these prelates and doctors have put before us, by the writings of the Apostles, and of the Holy Fathers and Doctors acknowledged by the Church, recognizing the Catholic, Apostolic, Roman Church to be God's true church, full of truth, unable to err, we have embraced it and have resolved to live and die in it.

HENRY.

He also wrote to the Pope:

Saint-Denis, August 9, 1593.

Very Holy Father,

Having recognized, by the inspiration that it has pleased God to give me, that the Catholic Church, Apostolic and Roman, is the true church full of truth, in which lies man's salvation, and, strengthened in this faith and belief by the enlightenment that the prelates and doctors of the sacred faculty of theology have given me, on the points which in the past have kept me separated, I am resolved to join this Holy Church and wholly determined to live and die in it, with the help of Him who has given me the grace to call me there. . . .

HENRY.

But among those who did not rejoice was his sister Catherine, who dearly loved her brother, in spite of his real indifference to her happiness. She wrote to Du Plessis-Mornay:

July, 1593.

Monsieur Duplessis:

I am very glad that you have so good an opinion of my constancy, in which I mean to persevere so that you and all who profess the same creed shall not be deceived. I do not doubt that the change of which you hear grieves you. For me I feel so badly that I can't describe it to you. But I hope that God who up to now has given us so much evidence of His Goodness, will not abandon us, and particularly not him, who, for the good of his people, is not afraid to relax his conscience a little. . . .

CATHERINE.

The ultramontane priests in Paris preached with fresh vigor. The Curé de Saint-André declared that he would not give a button for the soul of any man, priest, prelate, or spectator, who should be at Saint-Denis during the ceremony. Others called the King *"bougre," "Judas," "coquin," "pendard."* The Curé de Saint-Jacques de la Boucherie said that the three doctors who had instructed the Béarnais should be respectively burned, broken on the wheel and hanged. Other priests preached on wolves in sheeps' clothing, and so forth.

CHAPTER XXI

THE EDICT OF NANTES

THE game was won. The shrewd King had timed his conversion for the right juncture. The moderate Catholics had become disgusted with the bullying interference of the King of Spain and of the papal legate, and with the personal ambitions of the princes of the House of Guise, and were quite ready to accept the hereditary King now that he had become Catholic. The States-General, under the influence of Mayenne, of Rome and of Spain, continued to refuse acknowledgment; but all over France the tide turned, and gentles and commons came trooping in, one here, one there, in increasing numbers to offer allegiance. Cities and provinces followed the example; Meaux, Lyons, Orléans, Bourges, and on February 27, 1594, the King was crowned at Chartres, for Reims was still in the hands of the Guises.

Paris, the head and front of the Catholic League, showed signs of indecision and uncertainty. Quarrels between those who wished to acknowledge the King and the violent sectaries who would not, were of constant occurrence. Pierre de L'Estoile's diary tells of angry words, suspicions, conflicting hopes and purposes, fights, treacheries and murders. In the beginning of March, Mayenne left the city, ostensibly to confer with the Spanish army on the borders of Picardy, but contrary to his promise to the citizens, he took his wife and children with him and made arrangements for removing his personal property. Mayenne's flight determined the action of the

231

Governor of the city, the Comte de Brissac. He entered into secret negotiations with the King, and agreed to open the gates on the night of the twenty-first of March. A heavy mist and drizzle hung about the city, and, while still dark and the bells were ringing the angelus, the Kings troops arrived at the walls. Brissac opened the gates. There was no opposition. Except for one fight by the river, where some thirty German mercenaries of the League were killed, the occupation was effected without bloodshed. The King entered by the Porte-Neuve about seven o'clock in the morning, and sent word to the Spanish ambassador, the Duc de Feria, that his life and the lives of his men were in his power, but that he coveted neither, and handed them back on condition that, without delay or excuse, they should leave the city at once.

As the King rode through the Rue Saint-Honoré he saw a soldier taking bread by force from a baker, and was so indignant that he rode upon him and wanted to kill him. Passing on, he saw a man in a window who kept his hat on and stared at him insolently without a salutation; the crowd murmured angrily, but the King only laughed, and bade no one enter the house or trouble the man. As he crossed the bridge of Notre-Dame, the people shouted, *"Vive le Roi!"* He said: "I see how these poor people have been tyrannized over." He issued at once a proclamation of full pardon to everybody, and sent word to the ladies of the Guise family, Madame de Nemours, and Madame de Montpensier (mother and sister to Mayenne), who had both been wildly fanatical against him, to say that they and their property would be quite safe under his protection. They returned thanks with great humility. Poor Madame de Montpensier, when she heard that the King was in the city, had asked if there was no one to

Henry IV enters Paris

From the painting by Gérard in the Louvre

plunge a dagger into her heart. Then the King went to Notre-
Dame to render thanks. In the afternoon he placed himself
in a window over the Porte Saint-Denis, and watched the Duc
de Feria and the Spanish garrison march out. The Duke
saluted, after the Spanish fashion, gravely and slightly; the
King imitated him gaily, half taking his hat off, and called
out, "Give my regards to your master, but don't come back."
One of the Spanish women who accompanied the soldiers was
overheard to say that France was lucky to have so good, kind
and merciful a King, and when she saw him she cried out:
"I see him! I pray to God, good King, to give you all prosperity! And when I am in my own country, wherever I am,
I shall always bless you and praise your greatness, your goodness and your mercifulness."

There are various stories concerning the first few hours
after his entry. He asked one of the Leaguers what he thought
of seeing him in Paris; the Leaguer answered: "They have
given unto Cæsar the things that belong to Cæsar, as it was
right to give unto God the things that belong to God."
"Given!" the King exclaimed. *"Ventre-saint-gris!* They
haven't given Paris to me, they sold it at a jolly good price."
Some one spoke to him about some business, he replied: "I
must confess that I am so intoxicated to find myself here that,
I don't know what you are talking about, nor what I ought to
say." At dinner when he sat down, he laughed and said that
he could tell from his wet feet that he had gone through the
mud on his way into Paris; but that nevertheless his steps had
been worth while. He regretted very much that any men had
been killed, and said he would give fifty thousand crowns to
have them alive again, to be able to say to posterity that he
had taken Paris without the loss of a life. Even the Curé

de Saint-Jacques de la Boucherie, who had preached violent sermons on his conversion, admitted that "the King had been marvelously sweet and benign, especially as among those that he pardoned many had committed unforgivable deeds, and that one must say he is a good King." Henry himself said: "I recognize that all my victories are due to God who spreads His Hand over me, although I am not worthy, and as He forgives me, so do I, too, wish to forgive, and forgetting the faults of my people, to be still more merciful to them than I have been."

He called upon Madame de Nemours and Madame de Montpensier, and asked if they were not surprised to see him in Paris, and find that there had been no thieving or robbery, not an injury to the value of a straw, and that everybody down to the very lowest had paid for what they had taken. Turning to Madame de Montpensier he repeated: "What think you of that, my Cousin?" "Sire," she said, "we can think nothing but that you are a great King, very benign, very clement and very generous." The King replied with a smile: "I don't know whether I ought to believe that you say what you think. But I am sure of one thing, you are vexed with Brissac, aren't you?" "No, Sire, why should I be vexed with him?" "Yes, you are, yes, you are," the King answered. "I am sure of it. But some day when you have nothing else to do you will make it up with him." "Sire," she said, "since you wish it, it is already made up. There is one thing, however, about the surrender that I would have liked, and that is that my brother, Monsieur de Mayenne, might have been here to open the gates for you." "*Ventre-saint-gris!*" the King exclaimed, "perhaps he might have kept me waiting some time longer."

Then feeling hungry he asked her for some preserved fruits. She said, "I think you ask in mockery, for you think we have none left." "No," he said, "I ask because I'm hungry." She fetched a jar of apricots, and helping herself, was about to taste the jam in order to show that it was not poisoned. He stopped her and said: "My Cousin, you are not to think of doing that!" "What," she asked, "have I not done enough to arouse your suspicions?" "I have no suspicions of you, my Cousin." "Ah," she answered, "I see why people are loyal to you." Indeed, out of his abundant good-nature and policy, which happily went hand in hand, the King performed all the little acts that win popularity. In Easter week he followed the old ceremony of washing the feet of thirteen poor children and waited on them at dinner, and on Easter day he laid his hands on six hundred and sixty poor people, ill of the King's evil, the scrofula, and afterward, in the Louvre, on thirty more, being *personnes d'une condition plus honnête.*

Henry was right to rejoice in the possession of the capital. Other cities and towns followed its example; Rouen, Honfleur, Péronne, Troyes, Sens, Poitiers, Périgueux, Rodez, Agen, Amiens, Beauvais and so on. And young Charles de Guise, son to the murdered Henri, nephew to Mayenne and once talked of for King, surrendered Reims. Young Guise attempted to make a speech, when he was presented to the King. Henry laughed. "You are not much more of an orator than I. I know what you want to say. One word can do it. We are liable to youthful faults. I forget it all; only don't do it again. You shall recognize that I am the King and I will be a father to you. There is no man in my court on whom I shall look with more favor than you."

The city of Laon, however, had to be won by a siege, in the face of Mansfeld's army of relief. Sully joined the King there. He found him lying on a straw mattress, with his feet all bandaged up. The King said: "Welcome; I wager you are not a little surprised to find me in bed, for you have known me a long time and you know that it is not my custom to sleep overmuch on such occasions, and still less to be abed, when I should be up and doing. But I have had such a time this last night on the rough slopes of this mountain in order to visit all the outposts that I can hardly stand. And, so that you shan't think I am coddling myself, I'd like to have you look at my feet." The bandages and plasters were then taken off, and Sully found his feet all split and cut and blistered, and bleeding.

After his feet were well, the King took advantage of intermittences in active operations to amuse himself. One day he rode off to dine at Marle, a dozen miles away, where as a boy he used to go to one of his father's estates, for he wished to revive happy memories of fruits, cheese and cream, of boyhood and its pleasures; another day in a garden back of the lines, he was shaking a plum tree that bore the best plums when some of his retinue rode up in hot haste: "For goodness' sake, Sire, we have just seen some people coming up who seem to have in mind to prepare for you a breakfast of plums, quite different from these, and harder to digest if you don't ride off at once." Again and again his courage carried him into danger to the great alarm of his friends. Here is a special instance.

He had been obliged to declare war against Spain (January, 1595), for Philip II had continued to enable the League to keep in the field by supplies of men and money, and at the outset of the campaign Henry marched to meet the combined army of Leaguers and Spaniards (June, 1595). He was reconnoitering near Fontaine-Française, twenty miles northeast

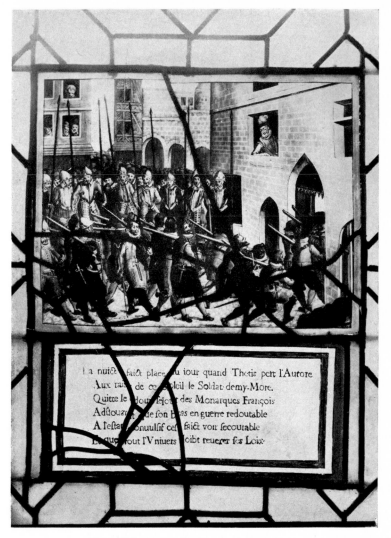

La nuict faict place au iour quand Thetis pert l'Aurore
Aux rais de ce Soleil le Soldat demy-More,
Quitte le iour séiour des Monarques François
Adiouzar que son Bras en guerre redoutable
A restablir onuulsif cest faict voir secourable
Lesque tout l'Vniuers doibt reuerer ses Loix.

Henry IV watches the Spaniards leave Paris

From the glass window in Troyes, which seems to have been executed after a painting by
Bollery

of Dijon with a small troop of horse, and came upon an outpost of the enemy. Thinking that their numbers were few, he charged. But Mayenne and the Constable of Castile were there with the main body of their army. The enemy were five to one. His companions urged him to beat a retreat, but his blood was up, and he charged. He wrote an account of the affair to his sister:

Dear Sister, the more I consider it the more I wonder at God's mercy to me in Monday's fight. I thought I had whipped twelve hundred horse, but they should be put down at two thousand. The Constable of Castile was there in person with the Duc de Mayenne. They saw me and recognized me perfectly, as I learned from their trumpeters and from prisoners. Many of my young gentlemen, seeing me everywhere with them, showed their mettle and much courage; among others I noticed Gramont, Termes, Boissi, La Curée and the Marquis de Mirebeau who all happened to be there; they had no armor but their jerkins and did wonders. There were some, who did not behave so well, and others who behaved very badly. Those who were not there will regret it. I had all my good friends on me, and you came very near to being my heir. . . . I am very well, thank God, and love you as I do myself. HENRY.

He also wrote to one of his old Béarnais companions who, if I am not mistaken, had been master of his hawks at Pau, and happened not to be present:

Dijon, June 13, 1595.

Harambure,

Go hang yourself, since you were not by my side in a

fight we have had with the enemy, in which we thrashed them. . . . I'll tell you all about it when I see you. . . . Join me as soon as possible. Hurry up, for I need you. Good-by, One-Eye!   HENRY.

His chaplain, Palma Cayet, says: "All those who have written how matters went that day, and particularly as to the charge, say that the King's escape was a miracle, that God took him under his special protection, for when the King saw three squadrons approach, though he had but sixty horse, he dashed into the first rank of the enemy composed of three hundred horse and routed them; then, rallying together what men he could, he broke the second rank which consisted of about two hundred, and again after that with twenty or twenty-five horsemen left (for the others had gone off in pursuit of the runaways) he broke the third squad that consisted of about one hundred and fifty." The affair was little more than a skirmish, but the moral effect was such that Mayenne and the Constable of Castile retreated across the border.

But his courage was not, strictly speaking, recklessness. In one of his appeals to the Parliament of Paris for money, he said: "You say that where I am, things go well. That is true, thank God for it. But I can not be everywhere. . . . You say that I run too much risk. I don't do it because I want to, but because I am obliged to; because, if I don't go into danger, nobody else will. They are all volunteers; I can't force them. If I had any money to hire soldiers with, I should have men whom I could trust and send to the front without going. I need money; and there is no way to get it so good as by means of the tax enactments that you must pass tomorrow. Say to those that raise objections, that it is they that oblige me to run risks." Sully expostulated, too; the King replied, "I am fighting for honor and for my crown, and there is no help for it."

In due course the King triumphed. Mayenne ate humble pie and was cordially received. When the King and he met— you remember that Mayenne was a large fat man—in the park of a château, the King made the Duke walk up and down at a very brisk pace, and the Duke, who also had sciatica, kept up with great labor. So they continued footing it to and fro, till the Duke, flushed, perspiring, and out of breath, begged for pity. "All right, Cousin, put her there," the King said, "for, by the Lord, that is all the revenge you will ever receive from me." And he bade Sully comfort him with two bottles of wine from Arbois, famous then as now (January, 1596).

The Duc de Joyeuse followed Mayenne's example, then the Duc d'Epernon, and the Duc de Mercœur; but the last was obliged to betrothe his only daughter to the King's little bastard, César, Duc de Vendôme, the four-year old son of Gabrielle. And in May, 1598, peace was made with Spain, without regard to England, although the King had made a treaty with Queen Elizabeth that contained the following article: "Fifth: The King and Queen aforesaid shall not make any treaty of peace or truce with the King of Spain, nor with his lieutenants or captains, without mutual consent, which shall be signified by the aforesaid King's or Queen's own hand." Monsieur Mariéjol, a distinguished French historian, says: "Henry could not really exhaust his kingdom for so inconstant an ally as Elizabeth." However, *Albion perfide* was scandalized. The terms of peace were virtually the same that had been fixed by the Treaty of Cateau-Cambrésis, nearly forty years before.

But one further act was necessary. Henry had accepted the national tradition that the King must belong to the Catholic Church, Apostolic and Roman, he had vanquished the League, he had put down civil war, and had made peace, but the status of his Huguenot subjects had still to be settled. This was not easy, for the Huguenots were large in their demands, and took what advantage they could of the Spanish war, but finally it was accomplished, liberty of conscience was to be universal, and liberty of worship according to Calvinistic ritual was granted, with certain differences under different circumstances, upon terms of reasonable liberality. The *Edict of Nantes* was signed on April 13, 1598. It has been estimated that during the thirty-odd years of civil war, near four millions had perished out of a population of from twelve to fifteen millions.

CHAPTER XXII

THE QUESTION OF AN HEIR

THE dominant political issue had been disposed of; France had adopted the policy of religious compromise. The religion of the State should be Catholic, Apostolic and Roman, but dissent should be tolerated, the individual might follow his bent, and either worship as his forefathers had done, or adopt the ritual that Calvin had deduced from his interpretation of the New Testament. In England the policy of Elizabeth and the Cecils had crushed Catholicism; in Spain Philip II and the Inquisition had suppressed the Protestants. The seamless garment of Christendom had been rent beyond repair. On one side had gathered those peoples and persons who abided by the ancient Christian tradition, fashioned by the contributing hands of fifty generations, with its acknowledgment of international brotherhood, of fellowship with the saints, of the sublimated influences of sex as set forth in the worship of the Virgin Mary, of a God present on the altar, beside his worshipers,

Verbum caro, panem verum
Verbo carnem efficit,

and of Divine Mercy, that might operate at the last minute; on the other side stood those who protested and denied, who rejected the magic of priestcraft and sacramental rights, who preferred an ancient Book to a living revelation, who exalted the idea of nationality above the ideal of Christendom, who

241

set the efficacy of faith above that of good deeds, and regarded
Purgatory as a superstition, the Papacy a tyranny, and auricular confession a device to control women and weak men.

Henry, himself, was inclined to think too lightly of these
differences of opinion, and ascribed them, as persons will, that
are not interested in supernatural things, to waywardness and
prejudice. In 1594, the year after his conversion, he said to
deputies from the city of Beauvais: "I promise you, in God's
name and by His grace that, before two years are out, you
shall see all the people of my Kingdom in one Church, Catholic,
Apostolic and Roman, and that I shall know how to handle the
Huguenots, whose chief I have been for twenty-two years,
with such gentleness, that I shall bring them all into the bosom
of the true Church." That hope he had been obliged to defer,
and to accept, for a time at least, the solution of an alien
church, with special political privileges, within his Kingdom.
At any rate, Henry's policy had stopped civil war and brought
peace to a long-suffering land; and his solution of that grievous
issue is his chief claim to fame and to the gratitude of his
people. And we may now turn to another matter that troubled
him considerably, the matter of an heir, of succession to the
throne. A son of his own would doubtless succeed peaceably
to the Crown; but suppose that he should have no legitimate
son? The next of kin was a boy, the son of that Prince de
Condé who had been poisoned by his wife, and some were
doubtful as to his legitimacy. Might not other claimants rise
up, might not Catholics and the fanatical Huguenots find
agreement impossible and come to blows again?

In 1585 Margot had left her husband and gone to Agen,
hated by him, and by her brother Henri III, and but little liked
by her mother, who said that "Margot was her scourge in

this world . . . that God had given her this creature in punishment of her sins . . . and that on her account she expected to die of vexation." The people of Agen liked her as little, for she acted with a high hand, and had driven her out. From there (riding behind a gentleman without any pad and skinning herself badly) she fled to Carlat, a castle in Auvergne, beyond Aurillac, where, according to some, she was bullied by adventurous gentlemen, who had aided her flight, and, according to others, she abandoned herself to her pleasures. A year later she fled from Carlat to take refuge in one of her mother's castles, but with no luck, for Henri III ordered her to be seized and locked in the Château d'Usson, a little fortress that Louis XI had found an excellent prison for those with whom he was displeased, situated near the southwest border of what is now the department of the Loire. It is a remote spot, and the modern guide-book merely notes "ruined fortifications and interesting houses." It is difficult to believe that even the houses were interesting in those days. Of the adventurous gentlemen who had aided and abetted her, he to whom she was most attached, d'Aubiac, lost his head. Henri III sent the order to the governor of Haute-Auvergne: "The Queen Mother," he said, "bids me have d'Aubiac hanged; let it be in the court of the castle of Usson in the presence of that miserable woman."

Scandal says that Catherine de Médicis suggested that Margot be put to death, and that Henry of Navarre should then marry Catherine's granddaughter, Christine de Lorraine. Benevolent historians doubt this, but Henri de Guise had believed it; he wrote to Don Bernardino de Mendoza that if he knew the details "his hair would stand on end." It is more charitable to believe that Catherine offered, in case Henry would turn Catholic, to confine Margot in a nunnery and procure an annulment of the marriage. Margot was frightened; she says: "Under my mother's assurance, I fled to her protection, but instead of the good treatment I expected I have experienced *honteuse ruine,* shameful misery. Patience! She brought me into the world; she wishes to take me out of it." There, however, she lived for over eight years, poor partly because she was very extravagant, and partly because the pension, allowed first by her brother and then by her husband, was irregularly paid, if at all. However, she made friends with the Governor of the fortress. Pierre Matthieu, the official chronicler, and Brantôme, always loyal to Margot, say: "The Governor thought to have triumphed over her, but the mere sight of her ivory arms triumphed over him, and thenceforth he lived in the victorious eyes of his beautiful captive." She seems to have bestowed her possessions and her affections upon him; at least, he allowed her for a good price to make herself mistress of the place. She herself, and some well-disposed friends, speak of Usson as a hermitage, and there she wrote her *Mémoires.* Joseph Scaliger, the great scholar, who saw her there, said that "she was free, did what she liked, and *a des hommes tant qu'elle veut"* but adds that she "took after her grandfather François I, liked intelligent men, was well educated and had many royal virtues, more so than the King." However that may be, Margot now became a person of some consequence, for she was the legal wife of the King, and he desired another wife, who should bear him issue, and could not divorce her without her consent. The question as to who should be that other wife had now come into the region of practical politics. Even before the King's conversion, the sagacious counselor, Du Plessis-Mornay, had been concerned

over the matter of succession, and the King had authorized
him to obtain from Queen Margot her consent to a divorce;
and an envoy, Monsieur de Erard, the *maître de requêtes* of
Navarre, went to Usson to see her about it. Margot professed
the greatest complaisance, but she had a long list of items that
she wished granted in consideration of her consent, and she
was both suspicious and wary; and though she signs her letters
to the King *votre très obéissante servante femme et subjecte,*
her formal consent was finally not executed until February
7, 1599.

As to the lady whom the King wished to put in the place
of his divorced Queen, there could be no doubt. Gabrielle was
now twenty-three or four, and as beautiful as ever, or more so.
A gentleman, one of the mob that write with ease, Guillaume
du Sable, whose taste is commended by Brantôme, described
her beauties: "His eye delighted to behold her lovely hair,
her forehead, her ebony eye-brows, her *beau nez décorant,*
her cheeks where Cupid played, her brilliant, tender eyes!
How happy he that might kiss her vermilion *(cinabrine)* lips,
her handsome double chin! How lovely her lily throat set on
alabaster! And what a delicious roguish laugh!" The King
agreed with the poet; and his love increased after the birth
of their first-born, César (June, 1594), subsequently Duc de
Vendôme. Of this his letters are the best evidence:

December, 1594.

Mes chères Amours,

I am writing at the foot of your portrait, which I adore,
not because it is like you, but because it was meant for you;
I am a competent judge, for I have your perfect picture in my
soul, in my soul, in my heart, in my eyes.   H.

Péronne, May 27, 1596.

Dear Heart,

This morning, as soon as I awoke, I had news of you, and that will make my day happier. . . . I shall not fail to commend myself twice a day to the favor of my dear love, for whose sake I shall take better care of myself than I have ever done. You will see César to-morrow; I envy you. Love your servant always, for he will adore no one but you until the grave. On this truth, I end, kissing you a million times, and as tenderly as yesterday morning.   H.

Amiens, October 22, 1597.

Mes chères Amours,

To tell truth, we love one another very much. Indeed, for a woman, there is none to equal you; and, for a man, no one can love as I do. My passion is as it was when I first loved you; my desire to see you again is still more violent than then; in short, I cherish you, and adore you and honor you marvelously. . . .

Good night, my Heart, I kiss your hands a million times.
H.

Fontaine, May 8, 1598.

Mon vrai Cœur,

La Varanne has just come bringing your letters, in which you tell me that you love me a thousand times more than I love you. You are a story-teller, and I will prove it in any way you like. . . . My darling, I shall not see you for ten days,—I shall die, I shan't tell you how it grieves me; you would be too proud. I never loved you as much as I do now; that's telling you too much. Good night, and millions of kisses.

H.

Rennes, May 14, 1598.

Mes chères Amours,

What joy to think that I shall see you in three days, and, Darling, how I shall make love to you. They have tried to frighten me about the road between here and Laval; but they are all wrong, for when I am going toward you, I don't run, I fly. You will have but one more letter from me. I kiss you a thousand times.

H.

May 21, 1598.

These verses will show you my state of mind better than prose. I wrote them off, and have not polished them. Last night we took a lot of rabbits in the park; it was great fun. I go round the walks to see what places are worthy to wish you there, I mean specifically, for I always want you everywhere where duty and destiny lead me. Love your subject, who will never adore anything but you, *Mes chères Amours,* I swear. . . . Keep your promise, and you shall be the happiest woman in the world. I kiss your beautiful eyes a million times.

H.

Verses enclosed.

Charmante Gabrielle,
Percé de mille dards,
Quand la gloire m'appelle
Sous les drapeaux de Mars.

Cruelle departie!
Malheureux jour!
Que ne suis-je sans vie,
Ou sans amour!

. . .

Partagez ma couronne,
Le prix de ma valeur;
Je la tiens de Bellone,
Tenez-la de mon cœur.

Charming Gabrielle,
Pierced by a thousand darts,
When glory calls me
To the flags of Mars.
Cruel parting!
Luckless day!
Why am I not without life,
Or without love?

Share my crown
The reward of my valor,
I receive it from Bellona
Take it from my heart.

On a day in that same month of May, just about the time
of the treaty of peace with Spain, with hopes of the rise and
restoration of the Kingdom before him, the King took Sully
apart and said to him: "There is only one defect in all these
fine plans. Who will profit by them? Unless my children succeed to me." And he wished that he could find a woman with
seven qualities, beauty, modesty, sweetness, intelligence, wealth,
royal birth and fecundity, who should make him forget his
first venture. Then he ran over possible wives, and the objections to them: The Infanta of Spain, Arabella Stuart of
Scotland, then various German princesses, "but the women
of that country are distasteful to me, I should always think
there was a wine-skin in bed with me," and so on. And he

asked Sully if he could not think of some lady. Sully, who
had been put on his guard for the King seemed *si rêveur* that
he guessed there was some secret sentiment that troubled him,
replied, that he was seeking too much and asked if he expected
to turn Queen Elizabeth into a young girl. "Oh, you know well
enough," the King went on, "you must have heard some little
whispers abroad. But I understand why you affect to be so
simple; it is to make me name her, and I will, for then you will
have to admit that the most important of the qualifications
that I enumerated are to be found in my mistress." Sully
protested; he spoke of the evil rumors concerning Gabrielle,
objected that César de Vendôme was born of double adultery,
that the second child was the son of single adultery, and if a
third son was born in wedlock, the three might quarrel as to
their claims. But the King was not affected by his objections
and merely asked if he thought that there would be a revolt
if he should marry her.

Sully, of course, as well as all the world, knew of the
King's disposition toward the favorite. He had flaunted her
in the public's face. Pierre L'Estoile in his diary makes
frequent references to this: "March, 1595: The King and
Gabrielle have been hunting in the neighborhood of the city,
she was dressed all in green, and rode astride like a man, the
King rode beside her, he held her hand. . . . January 13:
[during the Spanish war] The King returned to Paris, took
supper at Monsieur Zamet's, the banker, spent the night there,
and sent word to the Fair at Saint-Germain not to close their
booths as he would go out the next day. He did so and dined
at Monsieur Gondi's together with Madame la Marquise
[Gabrielle]. At the fair the King proposed to give her a ring
for which a Portuguese merchant asked eight hundred crowns,

the King bargained, but didn't buy it; he contented himself
with giving little César a silver sugar-plum box. He bargained
for various other articles; when the booth-keepers asked twenty
crowns, he offered six; they made nothing by his inspection of
their wares."

Except in the excitement of pursuing a new mistress, the
King always displayed his Béarnais thrift; on one occasion,
coming back from Fontainebleau with a company of friends,
he stopped at a restaurant, *Le Petit More,* for dinner and made
each man pay his scot. I quote L'Estoile's diary, again:
"February 23, 1596: On Sunday, the first day of Lent, the
King got up a masquerade party, and went around to various
houses, to the wife of the President of the court, to Madame
de Saint-André's, to Monsieur Zamet's, and elsewhere. The
Marquise was always at his side, and she kept taking off her
mask and kissing him wherever they went. They kept it up
all night, and did not get back to the Louvre till eight in the
morning. . . . March 5, 1596: The son of Connétable Montmorency was christened. The King held the baby at the font
and the Papal Legate baptised him. Madame la Marquise was
there, magnificently attired, all in green. The King amused
himself by taking note of her coiffure, and told her that she
had not enough diamonds in her hair, she had but twelve.
After the ceremony there was a most noble banquet at the
Montmorency mansion, for which all the cooks in Paris had
been impressed for more than a week."

There were ballets, masquerades, musical parties of all
sorts, buffooneries, as if everybody wished to bury their woes.
L'Estoile was scandalized: "God converted their merry-making
into a scourge." On the eve of *mi-carême,* word came that
the Spaniards had captured Amiens. The King, whose forti-

The surprise of Amiens by the Spaniards
From a contemporary drawing in the Bibliothèque Nationale

tude was not easily shaken, was like a man struck dumb. He cried out: "This blow comes from God. We've had enough of playing King of France, it's now time to be King of Navarre." He turned to Gabrielle who was weeping: "Mistress mine, we must forego the arms of Cupid. Come on, to horse, and fight other battles." Off he went, and Madame la Marquise, afraid to stay in Paris without the King's protection, for the people disliked her, left the city an hour before he did. Perhaps, to judge from the epigrams made at her expense, her apprehensions were not wholly without foundation.

During the siege to recover Amiens, "Henry did his duty as King, captain and soldier," nevertheless he found time to visit Gabrielle; he was seen to play tennis, while she and her much-talked-of aunt, Madame de Sourdis, looked on, not hesitating to kiss Gabrielle before everybody, and he also borrowed money from her. That summer he bought for her the duchy of Beaufort, and from that time "some people called her Duchesse de Beaufort, but others called her the *Duchesse d'Ordures* [the Duchess of Dirt]." And finally, after Amiens had been recaptured, and the war with Spain closed by the Peace of Vervins (May, 1598), a great celebration was held in Paris in honor of peace. The King with his own hand lighted a bonfire in the Place de Grève, in front of the Hôtel de Ville, where they burned War in effigy, together with a pile of trumpets, drums, spears, swords and other martial implements; and then a magnificent collation was served, at which the Duchesse de Beaufort was seated in a chair beside the King, and was waited on by the Duchesse de Guise, who with deep curtsies presented the dishes to her. Gabrielle helped herself with one hand, while she held the other out for the King to kiss.

In this public flaunting of his devotion to Gabrielle, the King was probably meaning to prepare his subjects for the step he was contemplating, and trying to discover how they would take it. As matters stood, there were numerous intimations of discontent with his mistress. The whole family were regarded as leeches. I have said how the King had given offices to her father, her quasi-uncle and her brother, how he made her first a marchioness and then a duchess; he also turned out the Abbess of Maubuisson, and put Gabrielle's sister, a lady who shared the family qualities, as Abbess in her place. For Gabrielle's sake he appointed Monsieur de Balagny governor of Cambrai, for Balagny had promised Gabrielle many things if he should be appointed; and afterward Balagny treacherously made only a sham defense against the Spaniards, and Cambrai was lost. And, at least so the people believed, Henry did many other things for her at the expense of the Kingdom.

Epigrams fluttered about. Respectable people murmured that the King would do well to imitate King David, and clear the court of its foulness. Wits passed about a story that the Grand Turk had won a great victory over his enemies, because he had killed his young mistress, whom both court and people detested; the King only laughed at the story and said that not only he should not stop kissing his mistress but that he would kiss her before everybody, and she him in the very middle of a Council meeting. Another story, of more precise details went the rounds, which L'Estoile says was at first disbelieved but turned out to be true. The King was going through the woods at Saint-Germain and met a poor peasant driving a cow; he was going to sell her in order that he might have money enough to pay the *taille*. The King fell into conversation with him, and the peasant, who did not recognize him, told him all the woes of the poor, of the terrible taxes laid upon them. Henry said that the King must certainly be bad to tax his poor people after that fashion. The peasant replied, "Well, they say that he is not one of the worst, but there is one Belle Gabrielle, who tickles him and ruins us all." The King laughed, and gave the man a dozen crowns, so that he need not sell his cow; the next day he repeated the story to Gabrielle, telling her that love of her had cost him twelve crowns.

There is another story to like effect, that L'Estoile also asserts to be true. It concerns a poor boatman, who ferried the King across the river on his return from the chase. As usual, the King, who was dressed very plainly, fell to talking, and asked the boatman what was thought about the peace. "I don't know what peace you're talking about," the fellow answered, "we are worse off than before; we pay more taxes than during the war. Everything, down to this miserable boat that I paddle, pays a tax, as if it weren't hard enough to make a livelihood without that." "And what does the King say about that?" Henry asked. "The King isn't a bad fellow," the boatman said, "I don't think the taxes are his doing; but there is a bad wh—e whom he keeps, who is the ruin of us all, for he gives her beautiful dresses and knickknacks every day, and the poor folk suffer from it, as they pay for it all. And if she were the only one, that would be something; but they say that there are lots of them who come in for their share." The King laughed, and then he and his retinue went off without paying. The boatman hallooed after them, and wished them to the devil. The King called back: "We are going away, we have something else to do." The next day he sent for the man, who, having learned that it was the King with whom he had to deal, was frightened to death.

The King made him repeat in the presence of Gabrielle just what he had said to him. She was greatly vexed and said that the fellow deserved to be hanged. "No, no, mistress mine," said the King, "on the contrary he is a good honest fellow, who has merely repeated what he has heard. I forgive him, and he shall not pay any further tax on his boat, for that was the beginning of the whole matter."

In spite of these and other unfriendly comments, the King determined to have his own way. He was a masterful man: "A king," he wrote to James I of England, "is only responsible to God and to his conscience." When the Parliament of Toulouse hesitated to register the *Edict of Nantes,* he called them before him: *"Je veux être obéi* [I mean to be obeyed]." And when the *Colonel-Général* of Infantry, the Duc d'Epernon, stood upon his rights as general, against the King's wish, the King wrote: "Come to me, but come with your mind made up to do my good pleasure; a servant who wishes his master's friendship obeys him. You write like an angry man; I am not angry yet, don't make me so."

In the beginning of 1599 he sent to Rome to obtain the Pope's consent to the annulment of his marriage. On February seventh Margot executed a full consent. In Paris preparations were begun for the ceremony. The bride's wedding-dress was ordered; and on Shrove Tuesday the King slipped a diamond ring on her finger, which he had worn at his coronation. In the beginning of April Gabrielle was at Fontainebleau; she left on the fifth in order to pass Easter in Paris. The King accompanied her part way. He never saw her again. She spent one night at Monsieur Zamet's house, and then went to her aunt's, the notorious Madame de Sourdis, who lived near Saint-Germain-l'Auxerrois. On Thursday the eighth she fell ill; on Friday, she gave birth to a child still-born. The King received the news of her illness that day and galloped to Paris; she was then in the first agony of death, an agony so terrible that they stopped him a few miles out and told him that she was dead. She died on Saturday. The King was stricken; he wrote to his sister:

Fontainebleau, April 15, 1599.

My dear sister,

I had much comfort from the person you sent. I had great need, for my affliction is as incomparable as she that causes it. Sorrow and mourning will accompany me to the tomb. Nevertheless, since God created me for this Kingdom and not for myself, all my wits and my care will be employed solely for its preservation and prosperity. The plant of love within me is dead, it will not flower again. But that of my friendship for you will always be green, my dear sister, I kiss you a thousand times.

HENRY.

Two months later, or a little less, in June, persons about the King spoke of a Mademoiselle Henriette d'Entragues, how pretty she was, how gay, how coquettish and quick-witted, "so that he wished to see her, then to see her again, and then fell in love." His wooing was impetuous. Sully was annoyed, for the exchequer had great expenses, and could ill spare the one hundred thousand crowns that the King squandered on her. The girl flirted, promised, evaded, brought in her father and mother, said that without their consent she could not escape their surveillance, but that she would help him to gain it. Her father was the Seigneur d'Entragues, her mother was

Marie Touchet, once mistress of Charles IX, and married by
him to Entragues whom he advanced in a worldly way. The
parents held off, for they had "a conscience toward God and
honor before the world." Henriette told the King, she had
hoped that his verbal promise of marriage would be sufficient
for them, but that her parents were stubborn and wished the
promise in writing, though to her that would be an unnecessary
formality, the word of such a man would be enough, and so
forth. The family carried her from place to place; he pursued, offered her presents, wrote her verses:

> *Je vous offre sceptre et couronne;*
> *Mon sincère amour vous les donne.*

But the prudent family preferred prose, and the King wrote:

"I, Henry the Fourth, by the grace of God, King of France
and Navarre, promise and swear before God, on the faith
and word of a King, to Monsieur François de Balzac, Seigneur
d'Entragues, knight of my order, that if he will give me as
companion Mademoiselle Henriette Catherine de Balzac, his
daughter, then in the case that within six months from to-day
she shall become pregnant, and that she shall give birth to a
son, at that moment I will make her my legitimate wife, and
I will solemnize the marriage publicly, in presence of our Holy
Church, according to the solemnities customary in such cases,
and in order to confirm this present promise more strongly
still, I promise and swear, as above, to ratify and renew it
under my seal, immediately after I shall have obtained from
our Holy Father the Pope, the dissolution of the marriage between me and the Lady Margaret of France, with permission
to remarry as I think best.

Henriette d'Entragues
After the portrait by Jérôme Wierix

In testimony of which I have written and signed these presents, at Bois-Malesherbes, October, 1, 1599.

HENRY.

This satisfied the parents' conscience toward God and honor toward the world, and Henriette became the King's acknowledged mistress.

CHAPTER XXIII

In the conversation with Sully in May, 1598, that I have cited, the King while enumerating the ladies, one of whom he might take to wife, remarked: "The Grand Duke of Florence has a niece who is said to be good-looking. But she belongs to one of the least important princely houses in Christendom. It is not more than sixty or eighty years since her forefathers were merely the most eminent of the Florentine bourgeoisie; besides it is from that family that the Queen Mother came who did so much harm to France and still more to me in particular. I am fearful lest such an alliance should bring evil to me, and mine, and to the Kingdom." Nevertheless, when the King sent Monsieur Brulart de Sillery to Rome on the matter of his divorce, in the early part of 1599, he instructed him to sound the Grand Duke as to a possible marriage between himself and the Duke's niece. There were good arguments in favor of such a marriage: the King owed the Grand Duke a great sum of money and thought by this means, not only to pay it, but also to obtain a great deal more; and it was the Duke's interest to secure an ally against the preponderant power of Spain in Italy.

Nevertheless, the Duke held off until the Pope had granted the divorce, and even then chaffered for the best bargain that he could make; there was a deal of expostulating, of demanding and rejecting, on both sides, and all this was going

on during the early period of the King's infatuation for Henriette d'Entragues.   On December 17, 1599, his Holiness dissolved the King's marriage with Margot; and on April 25,
1600, the contract for the King's marriage with Maria de
Médicis was duly executed.   But the course of Henry's second
matrimonial adventure did not at first run smoothly; Henriette
d'Entragues, now Marquise de Verneuil, announced that she
was pregnant and that she intended to hold the King to his
written promise.   The King, as a French scholar says, *avait
trop de sens politique pour prendre au sérieux les promesses
que lue arrachait la ténacité jalouse de sa nouvelle maîtresse*
(had too much political good sense to take the promises
seriously which his new mistress's obstinacy had wrenched
from him), so a few days before the signing of the marriage
contract he wrote her the following note:

Fontainebleau, Friday morning, April 21, 1600.
Mademoiselle,

Love, honor, or the benefits that you have received from
me, would have made the most frivolous soul in the world
refrain from what you are doing, were it not tenanted, like
yours, by a wicked disposition.   I shall say no more; although,
as you are aware, I could and should do so.   I beg you to send
me back the promise that you know of; do not put me to
the trouble of getting it back in some other way.   Send me
back also the ring that I gave you on the same day.   That
is the reason for this letter.   I wish to have an answer this
evening.

HENRY.

He also wrote to her father:

Fontainebleau, Friday morning, April 21, 1600.

Monsieur d'Entragues,

I am sending the bearer of this to bring back the promise
I handed to you at Malesherbes. I beg you not to fail to send
it back; but if you will bring it yourself, I will give you my
reasons, which are private not political. You will say that I am
right, and realize that you have been deceived and that my
disposition is rather too amiable than otherwise. I am certain
that you will obey my command, and I assure you that I am
your good master.

HENRY.

It was a pretty business; and unsavory words passed between the lovers. Not long afterward Henriette was delivered
of a boy, who lived but a few hours. French historians, as I
understand them, hold that the brevity of the baby's life relieved the King morally of his promise. But, in spite of
quarrels, Henriette had no intention of giving up the King,
nor had he any intention of wholly abandoning her. The
royal marriage took place by procuration in Florence on October fifth. The gentleman who carried the procuration to the
Grand Duke was no other than Bellegarde, whom the King
had royally supplanted in earlier days as Gabrielle's lover. Not
long afterward Marie de Médicis sailed from Leghorn to
Marseilles. The King went to meet her but was delayed by
war with Savoy, which necessitated a brief campaign. In the
meantime he wrote these letters:

To Madame, the Princess of Tuscany.

Paris, May 24, 1600.

The virtues and perfections that shine in you, and make
all the world admire you, kindled in me long ago a desire to

Marie de Médicis lands at Marseilles

From the painting by Rubens

honor and serve you according to your deserts. . . . As I can not in person lay before you my inviolable affection, I have, while awaiting that happiness (which shall be soon if Heaven blesses my vows) chosen my faithful servitor, Frontenac to do this in my name. . . . He will open my heart to you. You will find in it a passionate desire to cherish and love you all my life, as the mistress of my affections, and "to bow beneath the yoke of your command" [a phrase he borrowed from her]. Frontenac will present to you the homage of a Prince whom Heaven has created, and dedicated, for you and to you alone.

H. M.

On the original letter the King interlaced their two initials according to the gallant mode of the time. Marie de Médicis, who possessed very little French answered in Italian: *Christianissima Maestà . . . Humilissima et obligatissima serva Maria de Medici.* A little later he wrote:

To Madame the Princess of Tuscany.

July 11, 1600.

I have received news of you from Frontenac, to my great happiness. . . . He has described you so that I not only love you as a husband should love his wife, but as a passionate lover loves his mistress. I am going to give you that title until Marseilles when you shall change it for the more honorable one. I can not forego this occasion to assure you that my most violent desire is to see you, and have you beside me. Believe this, Mistress mine. Every month seems a century. I had a letter from you written in French this morning; if you wrote it without help, you are already very accomplished.

H.

To same.

Lyons, July 24, 1600.

Ma Maîtresse:

As you wish me to take care of my health, I wish the same for yours. Take care of it, so that when we meet we can compound a fine boy, who will make our friends laugh and our enemies weep. Frontenac tells me that you want some model to show you how ladies dress in France. I send you some doll models, and I will send you a very good tailor. I kiss your lovely hands a hundred thousand times.

H.

Chambéry, August 23, 1600.

Ma belle Maîtresse:

I never had a desire so violent as this to see you. May it be a spur to hurry your journey. . . . My love constrains me again to beg you to hurry as much as you can. I kiss your hands a hundred thousand times.

H.

September 3, 1600.

I have received your letter of August 16. . . . If it were good form to say that one is in love with one's wife, I would tell you that I am extremely in love with you; but I prefer to tell you that where there shall be no witnesses but you and me. I kiss your lovely hands a hundred thousand times.

H.

On September sixteenth, he writes to her from Grenoble and and again on the twenty-second, and on the thirtieth, this time as he has sent his procurator for the marriage, he addresses her as his wife, and "kisses her hands and mouth a hundred thousand times." Then come these letters:

To the Marquise de Verneuil
Beaufort, October 11, 1600.

My Pretty One,

We arrived here yesterday. . . . I was obliged to alight twenty times, and the road is a hundred times worse to-day. France is much indebted to me, for I am working hard for her. I have a thousand good stories to tell you, when I shall have the honor to see you, which will be on Sunday, I think. The time will seem longer to me than to you. Love me well, my own dear Love. I kiss you a million times.

H.

To the Marquise de Verneuil
October 11, 1600.

Deart Heart,

I started off early to reconnoiter the passes that I told you of, and that delayed me so that I have but just received your letter. I have kissed it (as you were not there) a thousand times. Don't imagine I have not much to say to you; we are too good friends for it to be otherwise, as I shall show you by my quick return. On my expedition the snow covered us for three hours, as thick as in France in January, but when we got down in the valley, it turned to rain. Men from Aiguebelette say that the road we took this afternoon is the highest and the worst. Indeed, in all the Alps there are none worse. I leave to-morrow, and I hope to be so near you on Friday that I shall call on you to fulfill the promise you made when I left (in case I should arrive without baggage). I have chattered too long, as I am very wet. Good night, dear Heart, I kiss you and kiss you again a thousand times.

H.

To my Wife, the Queen.

October 22, 1600.

My wife,

I am greatly disappointed to be obliged to postpone the pleasure I had hoped to receive from your presence, for the Duke of Savoy is making preparation to come to the relief of Montmélian. It is not the beauty of this country, nor the agreeableness of a stay here that detains me. The law of duty is superior to the law of love. . . . Love me dearly, and you shall be the happiest woman under heaven. I kiss you a million times.

H.

His letters to her are frequent, affectionate, and prodigal of metaphysical kisses.

Marie de Médicis was now twenty-six years old. She was not pretty. Her eyes were prominent and lacked vivacity; her eyebrows were very scanty; her mouth was expressionless, her face too full. In fact, she looked what she was, dull; in later life she showed herself to be both dull and obstinate. We know her best in the great pictures that Rubens painted for her Luxembourg palace, when she was forty-eight years old. The painter flattered her as best he could, but underneath the flattery and the weight of twenty-two added years, it is hard to discover any possibility of attractiveness or beauty. She landed at Marseilles in November; you will see how Rubens depicts the scene. The Queen disembarks from the splendid

The Marriage of Henry IV and Marie de Médicis
From the painting by Rubens

galley, upon a wharf like a Roman palace, while wonderful, buxom, Flemish mermaidens splash a tumultuous welcome. Rubens has not exaggerated. The galley was two hundred and ten feet long, with twenty-seven oars on either side, and all gilded to the water-line; the poop was inlaid with precious woods from India, with ebony, mother-of-pearl, ivory and lapis lazuli; hangings and appointments were in keeping. From Marseilles the Queen went by slow stages to Lyons, where her bridegroom met her on December ninth. In Rubens' picture, the royal pair sit on air high above the earth in ideal felicity. Henry, arrayed like Jupiter, takes Marie's right hand, while she, modestly and ineffectually, uses her left hand to eke out the scanty bodice of her French tailor-made gown. Peacocks perch upon her aerial chariot, a feminine Hymen holds a torch and little Cupids aloft manifest their pleasure, while on earth below a diademed lady, France perchance, sits in a chariot drawn by two lions, upon whose backs two torch-bearing Cupids ride. In real life matters took place a little differently. Henry arrived fresh from his campaign against Savoy, and coming upon Marie unannounced, for his first look at her concealed himself behind (of all people) Bellegarde; he then advanced and kissed her, as was reported to the Grand Duke, on both cheeks, *"da tutti i lati della faccia"*; he then went and dined, attended by the Princess's Italian gentlemen, with whom he chatted with his customary *domestichezza*.

The couple were afterward blessed by the Papal Legate, and when the King left on January twenty-first, he announced the prospective birth of an heir. Everything had gone off well, and even the arrangements as to the Queen's attendants were settled without any real friction. The Marquise de Guercheville, the Breton lady who had rejected Henry's addresses, was appointed one of the Queen's ladies of honor. *"C'est une des plus femmes de bien du monde."* (She is one of the best women in the world.) Henry also informed the Queen, "Our French cooking is better than yours," so it seems that he did not keep her Florentine cooks, but he permitted her to keep Leonora Dori, or Galigai, as *demoiselle d'atour.* The function of a *dame d'atour* was to go out driving with the Queen, carry her flowers and ribbons and so forth, in case of need. Such a lady, a *dame d'atour,* had always been of noble birth, whereas Leonora was but a *cittadina borghese,* a person of the middle class. Hence, the compromise upon the title *demoiselle d'atour.*

This done, and a treaty with Savoy made, the King hurried ahead to Paris and joined Henriette d'Entragues. He was in no hurry to have the Queen come. He writes to her:

[Verneuil?] January 30, 1601.

Dear Heart,

If I had not heard that you had recovered as soon as I heard of your indisposition, I should have felt badly. Be sure not to hurry on, so long as that might be bad for you. . . . Arrange to arrive on Monday and I shall go on Sunday afternoon to meet you at Nemours. I can't go sooner on account of the fête. You are awaited here with the liveliest possible expectation. Enough! I am off to play tennis. I kiss you a hundred thousand times. Kiss my son, César de Vendôme, for me.

H.

The Queen obeyed and traveled slowly. From Fontainebleau she went to Paris, where she arrived on February eighth. The meeting between her and Henriette was a delicate matter. The King told the Queen that he should be greatly displeased if she did not receive the Marquise de Verneuil graciously. Henriette was brought to the Louvre into the Queen's presence. The King said, "This woman has been my mistress; she now wishes to be your very humble servant." Henriette bent low and took the Queen's gown to kiss the hem. The King did not think that she bent low enough and roughly pushed her lower. That night the two ladies dined at the same' table. Matters however went smoothly on the outside. At Henriette's instance Leonora Galigai was made *dame d'atour.* Young César de Vendôme, Gabrielle's boy, aged seven and a half, called the King *babbo,* Italian fashion, and the Queen *maman.* The King seems to have been happier than at any other time of his life. On August twenty-seventh he was at Verneuil, but felt obliged to go to Calais to be near enough to watch the success of a Spanish attack on Ostend, and look to the fortification of the French frontier towns. From there he wrote to the Queen:

Calais, September 3, 1601.

My Love,

I have been waiting for your letter from hour to hour, I have kissed it as I read. . . . *Vive Dieu!* You could not have sent me more agreeable news than the pleasure you take in your reading. *Plutarque me sourit toujours d'une fresche nouveauté* [Plutarch always wears a fresh smile for me]. To love him is to love me, for he was my boyhood's teacher. My good mother, to whom I owe everything, and who took such pains to watch over my education, and did not wish, she said, to see her son an illustrious ignoramus, put this book in my hands when I was hardly more than weaned. He has been a conscience to me, and has taught me many lessons in honor, and excellent maxims for my behavior and also in the transaction of affairs. Adieu, my Heart, I kiss you a hundred thousand times.

H.

September 6, 1601.

Dear Heart,

Monsieur de Rosny [Sully] has just come. He has fulfilled your orders to bid me return at once. He found that I wanted to badly enough, and am doing all I can to hasten my business. Don't be afraid. I shall be one of your midwives. . . . I thank God that you are well, and I pray Him for you every day. I love you like my own life. I kiss you a hundred thousand times.

H.

On September 27, 1601, the Dauphin (Louis XIII) was born at Fontainebleau. The King was in the bedchamber and announced to her the sex of the baby: "My love, you have had a hard time. But God has done us the favor to grant our petitions. We have a fine son." He was overjoyed. That same day he bade the City of Paris celebrate the event, and issued a circular letter: "Among the miraculous evidences of divine assistance that have been noticeable in our behalf, since our coming to the throne et cetera, . . ." On October sixth, he wrote to Henriette that his wife was well and that the baby had gained half as much again in five days; that he himself was well and had no sorrow but absence from her. "Love your Lover always, I kiss your hands and mouth a million

Birth of the Dauphin (Louis XIII) at Fontainebleau

From the painting by Rubens

times." A little later he hurried to Verneuil, and spent four days by the side of the Marquise who also bore him a son, Gaston, Duc d'Entragues. This double paternity had not interfered with an outside flirtation with Mademoiselle de la Bourdaisière; to whom the King obliged Sully to pay fifty thousand crowns and to her father twenty thousand. The Queen's allowance is said to have been twelve thousand crowns a year. The amorous medal, however, had its reverse. The young Duc de Guise found his way into the good graces of Henriette d'Entragues; on hearing this, the King remarked philosophically: "So much has been taken away from these Lorrainers, that it is only right to leave them *le pain et les putains* [their bread and their b-tches]."

CHAPTER XXIV

KINGCRAFT

IN THE background the great rent of Christendom gaped as before. From the massacre at Vassy, in 1562, to the Peace of Vervins, 1598, France had been the arena of the contending forces; twenty years later, from 1618 to the Peace of Westphalia, 1648, Germany was destined to be; and, during the interim, Holland was the scene of conflict. On one side were ranged the Papacy, Austria, Spain and some states of Germany, on the other Holland, England, Denmark, Sweden and certain other German states, both sides mixing politics and religion, revenge and ambition, in stout contention. France, still raw and bleeding from her wounds, watched, expectant, on her guard. She had accepted the policy of toleration, as it was then understood, that Calvinism and Lutheranism had established themselves by the side of the Catholic Creed as legitimate branches of the Christian religion, and men might belong to any one of the three that they wished, and Henry IV, in his optimism, expected all Europe to adopt these principles; but the conservative half of Europe, faithful to the great tradition of a united Christendom, still clung to the idea of reestablishing a common creed, of bringing back the erring sheep into one fold, guided by one shepherd.

Under these circumstances, Henry IV, his Kingdom still heaving from the contention of civil war, was circumspect, and kept a watchful eye upon the Catholic Powers (for which

reason as we have seen, he had at one time gone to Calais).
On the other hand, he was compelled to be equally circumspect
within his Kingdom, in order to prevent any outbreaks that
might lead to a revival of civil war and the dismemberment of
France; for the fanatical Huguenots still wanted an *imperium
in imperio*, the surviving Leaguers still wished to stamp out
heresy, and great nobles, accustomed to the license of disorder,
looked back on what they considered happy feudal times and
were ambitious to become princes of independent principalities.
The task of preventing these evils fell on the King, and so,
though with no natural inclination for it, he was by force of
circumstances, swept into the position of absolute monarch.
His duty of restoring the Kingdom, mending its breaches,
healing its wounds, could not be accomplished otherwise. He
was obliged to be absolute, but he could not have become so
except for his character and disposition.

Henry's main faults hindered him but little; his love of
women wore at times an attractive aspect, as Queen Elizabeth
had remarked, "Among your admirable virtues I admire most
your valor in battle and your civility and courtesy to ladies"—
and at worst squandered but a small fraction of the State's
money; his ingratitude to old friends, whose services were
soon forgotten, often stood the State in good stead, for it left
him free to employ the best men for his political ends, and also
secured economies to the treasury. In other respects his
qualities served him well. His tastes for hunting, hawking,
riding at the ring, for the *jeu de peaume,* and other manly
sports, won him the approbation of the country gentlemen; his
military skill and his reckless valor that of his soldiers; and
his good fellowship and ready wit, that of all the chance people
high and low with whom he fell in. For instance: when his

gardener at Fontainebleau complained that in one spot he could make nothing grow, the King said: "Plant some Gascons; they take root anywhere." Once he invited himself unexpectedly to dine at Sully's:

H: Mr. Grand Master, I come uninvited to your banquet. Shall I get a poor dinner?

S: That may well happen, Sire, for I did not expect so exceeding an honor.

H: Well, I assure you that I shan't, for, while waiting for you, I went to your kitchens, and saw the finest possible fish, and many ragoûts cooked in the way I like, and I ate some of your little oysters, they were fresh as could be, and I drank some of your Arbois wine, the best I ever drank.

And, once in a village, he was told of a local wit, Jean Drake. "Fetch him up," the King said, and made him sit opposite him at the table. "What is the difference," he asked, "between Drake and rake?" "Sire," the peasant replied, "the width of this table." *"Ventre-saint-gris!"* and the King laughed. And he had a way of nicknaming his servants: his pastry cook *Cream,* his *valets de chambre, Bon enfant* and *le Brave,* his tailor *Beau-semblant,* his porter *Lesueur* (Sweat), his baker, *Poundcake* and so forth. His bold and charming personality won for him great personal popularity.

And he had a genius for handling men. He knew just what to say in order to win their affections:

October 10, 1598, Monceaux.

Brave Crillon,

You have forgotten your master and your friends. I haven't done like that. I love you more than you love me.

You will hear of me from Monsieur Pilles. But this note warrants you that my friendship continues. For a long time there have been reports that you were coming, but I shan't believe them till I see you. Good-by, brave Crillon,

HENRY.

While on a campaign, he wrote to Monsieur de Canisy: "I know how angry you would be if you lost the chance of a battle, and as I hope to have one in a few days with the Duc de Mayenne, I let you know, etc. HENRY."

Monsieur de Launay d'Entragues,

I hope that with God's help you have entirely recovered from the wound you received at Coutras, when you fought so valiantly by my side. . . . You will have sold your woods at Mezellac, as you told Du Plessis-Mornay you were going to do, and they must have realized several thousand pistoles. If so, don't fail to bring me all you can; for I was never so hard up in my life, and I don't know when, nor how, or if ever, I shall be able to pay you back. But I promise you honor and glory galore; money is no stuff that concerns gentlemen like you and me. . . . Yours affectionately,

HENRY.

It was perhaps less what he said than what he was that charmed his friends. His *vivacité miraculeuse* impressed d'Aubigné; and they all admired *le haut point de sa chevalerie et vaillance* (the fine temper of his chivalric valor), and felt that he was *un prince accoutumé à vaincre, à regner et à pardonner* (used to conquer, to rule and to forgive). "This Prince," Du Plessis-Mornay says, "was not born to yield to despair, he will unloose his cloak more readily to the south wind than to that from the north." And the contrast between his rank and his frayed and shabby clothes, heightened the effect of his manner; and his jokes were those of a boyish comrade. On a ceremonial entry into church, one member of the Parliament had come without his official dress. "There's Pontcaré!" the King exclaimed. "He's forgotten to put on his red robes, but he has not forgotten his jolly red nose." During a campaign he arrived, after a long hard ride, at Amiens; a delegation of citizens came out to pay their respects, and their orator began: "Your Majesty, very benign, very great, very merciful——" "—and very tired," the King interrupted. At another time he was stopped on his way to dinner, when he was hungry, by a petitioner, who began his address: "Sire, Agesilaus, King of Lacedæmonia . . ." "*Ventre-saint-gris!*" the King said, "I have heard of him; but he had dined and I haven't." And again, while a deputy from the Parliament in Britanny was proceeding with a carefully prepared speech, the King, who had twice hinted to cut it short, got up saying: "You will please tell the rest of it to my friend here, Monsieur Guillaume."

He was impatient of pomposity, tedious formalities and conventional methods, whether in members of Parliament, or the medical faculty, or anybody. During the Spanish war he had a quartan fever, and cured himself in the teeth of all his physicians, by eating a great quantity of raw oysters and drinking hippocras. Besides, he had a clever humorous way of meeting unreasonable demands. For instance, the magistrates of a Huguenot town came in a body to ask his permission to expel all Leaguers, and alleged that such a measure was necessary. "No," he replied, "I can't approve that. They are all my subjects, and I wish to treat and love them all alike, but you may keep a watch on the bad so that they shan't do any harm to the well-disposed." Nevertheless, he was not always in good humor. What he deemed lack of gratitude in the people depressed him: *"Ventre-saint-gris!* How could I be otherwise, to see a people so ungrateful toward its King, in spite of all I do and all I have done for it, and when I would sacrifice a thousand lives for their safety." And when the crowd cheered him on his way to Notre-Dame he said: "If my worst enemy were where I am, and the people saw him pass by, they would cheer louder than they do now. . . . The populace is a beast that lets itself be led by the nose, especially the Parisians." But those moments were rare, and he showed his innermost and truest self when he was successful and happy, *en mon char triomphant* (on my triumphant chariot), as he put it.

But if his charm, his wit and social readiness were important factors in making him a great king; more important factors still were his capacity for affairs, his power of taking infinite pains, his mastery of details, his executive ability, his quick anticipation of another's thought, his readiness for action, his skill in guerrilla fighting, got in long grim years of apprenticeship, his knowledge of his Kingdom from Languedoc to Picardy, for his habit was to question everybody, fishermen, plow-boys, tradesfolk, herdsmen, artizans, innkeepers, under-skinkers, private soldiers, and ask them of their work, their homes, their native territory, their tastes and amusements. And all the time under his familiarity, bonhomie and democratic manners, lay a commanding spirit, that spoke with authority and knew how to make itself obeyed. When the Parliament of Paris delayed to register the *Edict of Nantes,* he spoke to them roundly: "If obedience was due to my predecessors, devotion is due to me, inasmuch as I have reestab-

lished the State. . . . You people in Parliament would have
no seats but for me. I do not wish to brag, but if I should,
I can say that I have no example but my own to follow. I
know that there have been cabals in the Parliament, and that
seditious preachers have been stirred up, but I shall take care
of them without waiting for your help. That road led to the
Barricades and the murder of the late King. I shall guard
myself from all that; I shall cut faction at the root; I shall stop
seditious sermons; I shall hobble those that go to stir the
people up. I have leapt over town-walls, and I shall leap over
barricades; they are not as high."

And to the clergy, who remonstrated, he said: "The existing evils were introduced before I came. During the war, I
ran where the fire blazed up highest, to put it out. Now that
peace has come, I shall do what ought to be done in time of
peace. . . . I hope to discharge my conscience and to satisfy
you. That will be done little by little: Paris was not built in
a day. Set a good example and teach the people to be quick
to do right, as much as they were before to do wrong. You
exhort me to do my duty; I exhort you to do yours. Let us
both do good; you take one road, I'll take the other, and if we
meet, the thing will soon be done. My predecessors, in royal
robes, presented you with words; I, in my drab doublet, will
present you with deeds. I am drab without, but within I am
all gold."

Upon him personally, depended order, peace, even the unity
of France. Problems of all kinds confronted him: the nobles
had suffered greatly, their incomes had been pitifully reduced,
their rents were diminished or unpaid, their perquisites were
lost; the middle class had taken advantage of these misfortunes
to push themselves into posts and offices formerly confined to

the nobility, and so caused jealousy and ill-will; the agricultural class and poorer people of all sorts, especially in the country, had also met great distress, many were out of work, many had been forced to become beggars, vagabonds or highwaymen; the population had fallen off by millions; in towns, artizans lacked employment, business had gone to pot, many men had emigrated in search of a livelihood; prices had gone up, and the cost of living reduced poor families to the barest necessities. Taxes weighed more heavily than ever. Henry went to work with vigor; he started public building; he repaired roads, bridges, canals, all means of intercommunication; he reduced the *taille*, forgave back taxes, and supported Sully's attempts to bring order into the finances; he exempted cattle and agricultural implements from distraint; he reinstated on the tax-lists more than forty thousand shirkers; he used what means he could to get gentlemen back to their estates and to work; and so on. His desire to benefit the peasants earned him the name *"le Roi de la poule au pot,"* the King that wishes every subject to have a chicken in the pot on Sunday.

As he was the pillar and prop of the establishment of order, of religious toleration, of territorial unity and centralized authority, he was the object that malcontents aimed at. There were dozens of plots to assassinate him; as far back as 1590 he wrote to Corisande while off on a campaign, "I have escaped being killed thirty times in this farmhouse." All, or almost all, of these attempts came from fanatical Catholics. More important than these random plots, was a conspiracy in which the Maréchal de Biron was one of the plotters. Spain was malevolent to Henry IV and so was Savoy, and they found Biron ready to act with them. Biron was the most brilliant soldier of the civil wars after the King, who described him as "the

sharpest cutting implement of my victories," and had created
him marshal, duke, peer, and also Governor of Burgundy.
Biron was very ambitious; he believed that he had received less
than his deserts; he was indignant because the King had spoken
disparagingly of his father; he was restless; and though he
mocked at both religions, he listened to astrologers and weird
necromancers who predicted a crown. He agreed with Spain
and Savoy to overthrow Henry IV, or kill him; in return for
which he was to become virtually King of Burgundy, marry a
princess and receive one million two hundred thousand livres a
year. Of Biron's guilt there is no doubt; during the war with
Savoy the King imparted to him all his plans and Biron passed
on the information to the enemy. One of the underlings in the
conspiracy played false and revealed all to the King. Biron
was invited to Fontainebleau. He came. The King begged
him to confess, he refused, then he was arrested, convicted
and beheaded (1602).

Other great nobles among the malcontents were Turenne
now the Duc de Bouillon, a Huguenot, and the Comte d'Auvergne, bastard son of Charles IX, and half-brother to the
Marquise de Verneuil. Both were implicated in Biron's conspiracy, but d'Auvergne, who had been arrested, was set at
liberty, and Bouillon had been left undisturbed. D'Auvergne is
the villain of the second plot; he seems to have been a little
underwitted, or weak-minded, and full of vicious and criminal
propensities. His plan centered about the famous promise of
marriage given, or, as the King expressed it, "which they say
that I have given," to his half-sister. This promise, in spite of
the King's demands, had not been given up, but carefully kept
in a crystal box; a friendly Pope might declare the document
equivalent to a valid marriage and in that event the subsequent

Portrait of Henry IV by Pourbus
In the Louvre

Medici marriage would be null and void, and then Henriette's son, Gaston, would supplant the Dauphin, and, if by chance Henry IV should die, he would become King of France. In this plot Henriette d'Entragues and her father were accomplices. The promise of marriage was to be given to the King of Spain, who at the proper time would acknowledge Henriette's son as legitimate heir to the French Crown; Henriette and the boy were, in the meantime, to escape to the Spanish Netherlands; and the Comte d'Auvergne was to see to the deaths of the King and the Dauphin. An agent was caught, and confessed. Entragues, his daughter and the Comte d'Auvergne were arrested (1604).

All three did what they could to escape punishment. D'Entragues surrendered the famous promise, which he asserted he had kept solely for his own satisfaction, and certified that the paper he surrendered was the original and that he kept no copy. Henriette protested that she had done no more than seek protection, in case of the King's death, against the Queen, who, if she could, would destroy her and her son; she was not disturbed in mind, for she felt confident of her power over the King, and boldly told the judges that "the King would never wish it said that he had put his second wife to death." She was right; although, at this very time the King was seeking distraction. He coveted a pretty young lady. For the sake of propriety they found her a husband, by aid of a dot of fifty thousand crowns, who was—and here, as in the case of Bellegarde, we take a stitch that binds us to the past—no other than the nephew of our old acquaintance Champvallon, Margot's lover. As for the chief conspirator, the Comte d'Auvergne, he protested that he had been in close relations with Spain merely to learn Spanish secrets, and that, if the King would

set him free, he would creep closer and closer to the Spanish
bosom, and reveal all that he learned. Nevertheless, the three
were tried and convicted; the two men were sentenced to death,
and Henriette ordered to a nunnery. But at this point the
King's infatuation prevailed; d'Auvergne's sentence was com-
muted to imprisonment for life; d'Entragues, having given up
the promise, was soon set at liberty; and the Marquise, after a
few months' stay at Verneuil, was completely pardoned.

After that came Bouillon's turn. He held the little sovereign principality of Sedan, and was looked upon as the head of
the Huguenot party. The Protestant princes of Germany, and
the Swiss Reformed States interceded for him; Queen Elizabeth would not believe in his guilt; and the French Huguenots
declared that he was the victim of Catholic intrigue. Nevertheless, there was no doubt that he had been implicated in
Biron's plot. The King acted warily, he placated the Protestants abroad and at home in one way or another, and then
marched on Sedan with an army of sixteen thousand men.
Bouillon submitted, and was treated with great leniency; after
two years the principality was restored to him.

But these plots made it pretty clear that the maintenance
of peace, order and toleration in France was not merely a
national question, it was dependent upon the general situation
in Europe. The attempts at assassination had come from
fanatical Catholics, who looked to Spain and the Papacy for
comfort and abetting; the aspirations of the Huguenots for
virtual independence were supported by the sympathies of
German, Swiss, Dutch and English Protestants; and the efforts
of the great nobles to restore the old feudal system, to hold
provinces as little kingdoms, which involved the dismemberment of France, were favored by all the enemies of France,

and in especial by the House of Habsburg, masters of Austria
and Spain. Whether the King wished it or not, he could not
isolate France, he could not withdraw her from the political
perturbations of Europe; and those perturbations were caused
by the religious cleavage and by the power of the House of
Habsburg. If France was to tolerate Huguenots within her
borders, she must look to it that Protestants elsewhere were
tolerated; if she was to keep her King from assassination, she
must make herself feared in Rome and Madrid, where the
doctrine that it was lawful to kill tyrants was applauded; if
she was to carry out her domestic policy of centralizing power,
she must prevent the House of Habsburg from supporting her
rebel nobles. While the King was at Calais, when Sully made
his first trip to England, some vague motives of a large European policy were raised in interviews or in correspondence with
Queen Elizabeth, but for the time being immediate matters
required a policy of opportunism.

CHAPTER XXV

THE PRINCESS OF CONDÉ

UNFORTUNATELY for French foreign policy, whether conceived on broad principles or by attempted adaptation to rapidly shifting circumstances, the King's vagrant affections came in to trouble and confuse. Those vague affections during the conspiracy of Henriette d'Entragues, had wandered for a time to Mademoiselle de Bueil; then on to Mademoiselle de la Haye; then to Mademoiselle de Fontlebon, one of the Queen's maids of honor. The Queen threatened to send the girl away, but the King retorted that if she sent her out of the palace, he would pack the Queen out of the Kingdom, back to Italy. The court was indeed shameless. There were so many concubines and bastards, that the Florentine Ambassador said: *"Veddesi mai bordello più simile a questo di questa corte?"* (Was there ever a court more like a brothel than this?) Of these ladies, however, Henriette d'Entragues was the only one who played a large part in his life. Sully gives a picture of the poor King's domestic situation. The King talked openly to Sully about it: "After various talks he came back," Sully says, "to the good qualities of his mistress, when once she had come out of her fits of anger and caprice. He lavished praises upon the charm of her companionship, the gaiety of her wit, the vivacity and liveliness of her sallies. What the King said was not unfounded, and the contrast between that and the Queen's moods, rendered him all the more appreciative of it. 'I find nothing

282

of all that at home,' he said, 'from my wife I get neither companionship, nor amusement, nor happiness. There is nothing yielding in her disposition, no sweetness in her conversation; she never adapts herself in any way to my mood or my character. When I come in and wish to talk to her familiarly and go up to kiss her, she looks so cold, that I go away in disappointment, and I am forced to seek consolation elsewhere.' " And now a new and startlingly disturbing figure comes innocently to the front.

In January, 1609, but the dates here are somewhat confused, the Queen gave a ballet in which Mademoiselle de Montmorency appeared as a nymph; she was then fourteen years old. At one point of the dance she raised a javelin, and aimed at the King; he said afterward that it had pierced his heart, and at once asked the poet Malherbe to compose verses in her honor. The girl was beautiful, and was betrothed to Bassompierre, a gentleman of the court. The King, ill in bed of the gout, called Bassompierre to the bedside and informed him that he had not slept a wink for thinking of procuring him a wife, and that he had settled upon Mademoiselle d'Aumale. Bassompierre objected that he should then be having two wives. "Bassompierre," the King said, "I speak as your friend, I am madly in love with Mademoiselle de Montmorency. If you marry her and she loves you, I shall hate you; if she loves me, you will hate me. It is better that our friendship should not be broken, for I am very fond of you. I have decided to marry her to the Prince de Condé and keep her here by my wife. She will be the comfort of my old age." Bassompierre, whose heart was whole and whose mind was set upon advancement, acquiesced, and the King promised to assure his fortune as if he were one of his own bastard children.

The Prince de Condé was twenty and supposedly the son of the Prince de Condé who had been poisoned by his wife. He was commonly spoken of with contempt, and said to be of an ill-grained disposition. It was hardly his fault: his father poisoned by his mother, his legitimacy questioned, his importance as heir presumptive cut short at the age of thirteen by the birth of a Dauphin, and then he himself shifted from an admirable tutor to the charge of a mean-spirited fellow. When the King was reproached with this shift he replied: "When I wished to make a king of my nephew, I gave him Pisani, when I wished to make him a subject I gave him Belin." But subsequent events proved the Prince not to be so abject as he had been painted. He had no desire to marry, and hesitated to obey the King's wish. Henry heard that the lad's tutor, Belin, opposed the match, and berated him savagely. The Prince accordingly acquiesced, and the young couple were married in May (1609). Thereupon, the King took to handsome clothes, fashionable perfumes, had the girl's picture painted, and seemed a new man. The Prince became apprehensive and asked for permission for him and his wife to go into the country; the King refused and broke into threats; the Prince behaved with unexpected spirit, and spoke of tyranny and injustice. "Injustice!" said the King, "I never did but one unjust act in my life, and that was when I recognized you as a legitimate Condé. If you wish, I will point your father out in Paris." The Prince, however, left the court, taking his wife; the King, through Malherbe's aid, burst into poetical complaint. The Prince retired to a country house near Soissons; but the King was soon seen there dressed as a common huntsman, in livery, with a patch over his eye, holding dogs on a leash. The Princess, who was not in love with her husband, does not seem to have ob-

The Prince and Princess de Condé

From Montfaucon's *Monuments de la Monarchie françoise, 1733*

jected to this evidence of devotion, but her mother-in-law hurried her into a carriage and drove off to another estate; and from there the young Prince in hot haste carried his wife across the border into the Netherlands, which were then under the joint sovereignty of the Archduke Albert and his wife the Archduchess, a daughter of Philip II, and also under the suzerainty of Spain.

An eye-witness present when the King received the news, reports: "I never saw a man so cast down and so beside himself." Sully was at once sent for. When he arrived at the Louvre about eleven o'clock at night, the King was in the Queen's chamber, walking up and down, with sunken head, his hands behind his back. Various gentlemen were standing up against the wall without speaking. The King took Sully at once by the hand: "Our man has gone and taken all away. What do you say?" Sully: "There is nothing novel or strange about that. Ever since he spoke to me at the Arsenal, I expected such a flight." "But what shall I do?" "Nothing." "What, nothing?" "Nothing! If you do nothing at all and show no concern he will come back of himself within three months." But the King was in no mood to follow this excellent advice; he despatched messengers to stop the runaways if possible at the border, and to ask the Archduke and Archduchess to forbid Condé to remain in the Netherlands. He wrote the Princess love-letters, bade Malherbe mourn in poetry. He wrote to Montmorency, the girl's father: "*Mon compère,* Your son-in-law *faict icy bien le diable* (is cutting up like the deuce); we must talk to him together, *afin qu 'il soit sage.*"

And he issued highly colored explanations of his conduct to the world:

To the French Ambassador in Spain

Paris, December 5, 1609.

Monsieur de Vaucellas,

You know how I have always loved and cherished my nephew the Prince de Condé, what honors I have bestowed upon him, what special favors he has had from me from babyhood . . . and now I am disappointed of my hopes in his gratitude, not only as to my own pleasure but also as to the public good. . . . For two years he has had a fancy to travel out of the Kingdom; of which I heard so much that I was advised, nay constrained, publicly to refuse him permission, on account of his rank and of my knowledge of his restlessness. For this reason I decided to marry him, in order to stop him, especially because I discovered that he was obstinately bent on going to places little suitable to his rank. But he was no sooner married, than the same desire to travel and keep far from me has come over him with greater restlessness than ever, and neither remonstrances nor counsels have been able to affect him, nor even threats of my indignation and the loss of my favor. . . . [The letter then narrates the facts of the flight and says that the decision of the Archduke and Archduchess has not yet been given.] I am certain that if they don't grant my request, I have the right to be indignant with them, and to believe that the Prince concocted his escape with their connivance, and that perhaps the Spanish ambassador here had a hand in it. . . . [He also accused the Prince of fomenting disorders in Poitou.] Tell all the people, who ask about this (but as coming from yourself), that if the Prince is not sent back, or if his deportation is delayed, as no greater insult or injury could be done me, they must know that my friendship

for those involved will greatly abate, and that I shall try to
avenge myself by all the means that God shall counsel me.

HENRY.

To his ambassador at Rome he says: "If the Archduke and the
Archduchess, or the Spaniards think to get advantage from the
Prince's person to entertain practises against my Kingdom,
and hope to profit by them, I promise myself that they will be
mistaken, inasmuch as, by God's grace, I have more means and
more courage than ever, to show my resentment and to avenge
whatever insults and injuries that may be done me." It is
said that drawing up these documents gave some trouble to the
Ministry of Foreign Affairs.

The Prince de Condé, fearing for his safety, fled to Milan,
a Spanish possession, leaving his wife in charge of the Archduchess. The Archduke refused to surrender the Princess without an order from her husband; and his suzerain, Philip III of
Spain, and his advisers put their heads together, to see what
benefit they might derive from the situation; for the First
Prince of the Blood, more especially as some doubt had been
thrown on the legality of the King's second marriage, might
be of value in case the two kingdoms should come to war.

There had long been reason to expect war. After the Peace
of Vervins (1598) the two countries had been at rivalry to
extend their influence in Switzerland and in Italy; while in
Holland, Henry, under disingenuous subterfuges, in spite of
his treaty, was aiding the Dutch rebels with money and supplies, and encouraging Huguenot volunteers to join them. The
accession of James I and his treaty with Philip III, had induced
Henry to maintain outwardly friendly relations with Philip,
but he continued to intrigue with the Dutch, and had finally

thrown his influence on the Dutch side to compel Spain to agree
to a truce of twelve years. As Spain also was obliged to yield
on the question of acknowledging Dutch sovereignty, she felt
very angry with France. Other matters led up to difficulties
with Austria and Catholic Europe. On the Rhine in the corner
of Germany that juts up between Holland and Belgium, lies
the little state of Cleves. The lord of this territory died, and
the succession was disputed by a Catholic and a Protestant
claimant. The Emperor Rudolph asserted that as Emperor
and Suzerain it was for him to decide. Henry denied this, and
prepared for war; he proposed to raise an army of seven or
eight thousand men. He hired Swiss mercenaries (August,
1609), and bargained for the alliance of Savoy. But he hesitated; in October instead of marching, he merely declared that
he was ready to intervene, in case Spain and the Emperor
should.

Shortly after this, on November twenty-ninth, as I have
said, the Prince de Condé carried his wife across the border,
and put himself under the protection of the Archduke and
Archduchess. The war cloud thickened at once. In January,
1610, the King declared that he was resolved that if Spain and
the Emperor continued to uphold Condé in his refusal to return, "he would not endure the affront." In April after Condé
had fled to Milan, and the Princess had not been returned,
the Secretary of State, Villeroy, told the Flemish ambassador, that he had talked with the King about this matter, and
that he would report the interview frankly: The King was in a
passion; nevertheless, if the Archduke would *"remédier au fait
de la princesse* [would make it right as to the princess]," other
matters could be arranged on the basis theretofore discussed,
"but if the Princess stays where she is, we are on the eve of

an explosion that may set fire to the four corners of Christendom." The ambassador answered that he had thought as much; if war came, the Princess would be the principal cause of it. The interview ended on Villeroy's declaration that whoever discovered an expedient to send back the Princess would do the greatest good ever conferred on Christendom, as otherwise there was nothing to secure it against a universal war.

The King, in place of the army of eight thousand men, which he had had in mind when he expected merely to intervene in Cleves, proposed to levy an army of fifty thousand. All western Europe was agog, and ranged itself on one side or the other. Catholic Germany leagued together; Protestant Germany, but with diffidence, agreed to ally itself with France. England was ready to support the Protestant claimant in Cleves, but refused an alliance; King James said, "It is not love, but villainy, to wish to debauch another man's wife"; and he would not break with Spain. Holland strictly confined itself to the issue of the succession in Cleves; Venice held off; the Pope favored the Catholic powers. Henry made vast plans for a great struggle: thirty thousand men in Champagne, fourteen thousand in Dauphiné, another army at the Pyrenees. Taxation and financial expedients loomed up portentous. There was great dissatisfaction among taxpayers, and greater still among ardent Catholics, at the idea of going to war with Catholic princes for the sake of Protestant claimants to the principality of Cleves, or worse yet, on account of the King's infatuation for the Princess de Condé. Nobody was sure whether the war was for a great political ideal of relieving Europe from the preponderant power of the House of Habsburg and the safety of the Reformed religion, or to enable the King to lay hands on another man's wife.

CHAPTER XXVI

THE GREAT DESIGN

THE King's passion for the Princess de Condé appears to be the negation of statesmanship; nevertheless, behind this violation of the Commandment, "Thou shalt not covet thy neighbor's wife," behind intrigues, negotiations, pretenses, parleyings, behind opportunist jockeyings and bluffings, it is possible to discern the outline of a far-reaching, high-aspiring policy, not only for the good of France, but also of all Europe; and, though the details of it are uncertain, and the testimony, on which those details rest, depends in the main on one man, bears marks of untrustworthiness, and has been disbelieved by learned scholars, nevertheless, that policy, contemplating the brotherhood of Christendom and perpetual peace, remains the King's proudest title to statesmanship and enduring renown. Bear in mind that the King was no ordinary man, that he cared greatly for France, and had a high conception of a king's duties.

He knew well that the politics of France were inextricably bound up with the great religious and political movements elsewhere in Europe. As early as 1596 he confided to Sully his dearest wishes: that God should be good to him, deliver him from Margot so that he might marry a suitable wife; conquer Flanders and Artois, win a battle over the Spaniards, and defeat the Turks; and he added, "I wish before I die to carry out two magnificent designs, which I have in my mind, and have

290

never communicated to anybody (I don't doubt that you will be delighted with them) but I shall not tell you anything now, and perhaps never to anybody until I see the means to make their execution perfectly certain." Again, in a letter to Sully on the death of Queen Elizabeth, dated April 10, 1603, he writes (so Sully says) that she was the irreconcilable enemy of his irreconcilable enemies, and that he and she were making *great designs* against those enemies. And not long thereafter, in strict secrecy he told Sully of the plan: He and Elizabeth were to unite in close alliance, bring in Venice, the United Provinces (Holland), the Protestant princes and cities of Germany, and all together attack the House of Habsburg. Of course (he said), things were changed by the death of Queen Elizabeth, he could not tell what her successor would do; Sully should go, as his ambassador, ostensibly to carry his congratulations, but really to sound King James as to the plan, and to consider whether the attack should be in India, the Netherlands, Germany or Italy, or in all those places at once. Sully was to say nothing of communications which the King had already had with the people of Hungary, Bohemia, Upper Austria, Moravia, Silesia and Lusatia. At Sully's behest a memorandum of the King's instructions was drawn up under four heads:

1. France, England and Holland should try to seize the Indies or any islands in the Spanish main.

2. Wrench from the House of Habsburg, Hungary, Bohemia, Moravia, Silesia, Lusatia, Austria, Carinthia, Styria, and the Tyrol, and convert these provinces into independent principalities, giving to the peoples the right of election of their princes.

3. Blockade the Spanish Netherlands.

4. Confine the House of Habsburg to the Spanish peninsula; and, in order to accomplish this, to effect a union of France, England, Holland, Denmark, Sweden, the Protestant provinces and cities of Germany, Venice, Savoy, and other provinces, even the Pope, and that they should reassign the conquered provinces, but neither France nor England take anything.

Sully, accordingly, expounded these ideas to the English King, summing up the existing situation concisely as the struggle of Catholic Europe to subdue Protestant Europe in the interest of Spain. After Sully's return home, the Great Design was left in abeyance from 1605 to 1609. Then the question of the succession to the duchy of Cleves came up. In January, 1610, by the King's direction, Sully again drew up an elaborate statement of the design.

The evidence for all this consists of Sully's statements in his *Œconomies Royales,* compiled between 1611-1617. Agrippa d'Aubigné (in an Appendix to his *Histoire Universelle* published in 1620) contributes some corroboration to the story. D'Aubigné says that the object of the *grand dessein* was "to deliver from the Spanish dominion all those that groaned under it," that is to overthrow the House of Habsburg, take the Empire away from it, expel it from the Netherlands and Italy, and limit it to Spain and dominions over-seas. He adds that the King's plan had originally been merely to attack the Austrian branch of the Habsburgs, but that he bade the King strike at the heart, Spain, and advised the preparation of two armies of twenty-five thousand men each, one to invade Spain at San Sebastian, the other at Perpignan, and that he would undertake to feed those armies at prices current in Paris. In short d'Aubigné agrees in substance with Sully but as to this,

Henry IV at home

critics say that he must have got his information from Sully.
Bassompierre, however, in his *Memoirs* under date of September 12, 1609, also reports that the Duc de Bouillon warned the
King that all Christian princes must unite against Spain, which
was aiming at universal monarchy, and urged him to make
every effort to ruin her. And Du Plessis-Mornay as early as
1583 instructed Navarre's ambassador to Queen Elizabeth to
urge a league against the Catholic Powers: "She," he says,
"can unite the Protestant Princes in a counter league to oppose
the pernicious purposes of the enemies of the Religion." There
would be England, the King of Navarre, the Protestant Princes
of Germany, the Swiss, the King of Denmark, in short "a
general league of all the princes who have embraced the Reformation. . . . This league, which would be composed of
the most warlike peoples in Christendom, would be stronger
than any league the Roman Catholics could make. . . . As
to the conditions of the league, each should contribute according to his means."

Of a large but indefinite plan to overthrow the House of
Habsburg there can be no doubt; from Paris to Constantinople
reports made their way that some vast enterprise was on foot.
Remember, that at this time that House still bestrode Europe
like a colossus. Austria held the Empire. Spain ruled Belgium, Milan and Naples, and possessed dominions round the
world on which the sun never set; her soldiers were admitted
to be the best in Europe; her coffers were filled with gold and
silver from Mexico and Peru; and Spanish men were still of
the temper that have made Cortez and Loyola immortal. In
France the fear of Spain was like her fear of Germany before
the Great War.

This Great Design, as Sully finally describes it, consists

of two parts: first, a coalition between France and the Protestant states, to be followed by the downfall of the House of
Habsburg, and second, the reconstruction of Europe thereafter.
I now pass to the consideration of the second part of the plan.
This constructive half appears for the first time in the printed
copy of the *Œconomies Royales* published many years after the
date of the original manuscript; the first two parts in 1638,
the last two in 1662. In the manuscript of 1611-1617 there is
no hint of it. In substance the addition to the *grand dessein*
so set forth, is this: After the downfall of the House of
Habsburg and the consequent liberation of its subject states,
Europe should be politically rearranged. There should be
fifteen sovereign states: six hereditary monarchies, France,
England, Spain, Sweden, Denmark and Lombardy *(i. e.,* Savoy
and the duchy of Milan) ; six elective monarchies, Rome *(i. e.,*
the Papal States and the Kingdom of Naples), Venice, the
Empire, Poland, Hungary and Bohemia; three confederate
republics, the Helvetian (Switzerland, the Tyrol, Franche-
Comté, Alsace), the Belgian (Holland and Belgium), the
Italian (Genoa, Lucca, Florence, Modena, Parma and Pia-
cenza). There should be three religions, the Catholic, the
Lutheran and Calvinism. These fifteen states should constitute a confederacy of nations, governed by seven councils,
one that should embrace all the associated states, and six for
special zones; for these councils, the Amphictyonic League of
ancient Greece afforded the best historical precedent in ancient
times, the Hanseatic League in modern. The General Council
should consist of forty members, and should meet once a year
in each of the fifteen states in turn; it should have charge of
all matters of general interest concerning this "Christian Republic," including the determination of quotas for armed

forces, and so forth. The six subordinate councils should have charge of the affairs of special regions, and an appeal from their decisions would lie to the General Council. There should be no more war, except to expel the Turks and perhaps the Muscovites, from Europe.

This half of the *grand dessein* is usually thought to be the child of Sully's imagination, invented when he grew old and wished to clothe the past, in which he had been a leading actor, with a grandeur beyond that of the present, in which Richelieu had become the master architect. The chief arguments against its genuineness, that is against ascribing it to Henry IV, are these: It is not referred to, as I have said, in the manuscript which Sully prepared between 1611 and 1617, and appears first in the book printed twenty years later; it is not mentioned in any foreign archives; it is improbable in itself, even fantastic; various passages in the manuscript of 1611-1617 that refer to the first, or destructive, part of the plan, appear in the book changed, amplified and added to; there is no reference in the manuscript of 1611-1617 to Sully's alleged embassy to Queen Elizabeth in 1601 which is recounted at length in the printed book; in various statements, Sully has been proved, by his own letters, to have been untruthful or gravely mistaken. Some critics allege that the whole matter of secret instructions to King James in 1603 is a fabrication; in short Sully is thought to have wilfully ascribed his own imaginings to King Henry in order to glorify the monarch whom he had served and loved.

To these various objections there are, at least, partial answers; as to the honor of originating the design, Sully ascribes it to Queen Elizabeth; he states explicitly that in 1601 he went upon an embassy to her, and found her strongly set

on the plan; she talked, he says, of making the Holy Roman
Empire really elective, of uniting Holland and Belgium in a
republic, also Switzerland and neighbor provinces as another,
of rendering the chief European powers about equal, reducing
all religion to three, and so on. If all this is false, if Sully
was lying, he lied royally, *splendide mendax,* for he goes on
to assert that Henry talked to him about the plan from year
to year. And, as to the lack of confirmatory evidence: From
the beginning, there was every reason for secrecy, and no advantage to be got from communicating the plan to others, since
any outside knowledge of the plan might ruin it, more especially because Henry, as King of a Catholic country, was
contriving a great anti-Catholic policy. Next, Elizabeth's
death altered the whole situation; in 1604 James made a treaty
with Spain, and talked of marriages between English and
Spanish princes; without England's help the plan was moon-
shine. And at home Henry's hands were full; in 1602 came Biron's conspiracy, in 1604 that of the Comte d'Auvergne, in 1606
that of Bouillon, and before France could make the stupendous
effort that such a design required, her internal affairs must
recover from the hurts and dislocations of the civil wars; the
King must first put his own house in order. In any event the
preliminary half, the destructive half, of the design must be
accomplished first, and until that should be in a fair way of
success, until the House of Habsburg lay in ruins, it was worse
than idle to introduce a revolutionary plan of reconstruction.

As to the first part of the plan, there can be no question of
it in the main. France must come out of the shadow of the
House of Habsburg, but it was impossible for her to enter
upon so gigantic a struggle without allies, and in particular
without the Protestant states of Germany. For twelve years

Henry had been seeking their alliances; but united action was
difficult, because the German Protestants had become suspicious
of him after his abjuration; and in 1609, when the affair
of Cleves arose, the preliminary labors of bringing the Protestant countries into an alliance were still far from satisfactory.
Under these circumstances, it would have been surprising if
the King had suffered his attention to be diverted from the
practical task of fighting the House of Hapsburg to a Utopian
reconstruction of Europe on the basis of an overwhelming
victory. His common sense controlled his optimistic imaginings, and it is probable that he regarded the proposed
"Christian Republic" as no more than a glorious possibility.
But it seems more reasonable to suppose that he had given his
forgetive fancy rein, than that Sully wilfully invented the story
out of whole cloth.

Let us now go back to the close of the year 1609, when
preparations for a struggle with the House of Habsburg were
making. These preparations were not only not inconsistent with
the *grand dessein*, but were the necessary prologue to it. The
Protestant States of Germany had formed an Evangelical
Union, and in the presence of coming need turned toward
Henry IV; Holland was in accord up to a point; England refused to go farther than to support the Protestant claimants to
Cleves; Savoy alone was whole-hearted in the matter. The
forces to oppose the House of Habsburg seemed quite inade-
quate to any such task, and the quarrel unlikely to pass beyond
the confines of Cleves when the episode of the Princess de
Condé came dramatically to the fore. Contemporaries lay
stress on the King's thwarted passion as the efficient cause of
his sudden and immense preparations for the coming war.
Under date of December, 1609, Bassompierre states in his

Memoirs, that the Archduke's refusal to give up the Princess was "the cause that finally made the King decide to execute the *grand dessein,* to which he had long listened and had often given hope that it should be undertaken, but which until this time he had been unwilling to enter upon completely." The King had failed to get her back by persuasion, although he had made her father and other relations urge her to return, and now he was ready to resort to force. In March, 1610, d'Aubigné having, at least so he says, persuaded the King to strike at Spain, left for the province of Poitou, of which he was vice-admiral, in order to make his preparations. In April Monsieur Pecquius, the Archduke's ambassador, and Villeroy, the King's minister for foreign affairs, were discussing the urgency of the Princess's return. Henry, himself, announced to the Papal Nuncio that even then if the Archduke and the King of Spain should prove their friendship by sending the Princess back to her father, the affair of Cleves could be settled, or reduced to small proportion; and Pecquius says that Henry admitted to Father Coton that he made war on the Princess's account.

Let me now sum up what seems the most reasonable view of the King's plans and motives: He had long been of the opinion that, for the safety of France as well as of the rest of continental Europe, the House of Habsburg must be overthrown, but from Queen Elizabeth's death until the latter part of 1609, he had never regarded the attempt as an immediate matter; as to the reconstruction of Europe, he had thought of it and talked of it with Sully, as the best way of avoiding religious and international wars in the future, but he was well aware that until the overthrow of the House of Habsburg should have been accomplished, any question of building up

Henry IV confides the government to the Queen
From the painting by Rubens

Europe anew was not within the domain of practical states-manship; finally an imminent attack upon the Habsburgs would not have been planned, for conditions were not ripe, as Eng-land held aloof and without her the price and the risk were too great, had it not been for the King's overmastering passion for the Princess de Condé.

As it was, his passion put armies in the field, and he was ready to fight a world in arms. In May he appointed Marie de Médicis regent with a council to advise her. You will see this ceremony symbolized in one of Rubens' pictures in the Louvre; Henry hands the orb of authority to the Queen, while the young Dauphin, standing between them, looks up at her with appreciation and approval. On May thirteenth, at Saint-Denis, the coronation of the Queen, the *sacre,* was splendidly celebrated. The date of her ceremonial entry into Paris was set for the sixteenth; and immediately afterward the King was to join the army.

CHAPTER XXVII

THE END

THESE vast preparations for war aroused alarm at home as well as abroad. The extreme Catholics, heirs to the beliefs and fears of the League, heard reports and rumors that the King, who had been a heretic himself, who had abjured only for the sake of a crown, who protected heresy, was making alliances with all the Protestant powers in order to overthrow the House of Habsburg, the great bulwark of orthodoxy, to beat down Catholicism, and infringe still further upon the rights of the Holy See. Brooding monks, here and there, especially such as came under the influence of the Jesuits, pictured to themselves the King as Antichrist, and dreamed of delivering the world of such a monster. Among these wild-minded people was a certain François Ravaillac, a native of Angoulême who had led a patched and vagrant life, at one time a magistrate's clerk, at another, a monk and then a school-teacher, and had been for some months imprisoned for debt; this fellow was a little deranged in mind, saw visions, and wore next his skin a cotton heart, which he had been told held a bit of the true cross, and used to repeat to himself that he must "set the honor of God before everything else."

Ravaillac's first plan was to see the King in order to tell him that it was his duty to compel the Huguenots to become Catholics, or to leave the Kingdom; but, he did not succeed in obtaining an interview. He went back to Angoulême, and brooded; fresh rumors of what the Huguenot soldiers boasted they would do with the Pope brought his wild thoughts to a head. He would save the Pope and protect God's honor by killing the King. He went back to Paris,—it was now the end of April,—he lodged first at the inn of the Five Crosses in the Faubourg Saint-Jacques, then at that of the Three Pigeons in the Rue Saint-Honoré, and procured a weapon by stealing a carving knife. Again he left Paris in the beginning of May and started upon the road to Angoulême, but turned back, and then loitered about the Louvre watching his chance.

The Queen's coronation at Saint-Denis was performed on Thursday, May thirteenth. The King went out there the day before, and on Thursday after an early lunch had gone to the abbey, for the first time since his *saut périlleux*, to give final directions. He was in good spirits, very alert, and impressed those about him with his amazing quickness of observation and comprehension; he was constantly shifting his place, and talking to everybody. That evening after the ceremony he supped at Saint-Denis, and returned quietly to Paris in the same carriage with the Queen. She had her supper in the Louvre. The King sat beside her and chatted; twice he drank the rest of what wine she left in her glass, and went off early to bed. He did not sleep well, got up early, dressed, lay down again and sent for his prayer-book. He then received Villeroy, the Secretary of State, also the Ambassador to Spain, and one of his officers; walked a little in the Tuileries, said good morning to the Dauphin and went to the church of the Feuillants, Rue Saint-Honoré, to hear mass. Bassompierre and Guise met him in the Tuileries on his way back. Guise spoke of his loyal affection, the King embraced him and said: "You people don't know me yet; but I shall die one of these days, and when you have lost me, you will know how to value me and how different I am from other men." Bassompierre put in: "Good gracious, Sire, will you never stop worrying us by saying that you will die soon? That is not a nice thing to say. If God please, you will live for many happy years. There is no felicity in the world equal to yours; you are still in the prime of life, in perfect health and strength, full of honors, more than any other mortal, enjoying in perfect peace the most prosperous kingdom in the world, loved and adored by your subjects, endowed with riches, noble houses, a handsome wife, lovely mistresses, and fine children growing up, what more do you need, what more could you wish for?" The King sighed: "Ah, my friend, I must leave all that." "Likewise this subject of conversation," Bassompierre replied, "because I have a boon to ask, a couple of hundred muskets from your Arsenal which we need and can not get elsewhere at any price. It isn't for my troop, which is well equipped; but Monsieur de Varennes needs twenty-five, Monsieur des Bordes, twenty-five and the Comte de Charlus fifty." The King answered, "Bassompierre, I will give them to you; but don't say a word about it, for everybody would be asking, and I should have to strip the Arsenal." Bassompierre: "Sire, I will pay cash down to Monsieur de Sully for whatever they are worth, so that he can replace them." The King hummed the lines of a song,

Que je n'offre à personne,
Mais à vous je les donne!

and Bassompierre took his leave. Then the King had a consultation with some officers about the opening campaign, dined, and again talked with high officials. He then visited the Queen in her chamber; she was giving orders for her ceremonial entry into Paris for the day after next. Here the King talked gaily, but it was noticed that his face belied his words; nevertheless, he went on to talk nonsense and crack foolish jokes with the ladies there. He seemed nervous and restless. From there he went to his study, wrote a letter, got up, put his hand to his head and said, *"Mon Dieu!* I have something here that bothers me greatly." He went back to the Queen's chamber, played with two of his children and bade Vitry, the Captain of his Guards, go on an errand; but Vitry, on hearing that the King was going out to drive, asked leave to accompany him, saying that he was anxious about the King's safety, now that the city was so full of strangers. "Go along!" the King replied. "You're a sycophant! Do as I tell you! For more than fifty years I have guarded myself without the captain of my Guards, and I shall continue to do so without help." Nevertheless, he hesitated when it came to going out; "Shall I go, my love, or shan't I?" he repeated, twice or more, started to go and then stepped back. Finally he kissed his wife several times and went. The Maréchal de la Chastre, who was with him, said, "You are more and more in love with the Queen every day."

The King went down-stairs and got into a large carriage, together with several gentlemen. "What day of the month is it?" he asked. "The fifteenth," one said. "No," said another, "to-day is the fourteenth." "You are right," the King replied. "You know your almanac the best," and laughed; then he murmured, as if thinking of some prophecy, "Between the thirteenth and the fourteenth." The carriage drove away, into the Rue Saint-Honoré. It was followed by a tall man on foot with a melancholy face, large deep-set eyes and a reddish beard. Ravaillac had drunk that day more than his wont, and had loitered about the gate of the Louvre, sitting on the stone coping, waiting for the King to come forth. As the carriage drove out, the King was not seated as he expected, so he dared not risk a stroke, and holding back, followed. The carriage drove eastward along the Rue Saint-Honoré, crossing the street that led to the Pont Neuf, and on into the narrow Rue de la Ferronnerie. Here it nearly stopped, for the way was blocked by two carts, one of hay, one of wine. The coachman tried to pass, but was obliged to go very slowly. This was Ravaillac's opportunity; the King was sitting with his right arm round Monsieur d'Epernon's neck, his left elbow resting on Monsieur de Montbazon's shoulder. Ravaillac glided up on the left, his knife hidden under his cloak, and, stepping on the wheel, leaned forward into the carriage; then wielding the knife with his left hand, for he was ambidextrous, he struck the King on his chest. The wound was slight; a second stroke entered between the fifth and sixth ribs, close to the heart, so deep that the murderer's thumb touched the King's doublet. The King cried, "I am wounded!"; there was a hubbub, some leapt on Ravaillac, but d'Epernon bade them be careful not to kill him. The King was driven back to the Louvre, bleeding badly. It is uncertain whether he arrived there alive; some say that he opened his eyes, others think that he was already dead. The Queen shrieked, "The King is dead!"; but the Chancellor coming up with the Dauphin, said: "Your Majesty will excuse me, in France Kings do not die; here, Madam, is the living King." The King's heart, according to his wish, was given to the Jesuits to be put in their Collège de la Flèche, where it rested until the Lovers of Liberty, Equality and Fraternity, burned it during the Revolution, and his body was buried beside royal dust accumulated through centuries, in the abbey church of Saint-Denis. Paris, L'Estoile

Death Mask of Henry IV

From *Undying Faces*. Courtesy W. W. Norton & Co.

noted down, became a city of lamentation; and Matthieu says, that the people of France were like scattered sheep bleating and crying.

So perished the great King, and his *grand dessein,* and his passion for the Princess de Condé, and all his hopes, and loves and ambitions. His personal morals were those of a soldier in civil wars; his public morals did more for the welfare of France than any king had done since Charlemagne. He had put down civil war, he had established religious tolerance, he had let his fancy dwell on a League of Nations and European peace; he improved the national finances, suppressed abuses, abolished sinecures; he reformed the local government of towns, encouraged the manufacture of cloth and glass, introduced silk-making; he fostered agriculture, mended roads, dug canals; he reorganized the army, founded a school for cadets; he built the great gallery of the Louvre, completed the palace of the Tuileries, erected the Pont Neuf, the Hôtel de Ville, the Place Royale; in short he was a foresighted administrator and ruler.

As to his character let me quote Sully, who of all his servants and friends knew him best.

"As it now behooves me to speak of our great King, I will say boldly, without fear of being accused of flattery or falsehood, that, among the admirable virtues which Heaven and Nature favored him with, six of them became so usual and familiar, that they were converted into habits; to wit, in things spiritual, Faith, Hope and Charity, and in matters political, Generosity, Mercy and Prudence, and of these three Prudence so seasoned the other two that Mercy never degenerated into negligence or cowardice, nor Generosity into rashness or insolence. For, although his admirable courage, his good judgment, his long experience and exquisite skill in unraveling affairs of state, whether military, financial or political, made him meditate upon and devise high and magnificent designs and enterprises . . . nevertheless, he always showed that prudence and moderation were the seasoning of his enterprises. And he made it a rule never to undertake two difficult and important projects at once, nor any, unless he had prepared, labored and disposed the minds and interests of those whom he judged to be necessary associates, allies, and confederates in such a design, and on his own part had made all the preparations and provisions to execute his plans happily and successfully, and secure solid and abiding results."

But his best *apologia* is his own: "Some blame me," he said, "because I like building and expensive works; others, for hunting, for dogs and hawks; others for cards, dice and all sorts of games; others for women and the delights of love; others for festivities, banquets, sauces and dainties; others for receptions, plays, balls, dances, and riding at the ring. . . . But I may say, that, kept within measure, all this should be said rather by way of praise than of blame. And, besides, I shall show these people that I will forsake mistresses, love-making, dogs, hawks, games, cards, buildings, festivals and banquets, and all other pleasures and pastimes, rather than lose the slightest occasion or opportunity to acquire honor and glory; and these— after my duty to God, my wife, my children, my faithful servants and my people, whom I love as I do my children—consist in making a reputation as a loyal King, faithful and true, and to do deeds that at the end of my life shall make my memory live and crown it with glory and honor."

And, indeed, the memory of Henry of Navarre lives, crowned with glory and honor.

THE END

BRIEF BIBLIOGRAPHY

BRIEF BIBLIOGRAPHY

Contemporary

Lettres de Antoine de Bourbon et de Jehanne d'Albret
Lettres Missives de Henri IV, edited by Berger de Xivrey
Lettres inédites de Henri IV, edited by Augustin Galitzin
Lettres inédites de Henri IV à M. de Pailhes
Lettres de Catherine de Médicis, edited by La Ferrière
Mémoires et Lettres de Marguerite de Valois
Lettres inédites de Marguerite de Valois

Œconomies royales	Sully
Mémoires	Du Plessis-Mornay
Histoire Universelle	Agrippa d'Aubigné
Mémoires-Journaux	Pierre de L'Estoile
Histoire Universelle	Jacques Auguste de Thou
Mémoires	Bassompierre
Œuvres	Brantôme
Dell'istoria delle Guerre Civili di Francia	Davila
Histoire de Navarre	André Favyn
Histoire de France	Pierre Matthieu
Chronologie novenaire	Palma Cayet
Lettres	Estienne Pasquier

Archives historiques de la Gascogne (1576-1602)
Les Amours du Grand Alcandre
Memoires de Claude Haton (1553-1582)
Archives Curieuses de l'histoire de France, 1st Série, t. XII.
Relation de Miron
Mémoires de Henri de la Tour d'Auvergne, Vicomte de Turenne, Duc de Bouillon

Not Contemporary

Henri IV	Pierre de Vaissière
La Vie de Marguerite de Valois	Jean—H. Mariéjol (1928)

309

Catherine de Médicis	Jean—H. Mariéjol (1928)
Le Mariage de Jeanne d'Albret	A. de Ruble
Antoine de Bourbon et Jeanne d'Albret	A. de Ruble
Jeanne d'Albret et La Guerre	A. de Ruble
Quelques Assassins	Pierre de Vaissière
Histoire du règne de Henri IV	Poisson
Histoire des Princes de Condé	D'Aumale
La vie intime d'une reine de France (Maria de'Medici)	L. Batiffol

Observations on Sully's Œconomies Royales, Revue Historique, Volumes 54, 55, 56.

Histoire de France, Vol. VI   Lavisse
parts 1 and 2.

INDEX

INDEX

DATE DUE